The Outsider

Broadbent: . . . I find the world quite good enough for me—rather a jolly place, in fact.

Keegan (looking at him with quiet wonder): You are satisfied?

Broadbent: As a reasonable man, yes. I see no evils in the world—except of course, natural evils—that cannot be remedied by freedom, self-government and English institutions. I think so, not because I am an Englishman, but as a matter of common sense.

Keegan: You feel at home in the world then?

Broadbent: Of course. Dont you?

Keegan (from the very depths of his nature): No.

BERNARD SHAW: *John Bull's Other Island*, Act IV.

The Outsider

Colin Wilson

Foreword by Marilyn Ferguson

Jeremy P. Tarcher/Putnam
a member of
Penguin Putnam Inc.
New York

Most Tarcher/Putnam books are available at special quantity
discounts for bulk purchases for sales promotions, premiums,
fund-raising, and educational needs. Special books or book excerpts
also can be created to fit specific needs.
For details, write Putnam
Special Markets, 375 Hudson Street
New York, NY 10014

Jeremy P. Tarcher/Putnam
a member of
Penguin Putnam Inc.
375 Hudson Street
New York, NY 10014
www.penguinputnam.com

Library of Congress Cataloging-in-Publication Data

Wilson, Colin, date.
    The Outsider.

    Includes bibliographical references.
    I. Title.
PR6073.I4408   1982   823'.914   81-16702
ISBN 0-87477-206-0   AACR2

MANUFACTURED IN THE UNITED STATES OF AMERICA

26 28 30 29 27 25

ACKNOWLEDGMENTS

I THANK the following for giving permission to quote extracts:

Cambridge University Press: George Sampson, *Concise Cambridge History of English Literature;* George Fox, *Journals.*

Dodd, Mead & Company: Rupert Brooke, *Collected Poems;* Alexei Tolstoy, *The Death of Ivan Ilytch.*

Doubleday & Company, Inc.: *The Seven Pillars of Wisdom* by T. E. Lawrence. Copyright, 1925, 1936, by Doubleday & Company, Inc.

E. P. Dutton & Co., Inc.: *A Buddhist Bible* edited by Dwight Goddard. Copyright, 1938, E. P. Dutton & Co., Inc.; The Everyman's Library Edition of *The Idiot* by Fyodor Dostoevsky (translated by E. M. Martin); The Everyman's Library Edition of *Letters from the Underworld* by Fyodor Dostoevsky (translated by C. J. Hogarth); The Everyman's Library Edition of *Under Fire* by Henri Barbusse (translated by John Rodker).

Harcourt, Brace and Company, Inc.: *In Search of the Miraculous* by P. D. Ouspensky. Copyright, 1949, by Harcourt, Brace and Company, Inc.; *Speculations* by T. E. Hulme; *All and Everything.* Copyright, 1950, by G. Gurdjieff; *Collected Poems 1909–1935* by T. S. Eliot. Copyright, 1936, by Harcourt, Brace and Company, Inc.; *Selected Essays 1917–1932* by T. S. Eliot. Copyright, 1932, by Harcourt, Brace and Company, Inc. The above quotations are reprinted with the permission of Harcourt, Brace and Company, Inc.

Heritage Press: Leo Tolstoy, *War and Peace* (translated by L. and A. Maude). Copyright, 1938, by The Limited Editions Club.

Henry Holt & Company, Inc.: Hermann Hesse, *Steppenwolf; Magister Ludi.*

Alfred A. Knopf, Inc.: Albert Camus, *The Stranger* (translated by Stuart Gilbert); Thomas Mann, *Doctor Faustus,* "The Life of the German Composer Adrian Leverkuhn As Told by a Friend" (translated by H. T. Lowe-Porter).

Little, Brown & Company: Harley Granville-Barker, *The Secret Life.*

Longmans, Green & Company, Inc.: William James, *The Varieties of Religious Experience.* Permission to reprint granted by Paul R. Reynolds & Son, 599 Fifth Avenue, New York, N.Y.

FOR
ANGUS WILSON
WITH GRATITUDE

CONTENTS

CONTENTS

FOREWORD

THE OUTSIDER, first published in 1956 when Colin Wilson was only twenty-four, is a prophetic book as well as a literary *tour de force*. By tracing, analyzing and giving a context to the disaffection and struggle of creative thinkers from William Blake to Ernest Hemingway, Wilson anticipated many developments of the 1960s and 1970s. The trajectory of Outsider consciousness led naturally to the rising interest in Eastern philosophy, the human potential movement, and the proliferation of techniques designed to help individuals transcend a sense of alienation from self and society.

Wilson summarizes the problems of that alienation:

The Outsider wants to cease to be an Outsider.

He wants to be integrated as a human being, achieving a fusion between mind and heart.

He seeks vivid sense perception.

He wants to understand the soul and its workings.

He wants to get beyond the trivial.

He wants to express himself so he can better understand himself. He sees a way out via intensity, extremes of experience.

Surveys and polls in the United States reveal Outsider values in a significant and rapidly growing minority of the population. The "inner-directed" are the fastest-growing consumer group. Increasingly people say that meaning is a more important consideration in their work than economic incentives. Self-fulfillment and self-expression are high on the list of goals.

The atmosphere of conformity that made the Outsiders feel different from their peers is now under attack from the mainstream. Social norms are changing rapidly in the direction of greater personal freedom.

Those seeking the experiential, the spiritual, and the numinous are no longer a handful. Millions have recognized that they are harboring within themselves another dimension of consciousness and that many old social structures are deadly to this other self. The phenomenon Blake called "twofold consciousness" has become an increasingly common experience.

To an observer the way of the Outsider may appear excessive, difficult, even reckless. Wilson shows us, by example after example, why the Outsider cannot accept society as it is, why he "sees too much and too deep."

Outsiders seek to heal divisions: between conscious and unconscious, intellect and intuition, mind and body, self and society, spirit and sensuality. "The Outsider's chief desire is to be unified. He is selfish as a man with a lifelong raging toothache would be selfish."

Refusing to resolve life's difficulties by withdrawal or denial, Outsiders seek transcendence through headlong involvement. They believe with Hermann Hesse's Steppenwolf that "the way to innocence leads ... ever deeper into human life. Instead of narrowing your world and simplifying your soul, you will have at the last to take the whole world into your soul, cost what it may."

The Outsider's intensity is expressed in Goethe's poem, "The Holy Longing," with its image of the butterfly drawn to, and transformed by, the flame:

And so long as you haven't experienced
this: to die and so to grow,
you are only a troubled guest
on the dark earth.

Most of us accommodate to the cultural trance, but Outsiders continue to be appalled at inauthenticity and mechanicalness. They see through their own act and that of others. "The problem of the Outsiders is the unreality of their lives. They suddenly realize they are in a cinema. They ask: Who are we? What are we doing here? ... They are confronted with a terrifying freedom."

Because they have glimpsed another, deeper dimension to life, they are not satisfied to be automatons. They are driven to self-discovery, even self-inquisition. They put themselves to tests of imagination and action that awe more 'sensible' people. "I doubt whether such pain improves us," Nietzsche said, "but I know it *deepens* us." And Rilke wrote, "May I, emerging at last from this terrible insight, burst into jubilant praise...."

The Outsider, Wilson points out, does not wish to accept life merely because fate is treating him well at the moment *but because it is his Will to accept.* He wants to control his responses through understanding, to build affirmation into his vision. Freedom of response is the only authentic freedom. This search is essentially spiritual, but "religious truth cannot exist apart from intellectual rigor." The Outsider's stubborn intellect seeks to understand the whispers of his intuition.

For a hundred years or more, Wilson said, Outsiders have been slowly creating new values by implication. "The real issue is not whether two and two make four or whether two and two make five, but whether life advances by men who love *words* or by men who love *living*."

A thoughtful reading of *The Outsider* gives us a profound sense of our collective modern struggle: how to restore the timeless and visionary in a culture that has prided itself on divorcing reason from feeling. Understanding the historic roots of this struggle gives us a deeper understanding of the Outsider in ourselves.

—Marilyn Ferguson
Los Angeles, 1981

THE OUTSIDER,
TWENTY YEARS ON

CHRISTMAS DAY, 1954, was an icy, grey day, and I spent it in my room in Brockley, south London. I recall that I had tinned tomatoes and fried bacon for Christmas dinner. I was alone in London; my girlfriend had gone back to her family for the holiday, and I didn't have the money to return to my home town, Leicester. Besides, relations with my family were rather strained; my father felt I'd wasted my opportunities to settle down in a good office job, and prophesied that I'd come to a bad end.

For the past year I'd been living in London, and trying to write a novel called *Ritual in the Dark*, about a murderer based on Jack the Ripper. To save money during the summer, I'd slept out on Hampstead Heath in a waterproof sleeping bag, and spent my days writing in the Reading Room of the British Museum. It was there that I'd met the novelist Angus Wilson, a kindly and generous man who had offered to look at my novel and—if he liked it—recommend it to his own publisher. I'd finished typing out the first part of the book a few weeks before; he had promised to read it over Christmas. Now I felt at a loose end. So I sat on my bed, with an eiderdown over my feet, and wrote in my journal. It struck me that I was in the position of so many of my favourite characters in fiction: Dostoevsky's Raskolnikov, Rilke's Malte Laurids Brigge, the young writer in Hamsun's *Hunger:* alone in my room, feeling totally cut off from the rest of society. It was not a position I relished; I'd always been strongly attached to my home and family (I'm a typical Cancer), and missed being with them at Christmas. Yet an inner compulsion had forced me into this position of isolation. I began writing about it in my journal, trying to pin it down. And then, quite suddenly, I saw that I had the makings of a book. I turned to the back of my journal and wrote at the head of the page: 'Notes for a book "The Outsider in Literature".' (I have it in front of me now as I write.) On the next two pages, I worked out a fairly complete outline of the book as it eventually came to be written. I fell asleep that night with a feeling of deep inner satisfaction; it seemed one of the most satisfying Christmas Days I'd ever spent.

Two days later, as soon as the British Museum re-opened, I cycled there at nine o'clock in the morning, determined to start writing immediately. On the way there, I recalled a novel I had once read about, in which a man had spent his days peering through a hole in the wall of his hotel room, at the life that comes and goes next door. It was, I recollected, the first major success of Henri Barbusse, the novelist who had later become world famous for *Le Feu*, the novel of World War One. When I arrived at the Museum, I found the book in the catalogue. I spent the next few hours reading it from cover to cover. Then I wrote down a quotation from it at the head of a sheet of paper: 'In the air, on top of a tram, a girl is sitting. Her dress, lifted a little, blows out. But a block in the traffic separates us ...' During the remainder of that afternoon, I wrote the opening four pages of *The Outsider*.

It now strikes me as interesting that I chose this opening, with the man hoping to see up a girl's skirt, and being frustrated by passing traffic. For although I say very little about sex in the book, it was undoubtedly one of the major forces behind its conception. I understood precisely what Barbusse's hero means when he describes going to bed with a prostitute, then going through the banal ritual of copulation, and feeling as if he has fallen from a height. This had been one of the central obsessions of my teens: the fact that a glimpse up a woman's skirt can make her seem infinitely desirable, worth pursuing to the ends of the earth; *yet the act of sex cannot provide full satisfaction of this desire.* When he actually gets the girl into bed, all the perspectives have changed ...

This had been the main theme of my novel *Ritual in the Dark*. Like Barbusse's hero, my own Gerard Sorme finds himself continually surrounded by objects of sexual stimulation; the advertisements showing girls in their underwear on the London underground cause violent frustration, 'like a match tossed against a petrol-soaked rag.' And in the course of the novel he seduces a middle aged Jehovah's Witness (partly for the piquancy of overcoming her religious scruples) and her teenage niece; yet the basic sexual desire remains unsatisfied. One scene in the book had particularly deep meaning for me. Sorme has spent the afternoon in bed with Caroline—the niece—and made love to her six or seven times. He feels physically satiated, as if the sexual delusion has finally lost its hold over him. Then he goes out to the doorstep—it is a basement room—to collect the milk, and catches a glimpse up a girl's skirt as she walks past the railings. Instantly, he feels the stirrings of an erection ...

I was not concerned simply with the intensity of male sexual desire—although I felt that it is far more powerful than most men are willing to admit. It was this element of 'un-achievableness'. It reminded me of the feeling I used to get as a child if I was on a day-trip to the seaside, and the coach went over a river or past a lake: a curious, deep *longing* for the water that would certainly not be satisfied by drinking it or swimming in it. In the same way, C. S. Lewis has spoken of how he used to be convulsed with desire by the *idea of Autumn*—the brown leaves and the smell of smoke from garden bonfires, and that strange wet smell about the grass ... Sorme has the same suspicion about sex: that it is ultimately unattainable: that what happens in bed is a kind of confidence trick. For this reason, he experiences a certain abstract sympathy with his new acquaintance, Austin Nunne, when he begins to suspect that Nunne is the East End sex murderer. It seems to him that this *could* be a valid way to achieve the essence of sex: to grab a girl in the moment she arouses violent desire and rip off her clothes. Oddly enough, it never strikes him that this is unlikely to be Nunne's motive; he knows Nunne to be a homosexual, yet his own sexual obsession blinds him to its implications.

The theme is repeated in the first pages of *The Outsider*. Barbusse's hero watches a girl undressing in the next room; but when he tries to re-create the scene in imagination, it is only a poor carbon copy. 'These words are all dead. They leave untouched ... the intensity of what was.' Again, he is present at the dining table when someone describes the sex murder of a little girl. Everyone at the table is morbidly interested—even a young mother with her child; but they all try to pretend to be indifferent. The irony, of course, is that Barbusse cannot speak his meanings clearly. If, in fact, he watched a girl undressing in the next room, he would probably masturbate; as it is, he tries to convince the reader that it was an experience of spiritual beauty. For all his talk about truth, the narrator cannot be honest.

In *Ritual in the Dark*, this inability to grasp the essence of sexuality becomes the symbol of our inability to grasp the essence of anything important—of Autumn, of water ... This, it seemed to me, is the basic difference between human beings. Some are perfectly satisfied with what they have; they eat, drink, impregnate their wives, and take life as it comes. Others can never forget that they are being cheated; that life tempts them to struggle by offering them the essence of sex, of beauty, of success; and that she always seems to pay in counterfeit money. In the novel, Nunne—the purely physical type—pursues his will o' the wisp with a despairing ruthlessness. The painter, Oliver Glasp, is obsessed by a ten-year-old female model, but horrified at the idea of any physical lovemaking; he sublimates his desire in decadent romantic pictures. Sorme, the intellectual outsider, also pursues his desires with a touch of ruthlessness, but a fundamentally kindly nature makes him incapable of causing pain ...

Sometime shortly before that Christmas of 1954, I was walking along the Thames Embankment with my closest—and oldest—friend, Bill Hopkins, explaining to him the ideas of the novel. I explained that Sorme is an intellectual outsider; he has discipline of the intellect, but not of the body or emotions. Glasp, like Van Gogh, is the emotional outsider; he has discipline of the emotions, but not of the body or the intellect. Nunne, like the dancer Nijinsky, is a physical outsider; he has discipline of the body, but not of the emotions or the intellect. All three are 'lop sided'. And all three are capable of becoming insane. I went on to point out that Dostoevsky had used the same categories in the three Karamazov brothers. This, I believe, was the actual seed of *The Outsider*. In due course, the chapter contrasting the three types of outsider ('The Attempt to Gain Control') became the core of the book.

When it came to the actual writing, there was a certain amount of material that had to be scrapped. I had, for example, intended to write a chapter about the Faust figure, from Marlowe to Mann's Dr. Faustus—Mann's feeling about the un-attainableness of the ideal was obviously close to my own. There was a chapter on criminal outsiders that was abandoned after a few pages—the fragment was later reprinted in *An Encyclopedia of Murder*. And there was an interesting outline of a chapter on 'the weak outsider'—characters like Oblomov, the great Gatsby, Hamlet, the poets of the 1890s like Dowson and Johnson and Verlaine ... I was particularly fascinated by Gatsby because the essence he craved was the essence of 'success'. I was convinced that this, like all the other essences, is a fraud. Yet my romanticism found this hard to accept ...

A year and a half after writing the first page of *The Outsider,* I had a chance to find out for myself. I had written most of the book by the middle of 1955. (The most difficult parts, I found, were the links between the various sections; it cost me two weeks' hard work to write the link between Wells and Sartre in the first chapter; it finally came in a flash of inspiration as I was hitch-hiking on the back of a lorry near Oxford.) I tried sending a few pages, together with an outline, to the publisher Victor Gollancz. To my surprise, he replied almost immediately, saying that he liked the outline and would like to see the rest. At this time, I was working during the evenings in a coffee bar in the Haymarket, so that I could spend my days writing in the British Museum. In the Autumn I sent him the completed manuscript and he accepted it. That Winter, I gave up work for a few weeks—for the first time since I'd left school at 16—and lived on the £75 advance that Gollancz gave me. Somehow, I had no doubt that the book would be a success. I think I had too little doubt about the importance of what I had to say to feel misgivings. Gollancz, understandably, had no such confidence; he finally decided to take the risk of printing five thousand copies.

Publication day was set for Monday, May 26, 1956. Even before this, I was beginning to smell the breath of fame, and finding it exciting. Edith Sitwell, the poetess who had 'discovered' Dylan Thomas, had read the book in proof, and told Gollancz she thought I was going to be 'a truly great writer'. A journalist on one of the London evening newspapers asked to interview me; I spent an evening at his flat talking into his tape recorder—which struck me as a fabulous device—and listening to a record of the latest hit show, *My Fair Lady.* Gollancz told me he had been promised a review in the *Evening News* on the Saturday before publication. My girlfriend, Joy, was spending the weekend with me—I was now living in a room in Notting Hill Gate—and we bought the paper as soon as it appeared; but there seemed to be no review. I went to bed that night oddly depressed—my bicycle had been stolen a few hours before, and it seemed a bad omen. The next morning, we woke up early and rushed to the corner of Westbourne Grove to buy the two 'posh' Sunday papers. Both of them had devoted their lead review to *The Outsider,* and both were full of praise. When we got back to my room, someone told us that there *had* been a review in the previous evening's newspaper; we looked again, and found a headline: 'He's a major writer—and he's only 24'.

Before that day was out, I had no doubt that I was famous, whatever that meant. I had no telephone—naturally—but our neighbours in the basement had one, and it began to ring at about nine o'clock that morning—my editor ringing me up to congratulate me, and to ask my permission to give the telephone number to the press. Within a couple of hours I had agreed to be interviewed by half a dozen newspapers, and to appear on radio and television. Moreover, a playwright named John Osborne had achieved success on the same day; his play *Look Back in Anger* had been produced at the Royal Court a few days earlier, and reviews by Kenneth Tynan and Harold Hobson launched him to fame as the first 'Angry Young Man'. (The actual phrase was invented by J. B. Priestley, who wrote an article about the two of us under that title in *The New Statesman* the following week.) In fact, Osborne and I had only one thing in common—that both of us had been turned into 'outsiders' by our working-class backgrounds, and the suspicion that we would spend the rest of our lives stuck in dreary obscurity. But the fact that we appeared on the literary scene at the same time somehow doubled the furore.

It was a strange experience. On the 24th of May, 1956, I had been totally unknown. I had never doubted my own abilities, but I was quite prepared to believe that 'the world' would decline to recognize them. The 'famous' seemed to be a small and very exclusive club, and the chances of getting into it were about equal to those of winning the football pools. And then, suddenly, on the 25th, I had apparently been elected without opposition, and the pundits of the Sunday newspapers were assuring the public that I was at least as important as Sartre and Camus, a real British home-grown existentialist. And when the press got hold of the story about sleeping on Hampstead Heath, I became notorious as well as famous ...

The enormous publicity was partly due to the fact that I was one of a group, a 'new group', not just of writers, but of all kinds of personalities who were always worth a paragraph in a gossip column. It included Elvis Presley and Marilyn Monroe and Brigitte Bardot and Arthur Miller and Sandy Wilson and Pietro Annigoni (who had painted the Queen) and Francis Bacon and Stirling Moss and Mort Sahl, and a couple of dozen more assorted celebrities who somehow seemed typical of the mid-fifties. And it included a large-ish crop of young writers—Amis, Wain, Iris Murdoch, Brendan Behan, Françoise Sagan, Michael Hastings (who was eighteen), Jane Gaskell (who was fourteen), and even a nine-year-old French poetess called Minou Drouet. I have a feeling that the newspapers had an unconscious urge to manufacture an 'epoch'—like the 1890s or 1920s. And, for better or worse, I was in the middle of it, cast as the 'boy genius'. Somehow, Osborne and I were supposed to prove that England was full of brilliantly talented young men who couldn't make any headway in the System, and were being forced to go it alone. We were supposed to be the representative voices of this vast army of outsiders and angry young men who were rising up to overthrow the establishment.

Oddly enough, it was not particularly interesting or exciting to be involved in all this ferment. To begin with, the newspaper publicity was on such a moronic level (as it is more or less bound to be) that it seemed a travesty of what we were trying to do as individuals. It invited derision—and, of course, received it. I was delighted to know that I would never have to return to a factory or office. But otherwise, fame seemed to have no great advantages. It didn't bring any startling new freedom. I ate good food and drank wine, but since food and drink had never interested me much, this was unimportant. I wasn't fond of travel. If I hadn't been settled with Joy, the greatest bonus would probably have been the sexual possibilities; but since I had no intention of getting rid of her, I had to put that temptation behind me. I admit that this was my keenest regret.

What the newspapers really wanted from this new generation was scandal. Early in 1957, I inadvertently provided it, when Joy's parents turned up at the room we now shared in Notting Hill Gate, determined to drag her away from this life of sin; her father had even brought a horsewhip. Joy and I were giving supper to a villainous old queer named Gerald Hamilton, the original of Christopher Isherwood's Mr. Norris. As Joy's family tried to drag her off down the stairs, Gerald rushed to the nearest telephone and rang every gossip columnist he knew (and his acquaintance was wide). Ten minutes after I'd persuaded her family to leave (with some help from the police), the reporters and photographers started to arrive on the doorstep. After seeing the first ones, we sneaked out of the back door, spent the night with a friend, and then fled to Devon, to take refuge with the writer Negley Farson. The press caught up with us there after a few days, and then pursued us across to Wales and Ireland. The story occupied the front pages and gossip columns for about two weeks, until we returned to London. Victor Gollancz told me that my reputation as a serious writer was ruined, and that if I didn't get out of London, I'd never write another book. The man who lived in the room below us offered to rent us a cottage near Mevagissey, in Cornwall. We took Gollancz's advice, moved from London, and have been here ever since.

On the whole, Gollancz was right. The silly publicity made it impossible for Britain's intellectual establishment to take me seriously, and they showed their displeasure when my next book appeared. I had, it seemed, achieved 'recognition', and then lost it just as suddenly. I never had any great difficulty in finding publishers—my notoriety at least had that advantage—but the critics made sure that I had no more best sellers. Books like *Religion and the Rebel, The Age of Defeat* and *The Strength to Dream* were received with the kind of review that began: 'More pretentious rubbish from this intellectually confused and thoroughly overrated young man ...' *Ritual in the Dark* achieved a certain success when it finally appeared in 1960, but critics who had decided that I was a flash in the pan had no intention of reconsidering me as a novelist. *The Outsider* had made me about £20,000 in its first year— a considerable sum in 1956. Subsequent books seldom made more than £1,000. We were never poverty stricken, but invariably overdrawn at the bank. In the 1960s, I made several lecture tours of America to try and stabilize my finances. I usually returned to England with just enough money to pay all the outstanding bills, and start again from square one ...

I suppose this particular story has a kind of happy ending. When *The Outsider* appeared, T. S. Eliot told me that I had achieved recognition the wrong way; it was fatal to become known to too many people at once. The right way was to gradually achieve an audience of regular readers, and slowly expand from there, if at all. As the 1960s drew to a close, I realized that this was what was happening. Second hand shops told me that certain people were obsessive collectors of my books, and would pay fairly high prices for them. In the *New Statesman*, there was an advertisement asking for members for a Colin Wilson Society (apparently the founders were under the impression that I was dead). They succeeded in continuing for a couple of years (a remarkable feat, since they all regarded themselves as outsiders) during which time they met twice a week to study my books. I was becoming a 'cult figure'— but still having considerable difficulty making a decent living. In 1967, an American publisher commissioned me to write a book on 'the occult'. I had always enjoyed reading about such subjects, without taking them very seriously. The book, when finished, was a thousand pages long (in typescript) and I had now ceased to take the subject lightly. In fact, it was clear that my investigation into the mysteries of consciousness led straight into the heart of the 'paranormal'. Unfortunately, the English publisher who had also commissioned the book did not share my excitement; he gasped at the size of the manuscript, and asked me to take it elsewhere. Fortunately, a more enterprising publisher—Hodders—accepted it, and actually asked me to expand it. My editor, Robin Denniston, told me that he thought it was about time for a 'Colin Wilson revival'; he even decided to issue a pamphlet about me as advance publicity. I shook my head and thought: 'Poor devils, they'll lose their money'.

To my amazement, they proved to be right. The reviews had a serious and respectful tone that I hadn't heard since *The Outsider*. With a kind of dazed incredulity, I realized that I'd finally become an 'establishment' figure. I was no longer the 'boy genius' who'd proved to be a pretentious fraud. As if conveying the blessing of England's literary establishment, Cyril Connolly and Philip Toynbee—the two critics who had launched *The Outsider* on that bewildering Sunday fifteen years earlier, and then damned my subsequent books—produced lengthy and thoughtful reviews of *The Occult*, full of the kind of praise that can be extracted and used in advetisements. Apparently all was forgiven. In fact, publication week of *The Occult* was rather like that of *The Outsider*, but more dignified: interviews, appearances on television, requests for articles and book reviews. What was rather more important was that the book sold as well as *The Outsider*; and since it cost five times as much, royalties were correspondingly high—even enough to compensate for inflation. If *The Occult* didn't actually make me rich—few non-fiction books ever sell that well—it at least managed to give me a delightful sensation of not being permanently broke and overdrawn at the bank. It has also supported me during the six years I have taken to write a sequel, *Mysteries*, whose last chapter I have broken off to write this introduction ...

And how do I feel about *The Outsider* in retrospect? In order to answer that question I settled down the other day to re-read it—and found it impossible to gain a sense of perspective. It still produces in me the same feeling of excitement and impatience that I experienced as I sketched the outline plan on that Christmas Day of 1954. Why impatience? Because it aroused some enormous anticipation. At the time, I mistook this for anticipation of success (for somehow, I never had the slightest doubt that it would be a success). Now I recognize it for what it was: the realization that I had at last settled down to the serious business of living: that after the long-drawn-out and messy years of childhood, and the teenage agonies of self-consciousness, I had at last ceased to waste my time; I was starting to do what I was always intended to do. There was a feeling like leaving harbour. It made no difference that the critics later tried to take back what they'd said about the book. They couldn't take back the passport they'd given me.

Colin Wilson

CHAPTER ONE

THE COUNTRY OF THE BLIND

AT FIRST SIGHT, the Outsider is a social problem. He is the hole-in-corner man.

> In the air, on top of a tram, a girl is sitting. Her dress, lifted a little, blows out. But a block in the traffic separates us. The tramcar glides away, fading like a nightmare.
>
> Moving in both directions, the street is full of dresses which sway, offering themselves airily, the skirts lifting; dresses that lift and yet do not lift.
>
> In the tall and narrow shop mirror I see myself approaching, rather pale and heavy-eyed. It is not a woman I want— it is *all* women, and I seek for them in those around me, one by one. . . .[1]*

This passage, from Henri Barbusse's novel *L'Enfer*, pinpoints certain aspects of the Outsider. His hero walks down a Paris street, and the desires that stir in him separate him sharply from other people. And the need he feels for a woman is not entirely animal either, for he goes on:

> Defeated, I followed my impulse casually. I followed a woman who had been watching me from her corner. Then we walked side by side. We said a few words; she took me home with her. . . . Then I went through the banal scene. It passed like a sudden hurtling-down.
>
> Again, I am on the pavement, and I am not at peace as I had hoped. An immense confusion bewilders me. It is as if I could not see things as they were. *I see too deep and too much.*

Throughout the book, this hero remains unnamed. He is the anonymous Man Outside.

He comes to Paris from the country; he finds a position in a bank; he takes a room in a 'family hotel'. Left alone in his room, he meditates: He has 'no genius, no mission to fulfil, no

* See Notes on pp. 283-8.

remarkable feelings to bestow. I have nothing and I deserve nothing. Yet in spite of it, I desire some sort of recompense.'² Religion ... he doesn't care for it. 'As to philosophic discussions, they seem to me altogether meaningless. *Nothing can be tested, nothing verified.* Truth—what do they mean by it?'³ His thoughts range vaguely from a past love affair and its physical pleasures, to death: 'Death, that is the most important of all ideas.' Then back to his living problems: 'I must make money.' He notices a light high up on his wall; it is coming from the next room. He stands on the bed and looks through the spy-hole:

> I look, I see. . . . The next room offers itself to me in its nakedness.⁴

The action of the novel begins. Daily, he stands on the bed and stares at the life that comes and goes in the next room. For the space of a month he watches it, standing apart and, symbolically, above. His first vicarious adventure is to watch a woman who has taken the room for the night; he excites himself to hysteria watching her undress. These pages of the book have the kind of deliberate sensationalism that its descendants in post-war France were so consistently to be accused of (so that Guido Ruggiero could write: 'Existentialism treats life in the manner of a thriller').

But the point is to come. The next day he tries to recreate the scene in imagination, but it evades him, just as his attempt to recreate the sexual pleasures with his mistress had evaded him:

> I let myself be drawn into inventing details to recapture the intensity of the experience. 'She put herself into the most inviting positions.'
> No, no, that is not true.
> These words are all dead. They leave untouched, *powerless to affect it, the intensity of what was.*⁵

At the end of *L'Enfer*, its nameless hero is introduced to a novelist who is entertaining the company with an account of a novel he is writing. A coincidence ... it is about a man who pierces a hole in his wall and spies on all that happens in the next room. The writer recounts all of the book he has written; his listeners admire it: Bravo! Tremendous success! But the

Outsider listens gloomily. 'I, who had penetrated into the very heart of mankind and returned, could see nothing human in this pantomimic caricature. It was so superficial that it was false.' The novelist expounds: 'Man stripped of his externals . . . that is what I wish to show. Others stand for imagination . . . I stand for truth.' The Outsider feels that what he has seen *is* truth.[6]

Admittedly, for us, reading the novel half a century after it was written, there is not so much to choose between the novelist's truth and the hero's. The 'dramas' enacted in the next room remind us sometimes of Sardou, sometimes of Dostoevsky when he is more concerned to expound an idea than to give it body in people and events. Yet Barbusse is sincere, and this ideal, to 'stand for truth', is the one discernible current that flows through all twentieth-century literature.

Barbusse's Outsider has all of the characteristics of the type. Is he an Outsider because he's frustrated and neurotic? Or is he neurotic because of some deeper instinct that pushes him into solitude? He is preoccupied with sex, with crime, with disease. Early in the novel he recounts the after-dinner conversation of a barrister; he is speaking of the trial of a man who has raped and strangled a little girl. All other conversation stops, and the Outsider observes his neighbours closely as they listen to the revolting details:

> A young mother, with her daughter at her side, has half got up to leave, but cannot drag herself away. . . .
> And the men; one of them, simple, placid, I heard distinctly panting. Another, with the neutral appearance of a bourgeois, talks commonplaces with difficulty to his young neighbour. But he looks at her as if he would pierce deeply into her, and deeper yet. His piercing glance is stronger than himself, and he is ashamed of it. . . .[7]

The Outsider's case against society is very clear. All men and women have these dangerous, unnamable impulses, yet they keep up a pretence, to themselves, to others; their respectability, their philosophy, their religion, are all attempts to gloss over, to make look civilized and rational something that is savage, unorganized, irrational. He is an Outsider because he stands for Truth.

That is his case. But it is weakened by his obvious abnormality, his introversion. It looks, in fact, like an attempt at self-justification by a man who knows himself to be degenerate, diseased, self-divided. There is certainly self-division. The man who watches a woman undressing has the red eyes of an ape; yet the man who sees two young lovers, really alone for the first time, who brings out all the pathos, the tenderness and uncertainty when he tells about it, is no brute; he is very much human. And the ape and the man exist in one body; and when the ape's desires are about to be fulfilled, he disappears and is succeeded by the man, who is disgusted with the ape's appetites.

This is the problem of the Outsider. We shall encounter it under many different forms in the course of this book: on a metaphysical level, with Sartre and Camus (where it is called Existentialism), on a religious level, with Boehme and Kierkegaard; even on a criminal level, with Dostoevsky's Stavrogin (who also raped a small girl and was responsible for her death). The problem remains essentially the same; it is merely a question of discounting more or less as irrelevant.

Barbusse has suggested that it is the fact that his hero *sees deeper* that makes him an Outsider; at the same time, he states that he has 'no special genius, no message to bestow', etc., and from his history during the remainder of the book, we have no reason to doubt his word. Indubitably, the hero *is* mediocre; he can't write for toffee, and the whole book is full of clichés. It is necessary to emphasize this in order to rid ourselves of the temptation to identify the Outsider with the artist, and so to oversimplify the question: disease or insight? Many great artists have none of the characteristics of the Outsider. Shakespeare, Dante, Keats were all apparently normal and socially well-adjusted, lacking anything that could be pitched on as disease or nervous disability. Keats, who always makes a very clear and romantic distinction between the poet and the ordinary man, seems to have had no shades of inferiority complexes or sexual neuroses lurking in the background of his mind; no D. H. Lawrence-ish sense of social-level, no James Joycian need to assert his intellectual superiority; above all, no sympathy whatever with the attitude of Villiers De Lisle Adam's Axel (so much admired by Yeats): 'As for living, our servants can do that for us.' If any man intended to do his own living for himself, it was Keats. And he is undoubtedly the rule

rather than the exception among great poets.
may be an artist, but the artist is not necessa'
What can be said to characterize the Outsı.
strangeness, of unreality. Even Keats could write, i.
Browne just before he died: 'I feel as if I had died alrea
am now living a posthumous existence.' This is the sens
unreality, that can strike out of a perfectly clear sky. Gooq
health and strong nerves can make it unlikely; but that may
be only because the man in good health is thinking about other
things and doesn't look in the direction where the uncertainty
lies. And once a man has seen it, the world can never afterwards be quite the same straightforward place. Barbusse has
shown us that the Outsider is a man who cannot live in the
comfortable, insulated world of the bourgeois, accepting what
he sees and touches as reality. 'He sees too deep and too much',
and what he sees is essentially *chaos*. For the bourgeois, the world
is fundamentally an orderly place, with a disturbing element
of the irrational, the terrifying, which his preoccupation with
the present usually permits him to ignore. For the Outsider,
the world is not rational, not orderly. When he asserts his
sense of anarchy in the face of the bourgeois' complacent
acceptance, it is not simply the need to cock a snook at respectability that provokes him; it is a distressing sense *that truth must
be told at all costs*, otherwise there can be no hope for an ultimate
restoration of order. Even if there seems no room for hope,
truth must be told. (The example we are turning to now is a
curious instance of this.) The Outsider is a man who has
awakened to chaos. He may have no reason to believe that
chaos is positive, the germ of life (in the Kabbala, chaos—
tohu bohu—is simply a state in which order is latent; the egg is
the 'chaos' of the bird); in spite of this, truth must be told,
chaos must be faced.

The last published work of H. G. Wells gives us an insight
into such an awakening. *Mind at the End of Its Tether* seems to
have been written to record some revelation:

The writer finds very considerable reason for believing that
within a period to be estimated by weeks and months rather
than by aeons, there has been a fundamental change in the
conditions under which life—and not simply human life
but all self-conscious existence—has been going on since

its beginning. If his thinking has been sound . . . the end of everything we call life is close at hand and cannot be evaded. He is telling you the conclusions to which reality has driven his own mind, and he thinks you may be interested enough to consider them, but he is not attempting to impose them on you.[8]

This last sentence is noteworthy for its curious logic. Wells's conviction that life is at an end is, as he says, a 'stupendous proposition'. If it is true, then it negates the whole pamphlet; obviously, since it negates all life and its phenomena. Vaguely aware of the contradiction, Wells explains that he is writing 'under the urgency of a scientific training that obliged him to clarify the world and his ideas to the limits of his capacity'.

His renascent intelligence finds itself confronted with strange, convincing realities so overwhelming that, were he indeed one of those logical, consistent people we incline to claim we are, he would think day and night in a passion of concentration, dismay and mental struggle upon the ultimate disaster that confronts our species. We are nothing of the sort. We live with reference to past experience, not to future events, however inevitable.[9]

In commenting on an earlier book called *The Conquest of Time*, Wells comments: 'Such conquest as that book admits is done by time rather than man.'

Time like an ever rolling stream bears all its sons away
They fly forgotten as a dream dies at the opening day.[10]

This is the authentic Shakespearian pessimism, straight out of *Macbeth* or *Timon*. It is a surprising note from the man who had spent his life preaching the credo: If you don't like your life you can change it: the optimist of *Men Like Gods* and *A Modern Utopia*. Wells declares that, if the reader will follow him closely, he will give the reason for this change of outlook:

The reality glares coldly and harshly upon any of those who can wrench their minds free . . . to face the unsparing question that has overwhelmed the writer. They discover that a frightful queerness has come into life. . . . The habitual interest of the writer is his critical anticipation. Of everything he asks: To what will this lead? And it was natural for him to assume that there was a limit set to change, that new things and events would appear, but that they would appear consistently, preserving the natural sequence of life. So that in the present vast confusion of our world, there was always the assumption of an ultimate restoration of rationality. . . . It was merely the fascinating question of what forms the new rational phase would assume, what over-man, Erewhon or what not would break through the transitory clouds and turmoil. To this the writer set his mind.

He did his utmost to pursue that upward spiral . . . towards their convergence in a new phase in the story of life, and the more he weighed the realities before him, the less he was able to detect any convergence whatever. Changes had ceased to be systematic, and the further he estimated the course they seemed to be taking, the greater the divergence. Hitherto, events had been held together by a certain logical consistency, as the heavenly bodies have been held together by gravitation. Now it is as if that cord had vanished, and everything was driving anyhow to anywhere at a steadily increasing velocity. . . . The pattern of things to come faded away.[11]*

In the pages that follow, these ideas are enlarged on and repeated, without showing us how they were arrived at. 'A harsh queerness is coming into things', and a paragraph later: 'We pass into the harsh glare of hitherto incredible novelty. . . . The more strenuous the analysis, the more inescapable the sense of mental defeat.' 'The cinema sheet stares us in the face. That sheet is the actual fabric of our being. Our loves, our hates, our wars and battles, are no more than

* Readers of Professor Whitehead will probably feel that Wells is a bad example of Whitehead's old enemy, 'the bifurcation of nature', i.e. that as a man of science, he has gone to extremes of dividing nature into 'things as they are' (i.e. the things science is concerned with) and things as they are perceived by human beings (i.e. the things art and music are concerned with), and that Wells's feeling that mind and nature have ceased to run parallel is only an extreme consequence of his attitude. Certainly Whitehead's 'philosophy of organism' is concerned with making the same demands for a *wholeness* of conception of mind and nature that I am concerned with in this book; a parallel of the thought of Professor Whitehead with that of T. E. Hulme would probably shed a great deal of light on the problems of contemporary humanism.

phantasmagoria dancing on that fabric, themselves as in-substantial as a dream.'

There are obviously immense differences between the attitudes of Wells and Barbusse's hero, but they have in common the Outsider's fundamental attitude: non-acceptance of life, of human life lived by human beings in a human society. Both would say: Such a life is a dream; it is not real. Wells goes further than Barbusse in the direction of complete negation. He ends his first chapter with the words: 'There is no way out or round or through.' There can be no doubt that as far as Wells is concerned, he certainly sees 'too deep and too much'. Such knowledge is an impasse, the dead end of Eliot's Geron-tion: 'After such knowledge, what forgiveness?'

Wells had promised to give his reasons for arriving at such a stupendous proposition. In the remainder of the pamphlet (nineteen pages) he does nothing of the sort; he repeats his assertion. 'Our doomed formicary', 'harsh implacable hostility to our universe', 'no pattern of any kind'. He talks vaguely of Einstein's paradox of the speed of light, of the 'radium clock' (a method geologists use to date the earth). He even con-tradicts his original statement that *all* life is at an end; it is only the species *Homo sapiens* that is played out. 'The stars in their courses have turned against him and he has to give place to some other animal better adapted to face the fate that closes in on mankind.' In the final pages of the pamphlet, his trump of the last judgement has changed into the question: Can civiliza-tion be saved?

'But my own temperament makes it unavoidable for me to doubt that there will not be that small minority who will see life out to its inevitable end.'[12]

All the same, the pamphlet must be considered the most pessimistic single utterance in modern literature, together with T. S. Eliot's 'Hollow Men'. And Eliot's despair was essentially religious; we should be tempted to assume that Wells's despair is religious too, if it were not for his insistence that he is speak-ing of a scientific fact, an objective reality.

It is not surprising that the work received scant attention from Wells's contemporaries: to make its conclusions credible it would need the formidable dialectical apparatus of Schopen-hauer's *Welt als Wille und Vorstellung* or Spengler's *Decline of the West*. I have heard it described by a writer-contemporary of

Wells as 'an outburst of peevishness at a world that refused to accept him as its Messiah'. Certainly, if we accept it on the level on which he wrote it—acquiescing to every sentence—we feel the stirring of problems that seem to return into themselves. Why did he write it if he can hold out no hope of salvation? If the conclusions he has reached negate his own past life, and the possible futures of all the human race, where do we go from there? Wells's thesis is that we have never been going anywhere—we have been carried along by our delusions, believing that any movement is better than none. Whereas the truth is that the reverse, *no movement*, is the final answer, the answer to the question: What will men *do* when they see things as they are?

It is a long way from Mr. Polly's discovery (If you don't like your life you can change it) to: There is no way out or round or through. Barbusse has gone half-way, with his, Truth, what do they mean by it?, which has as a corollary, Change, what difference does it make? Wells has gone the whole distance, and landed us on the doorstep of the Existentialist problem: Must thought negate life?

Before we pass on to this new aspect of the Outsider's problem, there is a further point of comparison between Barbusse and Wells that deserves comment. Barbusse's hero is an Outsider when we meet him; probably he was always an Outsider. Wells was very definitely an Insider most of his life. Tirelessly he performed his duty to society, gave it good advice upon how to better itself. He was the scientific spirit incarnate: reviewing the history of the life and drawing conclusions, reviewing economics and social history, political and religious history; a descendant of the French Encyclopedists who never ceased to compile and summarize. From him: Truth, what do they mean by it? would have elicited a compendious review of all the ideas of truth in the history of the seven civilizations. There is something so shocking in such a man's becoming an Outsider that we feel inclined to look for physical causes for the change: Wells was a sick, a tired man, when he wrote *Mind at the End of Its Tether*. May we not accept this as the whole cause and moving force behind the pamphlet?

Unfortunately, no. Wells declared his conclusions to be objective; if that is so, then to say he was sick when he wrote them down means no more than to say he was wearing a dressing-gown and slippers. It is our business to judge whether the world *can* be seen in such a way that Wells's conclusions are inevitable; if so, to decide whether such a way of looking at things is truer, more valid, more objective, than our usual way of seeing. Even if we decide in advance that the answer is No, there may be much to learn from the exercise of changing our viewpoint.

*   *   *

The Outsider's claim amounts to the same thing as Wells's hero's in *The Country of the Blind*: that he is the one man able to see. To the objection that he is unhealthy and neurotic, he replies: 'In the country of the blind, the one-eyed man is king.' His case, in fact, is that he is the one man who knows he is sick in a civilization that doesn't know it is sick. Certain Outsiders we shall consider later would go even further and declare that it is human nature that is sick, and the Outsider is the man who faces that unpleasant fact. These need not concern us yet; for the moment we have a *negative position* which the Outsider declares to be the essence of the world as he sees it. 'Truth, what do they mean by it.' 'There is no way out, or round, or through.' And it is to this we must turn our attention.

When Barbusse made his hero ask the first question, he was almost certainly unaware that he was paraphrasing the central problem of a Danish philosopher who had died in 1855 in Copenhagen. Søren Kierkegaard had also decided that philosophic discussion was altogether meaningless, and his reason was Wells's reason: Reality negates it. Or, as Kierkegaard put it, existence negates it. Kierkegaard's attack was directed in particular against the German metaphysician Hegel, who had (rather like Wells) been trying to 'justify the ways of God to man' by talking about the goal of history and man's place in space and time. Kierkegaard was a deeply religious soul for whom all this was unutterably shallow. He declared: Put me in a System and you negate me—I am not just a mathematical symbol—I *am*.

Now obviously, such a denial that logic and scientific analysis can lead to truth has curious consequences. Our science is built on the assumption that a statement like 'All bodies fall at thirty-two feet per second in the earth's gravitational field' has a definite meaning. But if you deny the ultimate validity of logic, it becomes nonsensical. And if you don't deny logic, it is difficult, thinking along these lines, to pull up short of Wells and John Stuart Mill. That is why Kierkegaard phrases it: Is an Existentialist System possible; or, to put it in another way, Can one live a philosophy without negating either the life or the philosophy? Kierkegaard's conclusion was No, but one can live a religion without negating life or religion. We need not pause here over the reasoning that led him to this conclusion (readers interested enough can consult the *Unscientific Postscript*). What is worth noticing at this point is that his affirmation of Christian values did not prevent him from violently attacking the Christian Church on the grounds that it had solved the problem of living its religion by cutting off its arms and legs to make it fit life. It is also an amusing point that the other great Existentialist philosopher of the nineteenth century, Frederick Nietzsche, attacked the Christian church on the opposite grounds of its having solved the problem by chopping down life to fit the Christian religion. Now, both Kierkegaard and Nietzsche were trained thinkers, and both took a certain pride in stating that they were Outsiders. It follows that we should find in their works a skilled defence of the Outsider and his position. And this in fact is what we do find.

Nietszche and Kierkegaard evolved a philosophy that started from the Outsider; nowadays, we use Kierkegaard's phrase in speaking of it, and call it Existentialism. When, in the nineteen-twenties, Kierkegaard was re-published in German, he was taken up by the professors, who discarded his religious conclusions, and used his methods of analysis to construct the so-called *Existenzphilosophie*. In doing so, they removed the emphasis from the Outsider and threw it back again on to Hegelian metaphysics. Later, in France, Existentialism was popularized by the work of Jean-Paul Sartre and Albert Camus, who once more restored emphasis to the Outsider, and finally arrived at their own conclusions upon the question of how to live a philosophy: Sartre in his 'doctrine of commitment' (which we shall touch upon later) and Camus with the belief: Remain an Outsider. We must examine each of these in turn.

* * *

In his early novel, *La Nausée*, Sartre skilfully synthesizes all the points we have already considered in connexion with Wells and Barbusse: the unreality, the rejection of people and civilized standards, and, finally, the 'cinema sheet' of naked existence, with 'no way out or round or through'.

La Nausée purports to be the journal of an historian named Roquentin: not a full-fledged scientific historian like Wells, but a literary historian who is engaged in unearthing the life of a shifty diplomat-politician named Rollebon. Roquentin lives alone in a Hotel in Le Havre. His life would be a quiet record of research, conversations in the library, sexual intercourse with the café *patronne*: 'I live alone, entirely alone; I never speak to anyone, never; I receive nothing, I give nothing. . . .'

But a series of revelations disturb him. He stands on the beach and picks up a flat stone to skim on the sea, and suddenly . . . 'I saw something which disgusted me; I no longer know whether it was the stone or the sea.' He drops the stone and walks off.[13]

Roquentin's journal is an attempt to objectify what is happening to him. He searches his memory, examines his past. There was something that happened in Indo-China; a colleague had asked him to join an archaeological mission to Bengal; he was about to accept—

> . . . when suddenly I woke up from a six-year slumber. . . .
> I couldn't understand why I was in Indo-China. What was I
> doing there? Why was I talking to these people? Why was
> I dressed so oddly? . . . Before me, posed with a sort of
> indolence, was a voluminous, insipid idea. I did not see
> clearly what it was, but it sickened me so much I couldn't
> look at it.[14]

Certainly something is happening. There is his ordinary life, with its assumptions of meaning, purpose, usefulness. And there are these revelations, or, rather, these attacks of nausea, that knock the bottom out of his ordinary life. The reason is not far to seek. He is too acute and honest an observer. Like Wells, he asks of everything: to what will this lead? He never ceases to notice things. Of the café *patron*, he comments: 'When his place empties, his head empties too.' The lives of these people are contingent on events. If things stopped happening to them, they would stop being. Worse still are the *salauds* whose pictures he can look at in the town's art gallery, these eminent public men, so sure of themselves, so sure that life is theirs and their existence is necessary to it. And Roquentin's criticism is turning back on himself; he too has accepted meanings where he now recognizes there were none. He too is dependent on events.

In a crowded café, he is afraid to look at a glass of beer. 'But I can't explain what I see. To anyone. There: I am quietly slipping into the water's depths, towards fear.'[15]

A few days later, again, he describes in detail the circumstances of an attack of the nausea. This time it is the braces of the café *patron* that become the focus of the sickness. Now we observe that the nausea seems to emphasize the sordidness of Roquentin's surroundings. (Sartre has gone further than any previous writer in emphasizing 'darkness and dirt'; neither Joyce nor Dostoevsky give the same sensation of the mind being trapped in physical filth.) Roquentin is overwhelmed by it, a spiritual counterpart of violent physical retching.

... the nausea is not *inside* me; I feel it *out there*, in the wall, in the suspenders; everywhere around me. It makes itself one with the café; I am the one who is within it.[16]

Like Wells, Roquentin insists on the objective nature of the revelation.

Somebody puts on a record; it is the voice of a Negro woman singing 'Some of These Days'. The nausea disappears as he listens:

When the voice was heard in the silence I felt my body harden and the nausea vanish; suddenly it was almost unbearable to become so hard, so brilliant.... I am *in* the music. Globes of fire turn in the mirrors, encircled by rings of smoke.[17]

There is no need to analyse this experience; it is the old, familiar aesthetic experience; art giving order and logic to chaos.

I am touched; I feel my body at rest like a precision machine. I have had real adventures. I can recapture no detail, but I perceive the rigorous succession of events. I

have crossed seas, left cities behind me, followed the course
of rivers or plunged into forests, always making my way
towards other cities. I have had women; I have fought with
men, and never was I able to turn back any more than a
record can be reversed.

Works of art cannot affect him. Art is thought, and thought
only gives the world an appearance of order to anyone weak
enough to be convinced by its show. Only something as
instinctively rhythmic as the blues can give him a sense of
order that doesn't seem false. But even that may be only a
temporary refuge; deeper nervous exhaustion would cause the
collapse of the sense of order, even in 'Some of These Days'.
   In the Journal, we watch the breaking-down of all Roquentin's values. Exhaustion limits him more and more to the
present, the here-now. The work of memory, which gives
events sequence and coherence, is failing, leaving him more
and more dependent for meaning on what he can see and touch.
It is Hume's scepticism becoming instinctive, all-destroying. All
he can see and touch is unrecognizable, unaided by memory;
like a photograph of a familiar object taken from an unfamiliar
angle. He looks at a seat, and fails to recognize it: 'I murmur:
It's a seat, but the word stays on my lips. It refuses to go and
put itself on the thing. . . . Things are divorced from their
names. They are there, grotesque, stubborn, huge, and it
seems ridiculous to call them seats, or to say anything at all
about them. I am in the midst of things—nameless things.'[18]
   In the park, the full nature of the revelation comes to him as
he stares at the roots of a chestnut tree:

   I couldn't remember it was a root any more. The words
   had vanished, and with them, the significance of things, their
   methods of use, and the feeble points of reference men have
   traced on their surface. I was sitting . . . before this knotty
   mass, entirely beastly, which frightened me. . . . It left me
   breathless. Never, until these last few days, had I understood
   the meaning of *existence*. I was like the others. . . . I said with
   them: The ocean *is* green, that white speck up there *is*
   a seagull, but I didn't feel that it existed. . . . And then
   suddenly existence had unveiled itself. It had lost the look
   of an abstract category; it was the very paste of things; this

root was kneaded into existence. . . . These objects, they inconvenienced me; I would have liked them to exist less imposingly, more dryly, in a more abstract way. . . .[19]

He has reached the rock bottom of self-contempt; even things negate him. We are all familiar enough with his experience in the face of other human beings; a personality or a conviction can impose itself in spite of resistance; even the city itself, the confusion of traffic and human beings in Regent Street, can overwhelm a weak personality and make it feel insignificant. Roquentin feels insignificant before things. Without the meaning his Will would normally impose on it, his existence is absurd. Causality—Hume's bugbear—has collapsed; consequently *there are no adventures*. The biography of Rollebon would have been another venture of 'bad faith', for it would have imposed a *necessity* on Rollebon's life that was not really there; the events didn't really cohere and follow one another like a story; only blindness to the fact of raw, naked existence could ever produce the illusion that they did.

What then? Is there no causality, no possible meaning? Sartre summarizes life: '*L'homme est un passion inutile.*' There is no choice, in Roquentin's reckoning; there is only being useless and knowing it and being useless and not knowing it.

Yet Roquentin had had his glimpse of meaning and order; in 'Some of These Days'. There was meaning, causation, one note following inevitably on another. Roquentin wonders: why shouldn't he create something like that; something rhythmic, purposive—a novel, perhaps, that men could read later and feel: There was an attempt to bring order into chaos? He will leave Havre and the life of Rollebon; there *must* be another way of living that is not futile. The Journal comes to an end on this note.

*   *   *

Roquentin lives like Barbusse's hero; his room is almost the limit of his consciousness. But he has gone further and deeper than the hole-in-the-wall man. His attitude has reached the dead-end of Wells; 'Man is a useless passion': that could be taken as a summary of *Mind at the End of Its Tether*. Complete denial, as in Eliot's 'Hollow Men': We are the hollow men, we are the *salauds*. Roquentin is in the position of the hero of

The Country of the Blind. He alone is aware of the truth, and if all men were aware of it, there would be an end of life. In the country of the blind, the one-eyed man is king. But his kingship is kingship over nothing. It brings no powers and privileges, only loss of faith and exhaustion of the power to act. Its world is a world without values.

This is the position that Barbusse's Outsider has brought us to. It was already explicit in that desire that stirred as he saw the swaying dresses of the women; for what he wanted was not sexual intercourse, but some indefinable freedom, of which the women, with their veiled and hidden nakedness, are a symbol. Sexual desire was there, but not alone; aggravated, blown-up like a balloon, by a resentment that stirred in revolt against the bewilderment of hurrying Paris with its well-dressed women. 'Yet in spite of this I desire some compensation.' In spite of the civilization that has impressed his insignificance on him until he is certain that 'he has nothing and he deserves nothing', in spite of this he feels a right to . . . to what? Freedom? It is a misused word. We examine *L'Enfer* in vain for a definition of it. Sartre and Wells have decided that man is never free; he is simply too stupid to recognize this. Then to what precisely is it that the Outsider has an inalienable right?

The question must take us into a new field: of Outsiders who have had some insight into the nature of freedom.

CHAPTER TWO

WORLD WITHOUT VALUES

THE OUTSIDER TENDS to express himself in Existentialist terms. He is not very concerned with the distinction between body and spirit, or man and nature; these ideas produce theological thinking and philosophy; he rejects both. For him, the only important distinction is between being and nothingness. Barbusse's hero: 'Death, that is the most important of all ideas.'

Barbusse and Wells represent two different approaches to the problem. Barbusse's approach can be called the 'empirical'. His hero is not a thinker; he accepts *living*; it is its values he cannot accept. Wells goes much further in rejection; his conclusions have been pushed to nihilism; his approach is, like Hume's, rationalist.

In Roquentin's case, the conclusions are reached through an interaction of reason and experience. Again, it is the rational element that pushes him into nihilism; his only 'glimmer of salvation' comes from a level of experience untouched by discursive thought, from a Negro woman singing 'Some of These Days'. Reason leads into an impasse. If a solution exists, it must be sought, not in reasoning, but in examination of experience. We must keep in mind the logical possibility that a solution may not exist. In any case, it is the empirical approach that must be examined now.

Albert Camus's Outsider is even more of an empiricist than Barbusse's. He thinks even less; he has 'no genius, no unusual feelings to bestow'; in fact, he has hardly any feelings at all.

'Mother died today. Or maybe yesterday. I can't be sure.'[1]

This tone of indifference persists throughout the novel *L'Etranger*. Like *L'Enfer* and *La Nausée*, it observes the convention that the hero is keeping a diary. Meursault is an Algerian. The first page establishes his character. When he asks his employer for time off to attend his mother's funeral, he says:

'Sorry, sir, but it isn't my fault, you know.'
Afterwards it struck me that I needn't have said that . . .
it was up to him to express his sympathy and so forth.[2]

If Meursault had 'felt' his mother's death he wouldn't have apologized. As the reader soon discovers, he feels very little.

This is not to say that he is disillusioned or world-weary. His type of light-headedness bears more relation to P. G. Wodehouse's 'Young men in spats'. He enjoys eating and drinking, sunbathing, going to the cinema. He lives in the present. He tells of his mother's funeral, objectively but unfeelingly; it exhausted him because he had to sit up all night, but did not otherwise affect him. The next day he goes swimming and begins an affair with a girl. In half a page he outlines the development of the relation; they go to see a comic film, then return to his room and sleep together. In the morning, after she has gone: 'I slept till ten. Then I stayed in bed until noon, smoking cigarettes.'[3]

This is the atmosphere of Eliot's 'Waste Land':

I read much of the night and go south in the winter.

What surprises us, by comparison, is the lack of moral disapproval in Camus's book; there is no suggestion that the author intends us to condemn Meursault as a futile idler.

The unusual quality about Meursault is his honesty. The girl asks him to marry her and he promptly agrees:

Then she asked me again if I loved her; I replied, much as before, that her question meant nothing or next to nothing, but I supposed I didn't.[4]

This honesty springs out of indifference to issues of feeling; he does not attach importance to anything; why should he lie?

Meursault becomes friendly with a pimp, and finds himself involved in a feud between the pimp and an Arab. A day spent lounging on the beach culminates in the shooting of the Arab by Meursault. It was self-defence, but the Arab was unarmed, and there were no witnesses. Meursault finds himself on trial for murder.

And it is now that his strange qualities as an Outsider are against him. A man who has committed a murder should at least show some interest in what he has done; his best chance of acquittal lies in his weeping, protesting, showing himself overwhelmed by this terrible accident. But from the beginning,

Meursault's indifference disconcerts his questioners. They can only put it down to callousness. And then there was the affair of the funeral. Why was he so unaffected by his mother's death? Didn't he love her? Again his honesty is against him:

> I could say quite truthfully that I'd been fond of my mother, but that didn't mean much.

The magistrate is a humane and religious man who would be only too happy to find grounds for acquitting Meursault, for 'There is more joy over one sinner that repenteth. . . .' With tears in his eyes, he shows Meursault a crucifix and exhorts him to repent. But Meursault looks on with mild surprise. All this is meaningless. It is so completely beside the point. Repent of what?

Finally Meursault is tried. Now Camus no longer bothers to disguise the irony. Meursault, as innocent as Mr. Pickwick, hears the prosecutor summing up in a deeply moved voice:

> 'Gentlemen of the jury, I would have you note that, on the day after his mother's funeral, that man was visiting a swimming pool, starting a liaison with a girl and going to see a comic film. That is all I wish to say.'[6]

That is all he needs to say, for Meursault is condemned to death.

In his cell, the chaplain visits him, with more exhortations to repent. Suddenly, Meursault can stand the stupidity no longer; he seizes the priest by the collar and pours out his irritation:

> He was so cocksure, you see. Yet not one of his certainties was worth one strand of a woman's hair.
>
> . . . Nothing, nothing had the least importance, and I knew quite well why. . . . From the dark horizon of my future, a sort of slow, persistent breeze had been blowing towards me . . . and on its way, that breeze had levelled out all the ideas people had tried to foist on me *in the equally unreal years I was then living through.*
>
> . . . all alike would be condemned to die one day; his turn too would come like the others. And what difference did it make if, after being charged with murder, he were executed

because he didn't weep at his mother's funeral, since it all
came to the same thing in the end.'⁶ [Italics mine.]

His last reflections, as he falls asleep on the eve of his execution, bring him a sort of insight:

> With death so near, mother must have felt like someone on
> the brink of freedom, ready to start life again. . . . And I too
> felt ready to start life again. It was as if this great rush of
> anger had washed me clean, emptied me of hope, and,
> gazing up at the dark sky. . . . I laid my heart open to the
> benign indifference of the universe. To feel it so like myself . . .
> made me realize I had been happy, that I was happy still.
> For all to be accomplished, for me to feel less lonely, all that
> remained to hope was that, on the day of my execution
> there should be a huge crowd of spectators, and that they
> should greet me with howls of execration.⁷

The last pages of the novel have revealed Meursault's
secret; the reason for his indifference is *his sense of unreality*.
All his life he has lived with the same sense as Roquentin:
All this is unreal. But the sense of unreality doesn't torment
him, as it tormented the Outsiders of our first chapter. He
accepts life; sunlight, food, girls' bodies; he also accepts the
unreality. It is the trial that pulls him up, 'with a brutal
thunderclap of Halt' (Wells's phrase). The prospect of death
has *wakened him up*, thereby serving the same function as
Roquentin's nausea. It has, admittedly, wakened him up too
late as far as he is concerned. But at least it has given him a
notion of the meaning of freedom. Freedom is release from
unreality. 'I had been happy and I was happy still', but where
is the point in being happy if the happiness is hidden from the
consciousness by a heavy grime of unreality?

Sartre's later formulation of Meursault's realization is:
'Freedom is terror.' He observes, in his *Confederation de la Silence*,
that it was during the war, working in the Underground
resistance, in constant danger of betrayal and death, that he
felt most free and alive. Obviously, freedom is not simply
being allowed to do what you like; it is *intensity of will*, and it
appears under any circumstances that limit man and arouse
his will to more life.

The reader cannot fail to be struck by the similarity between Camus's work and Franz Kafka's. In Kafka, the sense of unreality is conveyed by deliberately using a dream-technique. In *The Metamorphosis* the hero awakens one morning to find himself changed into a gigantic beetle; in *The Trial* he is arrested and finally executed without knowing why. Destiny seems to have struck with the question: If you think life is unreal, how about *this*? Its imperative seems to be: Claim your freedom, *or else* . . . For the men who fail to claim their freedom there is the sudden catastrophe, the nausea, the trial and execution, the slipping to a lower form of life. Kafka's *Metamorphosis* would be a perfectly commonsense parable to a Tibetan Buddhist.

Camus's *L'Etranger* reminds us of another modern writer who has dealt with the problem of freedom, Ernest Hemingway. The parallel that *L'Etranger* brings to mind is the short story 'Soldier's Home', but comparison of the two makes it apparent that all of Hemingway's work has its relevance to the problem of the Existentialist Outsider. Hemingway's contribution is worth examining at length at this point.

'Soldier's Home' deals with an American soldier who was returned from the war some time in late 1919. Krebs had been to a Methodist college before he joined up; when he comes back home, it is to realize that he has lost contact with his family and his former self. No one wants to hear about his war experiences—not the true stories, anyway.

A distaste for everything that had happened to him in the war set in, because of the lies he has told. All the times that had been able to make him feel cool and clear inside him when he thought about them; the times when he had done the one thing, the only thing for a man to do, easily and naturally, when he might have done something else, now lost their cool, valuable quality, and then were lost themselves.[8]

At home, a kind of apathy makes him spend his days reading or playing pool. He would like a girl, but cannot overcome the apathy enough to go to the trouble of finding one. One morning his mother talks to him during breakfast:

'God has some work for everyone to do,' his mother said. 'There can be no idle hands in his kingdom.'

This sort of thing is notoriously meaningless to the Outsider. Krebs tells her:

'I'm not in his kingdom.'
'We are all of us in his kingdom.'
Krebs felt embarrassed and resentful, as always.

His mother asks him:

'Don't you love your mother, dear boy?'
'No,' said Krebs.
His mother looked at him across the table. Her eyes were shiny. She started crying.
'I don't love anybody,' Krebs said.
It wasn't any good. He couldn't tell her; he couldn't make her see it. It was silly to have said it. . . .
'I didn't mean it,' he said. 'I was just angry at something. I didn't mean I didn't love you.' . . .
'I'm your mother,' she said. 'I held you next to my heart when you were a tiny baby.'
Krebs felt sick and vaguely nauseated.⁹

She insists on their kneeling together to pray. He submits, but cannot pray when she asks him to. Afterwards he reflects:

He had tried to keep his life from being complicated. Still, none of it had touched him. He had felt sorry for his mother and she had made him lie about it. He would go to Kansas City and get a job there. . . .

Krebs's similarity to Camus's Meursault is immediately striking. With the difference that Krebs's state of mind is the result of specific experiences, while Meursault's is natural to him, Krebs and Meursault would be almost interchangeable in their two stories. The difference is important though. Meursault reached a state of being 'cool and clear inside' on the eve of his execution; it came too late. Krebs had been through experiences during the war that had given him the sense of freedom; now, back in his home town, he knows that this way of life is *not* freedom. The times when he has done 'the one thing, the only thing for a man to do, easily and naturally' has given him a glimpse of meaning, of a part of himself that is not contented with the trivial and unheroic. *Freedom lies in finding a course of action that gives expression to that part of him.*

This is the theme of a great deal of Hemingway's early work. The first novel, *The Sun also Rises* (the title taken from the Book of Ecclesiastes) has a stifling atmosphere of the trivial and unheroic. The hero, Jake Barnes, has been through the war, and a serious wound in the genitals has made him incapable of consummating sexual union with a woman. The wound is symbolic of the whole tragedy of unrealized freedom. The woman he loves has to take other men for physical satisfaction. Paris of the nineteen-twenties is a futile round of drinking and dancing; the futile people of the 'Waste Land': 'I see crowds of people walking around in a ring.' Hemingway does not turn to the past, to the Biblical prophets or Dante's *Commedia*, for meaning. He is much less an intellectual than Eliot. He finds his memories of the heroic in his own past; in the war, in hunting and fishing in the Michigan backwoods. He finds it in the bullfighter who risks his life every day. But certainly he would agree with Sartre that 'Freedom is terror'; or possibly: Freedom is crisis. Jake Barnes goes on a fishing trip to Spain, and sees the running of the bulls, and in spite of his unhappy love affair, he is not too discontented with life. As with Meursault the pleasures of eating and drinking and sunlight make up for a great deal. Hemingway's answer to the indictment of Eliot's 'Waste Land' is: Seek out the heroic. Jake Barnes says in *The Sun also Rises* 'Nobody ever lived their life all the way up except bull-fighters.'[10] The facts of Hemingway's life fill in the picture that his work outlines. Everything he writes has a more or less immediate bearing on his own experience. The early stories ('In Our Time') deal with his childhood in the Michigan backwoods, and with later incidents in the war. The hero, Nick Adams, goes fishing or ski-ing or canoeing, or possesses a little Indian girl on a carpet of pine needles, and there is no shadow on his world; he reads Maurice Hewlett, G. K. Chesterton and Mark Twain. Everything is fun. The war makes the difference. When he returns from it, the notion of evil has entered his life, the idea of a fundamental disharmony that cannot be evaded in sport or whoring. In various stories and novels, Hemingway gives different versions of how the 'fall' took place. The voice telling the stories is always personal enough to excuse us for

regarding them as all part of the same legend. Nick Adams is
wounded and shell-shocked. Propped up against a wall in a
retreat, he comments: 'Senta, Rinaldi, senta. You and me, we've
made our separate peace.' The nameless hero of 'A Very Short
Story' has a love affair with a nurse in hospital in Padua; later,
when she betrays him, he contracts gonorrhoea from a shop-
girl in Chicago. Jake Barnes was made sexually impotent.
Frederick Henry of *A Farewell to Arms* has the love affair with
the nurse that was sketched in 'A Very Short Story', but loses
her when she dies in childbirth. After the publication of *A
Farewell to Arms* in 1929, Hemingway's work takes on the
nihilistic colouring of Wells's *Mind at the End of Its Tether*;
the stifling feeling of thought turning on itself.

After the war, Hemingway found himself in somewhat the
same position as Corporal Krebs, with the past dead on his
hands, the future a possible 'posthumous existence'. The early
stories begin the attempt to reconstruct the past; the Nick
Adams cycle are his Garden of Eden legend. Then follows the
major attempt at reconstruction, *A Farewell to Arms*. This is
Hemingway's most satisfying single performance; more than
anything before, it conveys a sense of warmth, of excitement in
reliving a fragment of *temps perdu*. In the novels that followed,
the early spring quality was lost; they seem cold in comparison. *A Farewell to Arms* opens with a skilful evocation of the
sense of meaninglessness, of confusion, of the soldier in a strange
country. Drinking in cafés 'when the room whirled and you
needed to look at the wall to make it stop' and 'Nights in bed,
drunk, when you knew that was all there was, and the strange
excitement of waking and not knowing who it was with you,
and the world all unreal in the dark. . . .'[11] And when Frederick
Henry starts an affair with a nurse, it is all happening at three
removes from him:

> 'You did say you loved me, didn't you?'
> 'Yes,' I lied, 'I love you.' I had not said it before.[12]

He is in the same position as Meursault and Krebs. Love is
impossible when there is a prevailing sense of unreality. It is
only later, when he lies wounded in the hospital in Milan, and
the nurse is posted there too, that he suddenly realizes he loves
her. The unreality is dispersed; the atmosphere of *L'Etranger*

is replaced by the atmosphere of a strange modern *Tristan und Isolde*. (Hemingway, in point of fact, liked to refer to it as his *Romeo and Juliet*.) It is a masterly achievement, beyond comparison in its kind with anything else in modern letters. Scene after scene has a poignant vividness; the climax, with Catherine's death in childbirth, is as emotionally exhausting as the last act of *Tristan*.

Hemingway had taken a firm grip on those experiences that made him feel 'cool and clear inside', and the novel has the power of conveying the reader into the sensation spoken of by Sartre: I am touched: I feel my body at rest like a precision machine.

The subsequent stages in Hemingway's work are far less satisfying. With this major evocation of the war behind him, the artistic problem was then how to go forward from such a level of seriousness and intensity. His various solutions—big-game hunting, deep-sea fishing and, later, rushing off to Spain as soon as the civil war broke out—betray his failure to get at the roots of the problem. His formulae for the later books would seem to have been arrived at by considering the elements that he supposed made the early books an artistic success—realism, violence, sex, war—and repeating them with variations. The elements that give the early books their unique atmosphere, the blending of a sort of religious despair with a rudimentary nature mysticism, have disappeared, and have been replaced by elements that could be found in half a dozen other American writers or, indeed, Soviet Russian 'historical realists'.

In spite of this, some of the later work succeeds in taking the Outsider problems a stage beyond Meursault and Corporal Krebs. For Frederick Henry, the sense of unreality is dispersed by the physical hardships of the war, and then by his falling in love with Catherine Barkely. (It is to be noted that Catherine Barkely was in love with Henry long before he realized he was in love with her; the woman is always more instinctively well-adjusted, less susceptible to the abstract, than the man.) The feeling that the final Negative gets the last word, Catherine's death, is a maturer realization than the feeling that nothing matters.

The short stories after 1930 often contain sentences that can be taken as fragments of the Hemingway Credo; there is, to begin with, Frederick Henry when Catherine is dying:

> Now Catherine would die. That was what you did. You
> died. You did not know what it was all about. You never had
> time to learn . . . they killed you in the end. You could
> count on that. Stay around and they would kill you.[13]

Or the Major of 'In Another Country', whose wife has
died:

> A man must not marry. . . . If he is to lose everything, he
> should not place himself in a position to lose that. . . . *He
> should find things he cannot lose.*[14]

Or the reflections of the heartless cripple in 'The Gambler,
the Nun and the Radio':

> Religion is the opium of the people . . . and now economics
> is the opium of the people, along with patriotism. . . . What
> about sexual intercourse, was that an opium of the people?
> But drink was a sovereign opium, oh, an excellent opium. . . .
> Although some people prefer the radio, another opium of the
> people.[15]

There is the old waiter of 'A Clean, Well-lighted Place', who
prays: 'Hail nothing, full of nothing, nothing is with thee.'
Here the encounter with death has become an encounter with
the meaninglessness of life, an encounter with nothingness.
The only value that remains is courage; Santiago in *The Old
Man and the Sea* with his 'A man can be destroyed but not
defeated'. And the value of courage is doubtful. Death negates it,
and the causes that inspire it are usually 'opium of the people'.
There is a short story written before 1933 that expresses
Hemingway's *Weltanschauung* briefly. This is the unsuccessful
experiment in style called 'The Natural History of the Dead'.
He opens by quoting Mungo Park's argument for 'a divinity
that shapes our ends': how, when fainting from thirst in the
desert, he noticed a small moss flower and reflected: 'Can that
Being who made, watered and brought to perfection . . . a
thing that appears so unimportant, look with unconcern upon
the suffering of creatures made in his own image?' Encouraged

by this thought, he travelled on, and soon found water. Hemingway asks: 'Can any branch of Natural History be studied without increasing that faith, love and hope which we also, every one of us, need in our journey through the wilderness of life? Let us see therefore what inspiration we may derive from the dead.'[16]

The story then becomes a ponderously ironic account of war experiences. He recalls the mules at Smyrna, their legs broken, pushed into the shallow water to drown: ... 'Called for a Goya to depict them. Although, speaking literally, one can hardly say they called for a Goya, since there has only been one Goya, long dead, and it is extremely doubtful if these animals, were they able to call, would call for pictorial representation of their plight, but more likely would, if they were articulate, call for someone to alleviate their condition.'[17]

The examples Hemingway selects for his 'field of observation' are all violent and bloody:

The first thing you found about the dead was that, hit quickly enough, they died like animals. . . .
I do not know, but most men die like animals, not men.[18]

Speaking of natural death, he comments: 'So now I want to see the death of any so-called humanist . . . and see the noble exits they make.'

'The Natural History of the Dead' is Hemingway's clearest exposition of his Existentialist position, and the key sentence, 'most men die like animals, not men', is his answer to the humanist notion of the perfectibility of man. He cannot believe in the God of Bishop Butler's or Paley's arguments, because the idea looks thin against the raw facts of existence. The nearest approach to religious ideals in his work is the sentence 'He should find things he cannot lose'. This idea is not followed up, or rather, is followed up by a protracted demonstration that there is nothing that man cannot lose. This doesn't mean that life is of no value; on the contrary, life is the only value; it is ideas that are valueless.

*   *   *

At first sight, Hemingway's contribution to the Outsider would seem to be completely negative. Closer examination shows a great many positive qualities; there is honesty, and intense love of all natural things. The early work especially seems to be Hemingway's own *Recherche de Temps Perdu*, and frequently the reader is picked up in a rush of excitement that the search is really leading somewhere. It is after 1930 that the direction seems to have been lost, the time of Hemingway's great commercial success, when he had become a public figure and something of a legend. The stoicism of *A Farewell to Arms* should have led to something, and it didn't. In none of the novels after 1929 do we feel ourselves in the hands of Hemingway the supremely great artist. And Hemingway the thinker, who had so far sifted and selected his material to form a pattern of belief, has disappeared almost entirely.

Perhaps Hemingway's susceptibility to success is not entirely to blame. The problem is difficult enough. In the whole of *L'Etre et le Néant* Sartre says little more than Hemingway in *A Farewell to Arms*. Subsequently, Sartre, for all his intellectual equipment, has failed to advance to a satisfyingly positive position. His philosophy of 'commitment', which is only to say that, since all roads lead nowhere, it's as well to choose any of them and throw all the energy into it, was anticipated by Hemingway in Henry's finding that the feeling of unreality disappears as soon as he plunges into the fighting.

Compared with Sartre, neither Hemingway nor Camus is a penetrating thinker. Camus's *Mythe de Sisyphe* enlarges on the conclusions of the last pages of *L'Etranger*, and concludes that freedom can be most nearly realized facing death: a suicide or a condemned man can know it; for the living, active man it is almost an impossibility. In the later book, *L'Homme Revolté*, he studies the case of the revolt against society, in men like de Sade and Byron, and then examines the attempt of various social ideologies to realize the rebel's ideal of freedom. It would be an impossibility to advance from *L'Etranger* and *Le Myth de Sisyphe* to acceptance of a sociological answer to the problem of man's freedom; and Camus faces this conclusion squarely at the end of *L'Homme Revolté*. In this matter he clashed violently with Sartre, whose theory of commitment or 'engagement' had led him to embrace a modified communism; thereafter Sartre and Camus, once comrades in Existentialism, went their separate ways.

Hemingway had never thought in terms of a social answer,

or in fact, of any answer except that of his semi-stoic philosophy. This has been the most constant complaint of Marxist critics against Hemingway.

Our foregoing considerations have made it clear, however, that the question of freedom is *not* a social problem. It may be possible to dismiss Barbusse's Outsider as a case of social maladjustment; it may be possible to dismiss Wells's pamphlet as a case for a psychiatrist. But the problem of *La Nausée* is unattackable except with metaphysical terminology, and Camus and Hemingway tend to fall into very near-religious terms. This is a point that I must return to later in the chapter, after further consideration of our terms: freedom and un-reality.

Freedom posits free-will; that is self-evident. But Will can only operate when there is first a motive. No motive, no willing. But motive is a matter of *belief*; you would not want to do anything unless you believed it possible and meaningful. And belief must be belief in the *existence* of something; that is to say, it concerns what is *real*. So ultimately, freedom depends upon the real. The Outsider's sense of unreality cuts off his freedom at the root. It is as impossible to exercise freedom in an unreal world as it is to jump while you are falling.

*   *   *

For an enlargement of the position established by Camus and Hemingway regarding human freedom, it is necessary to turn to a neglected play of the 1920's, Harley Granville-Barker's *Secret Life*. A quotation from George Sampson's *Concise Cambridge History of English Literature* will make clear its relevance at this stage:

[The Secret Life] is a puzzling, disturbing post-war play [that] shows us the intellectual world reduced to spiritual nihilism. There is no clear centre of dramatic interest. The characters just come and go, and what 'love interest' there is seems entirely gratuitous. The dialogue is sometimes normally dramatic, sometimes philosophically enigmatic, as if the speakers had no other purpose than to ask riddles to which there can be no answer. Perhaps in no other volume is there so complete a revelation of the spiritual bankruptcy produced by the war.[19]

The background of the play is the post-war party politics of
the Liberal party. The interest centres around two main
characters, the middle-aged ex-politician Evan Strowde, and
Oliver Gauntlett, his natural son, who has returned from the
war minus an arm. What plot the play has can easily be
outlined. Before the war, Strowde had been in politics. He
had quarrelled with the party leader and resigned. Now the
party wants him back.

Oliver Gauntlett has been invalided from the war, gone into
the City, and started to make a business career. When he is
arrested at an anarchist meeting, he is glad to make the
scandal an excuse for escaping from the futility of the City.
It is Evan Strowde who puzzles him most. (At the beginning of
the play he is not aware that Strowde is his father.) Strowde's
powerful intellect and great will-power should have made him a
success in some field. Oliver wants to know why he has failed.

The play opens with a curious scene at Strowde's house by
the sea; Strowde and a group of old schoolfriends have gathered
to perform *Tristan und Isolde* on the piano, singing the parts
themselves. The performance over, they talk reminiscently of
their younger days, and Salomons states his creed as a practical
politician:

> Salomons: Never be carried off on crusades you can't
> finance. . . . Don't, for one moment, let art and religion and
> patriotism persuade you that you mean more than you do.
> Stand by Jerusalem when it comes to stoning the prophets.
> I must be off.
> Eleanor: Before you're answered?
> Salomons: Answers are echoes.[20]

Joan Westbury, with whom Strowde had had a love affair
sometime long before the war—who represents for him the
clearest vision of certainty that he ever achieved—leans on the
parapet of the loggia and stares at the moon:

> Joan: I must pray now to the moon . . . as one burnt-out
> lady to another, to teach me to order my ways.[21]

She has lost her two sons in the war. More recently, her
home was destroyed by fire. She leans, staring at the moon, as

the guests leave; from inside float snatches of the Second Act of *Tristan*—the love duet. The curtain descends on the first scene.

The fact that the play has no 'clear centre of dramatic interest' makes it difficult to summarize. Certain conversations stand out as being important to the exposition. There is the long scene between Strowde and Joan, when Strowde's sister Eleanor is in London and they have spent the day together. They pick up the threads of their old romance, and Joan admits that she is still in love with Strowde; nevertheless, she insists they were right to separate instead of marrying. She could not have lived her love for Strowde; it would have killed her. Now she asks him the question which also puzzles Oliver: why is he not a success? Why is he not in power instead of these bungling, well-meaning politicians? His answer is the essence of the play:

Strowde: Save me from the illusion of power! I once had a glimpse—and I thank you for it—of a power that is in me. But that won't answer to any call.

Joan: Not even to the call of a good cause?

Strowde (*as one who shakes himself free from the temptations of unreality*): Excellent causes abound. They are served—as they are—by eminent prigs making a fine parade, by little minds watching what's to happen next. . . . Search for their strength—which is not to be borrowed or bargained for—it must spring from the secret life.[22]

He scouts Joan's suggestion that perhaps it would have been better if they had never met:

Strowde: No, that's blasphemy. At least don't join the unbelieving mob who cry: Do something, anything, no matter what . . . all's well while the wheels go round—while something's being done.

Joan (*with . . . irony*): But seek first the kingdom of God, and the desire of all other things shall be taken from you?

Strowde (*very simply*): It has been taken from me. I don't complain and I don't make a virtue of it. I'm not the first man who has found beliefs that he can't put in his pocket like so much small change. But am I to deny them for all that?

This passage shows Strowde's affinity with the other Outsiders we have considered. There is the 'glimpse of power', of contact with some reality, awareness of a new area of his own consciousness, that came in a time of emotional stress (as with Corporal Krebs and Camus's hero). There is the constant searching of motive; analysis of other people's and his own driving force (politicians are 'little minds' etc.; Roquentin: *salauds*). In one passage he even speaks with the accents of Wells's pamphlet:

> Joan: Evan—stir yourself out of this hopelessness of unbelief.
> Strowde (*grimly*): When the donkey's at the end of his tether and eaten his patch bare, he's to cut capers and kick up dust, is he?[23]

It is motive that has collapsed. The Outsider has glimpsed a higher form of reality than he has so far known. Subsequently he loses that glimpse and has to accept a second-best. But the 'first-best' is known to exist. Joan admits that she accepted marriage to a civil servant and 'housekeeping in odd corners of the world' because the strain of living on the level of 'first-best' would have been too much for her. Strowde has not given up the aspiration to the first-best, but he has preferred to do nothing when it seemed out of reach.

When, at the close of the scene, Eleanor returns with the news that Joan's husband has died of a heart attack, the full implication of the scene has been hammered home. It was Joan who accepted second-best; now she has lost even that.

In the Second Act, Strowde decides to return to politics; Oliver wants the job of his secretary, and when Strowde refuses, he automatically turns to the woman they are both in love with, Joan Westbury. There is an important scene between Oliver and Joan. He explains to her the reason he wants the close contact with Strowde. He wants to know why Strowde has failed. Joan points out that Strowde can hardly be said to have failed as a politician; but Oliver was not referring to that kind of success:

> Oliver: Nothing's much easier, is it, than to make that sort of success if you've the appetite for it. . . . But Evan set out

to get past all tricks, to the heart of things. . . . Is it a stone-dead heart of things, and dare no one say so when he finds out?[24]

Oliver has a symbol for this state of moral emptiness:

A shell missed me outside Albert and did for my watch. I could shake it, and it would tick for a bit, but the spring was gone. I've an idea I don't grow any older now, and when I come to die, it'll seem an odd, out-of-date sort of catastrophe.[25]

This is Keat's 'posthumous existence' of the last letter to Brown. Oliver's solution to the question is simple: destruction.

Oliver: Save me from weary people with their No More War. What we want is a real one.
Joan: And where's the enemy?
Oliver: If I knew where, I shouldn't be sitting here helpless. But we're tricked so easily.[26]

In spite of this, certain notions still have value for him: courage and discipline. When Joan asks him: 'Tell me how one soberly hates people—I don't think I know.'

Oliver: Well, you can't love a mob, surely to goodness? Because that's to be one of them, chattering and scolding and snivelling and cheering—maudlin drunk if you like. I learned to be soldier enough to hate a mob. There's discipline in heaven. . . . [27]

Both Oliver and Strowde are obsessed by a Pascalian world-contempt, an insight into 'the misery of man without God'. But for either of them to accept God would be bad faith; the Existentialist must see and touch his solution, not merely accept it.

Strowde's problem is not a dramatic problem; it can produce none of the violent emotions and make 'good theatre'. And with the problem fully set out in these two important conversations, Granville-Barker has very little more to do than devise further situations that will show Oliver and Strowde in

their characters of world-contemners. Strowde begins election-
eering, with Oliver as his secretary; in America, Joan Westbury
is dying. It remains for Strowde to throw over the politics and
sail for America; renounce the meaningless and turn towards
his symbol of meaning. He leaves London on the eve of
the election. But Joan Westbury is dead before he gets to
Southampton. The reader is left feeling oddly 'up in the air'
about it all. No happy finale, no dramatic tying up of loose
ends.

The last scene of the play recalls echoes of the first. When
Strowde has gone, Oliver talks to the millionaire businessman,
Lord Clumbermere. Clumbermere is another symbol of
material success, like Salomons. But his philosophy is not so
brutal; he is a vague, rather shy idealist, as well as a vastly
successful businessman:

> Clumbermere: You think you're all for truth and justice.
> Right—come and run my pen factory and find out if that is
> so.
> Oliver: If I ran your pen factory, I'd be for the pen, the
> whole pen and nothing but the pen.
> Clumbermere: Then you'd be of little use to me. If we
> want a good gold nib, it's religion we must make it with. . . .
> Oliver: But are you a devil then, my lord, that you want to
> beat the souls of men into pen nibs?
> Clumbermere: I hope not, Mr. Gauntlett, but if I am,
> please show me the way out of the pit. . . .[28]

Afterwards Oliver and the American girl Susan argue about
whether to recall Strowde with the news that Joan is dead.
Oliver finally gives way, with a bad grace. And when Susan
tells him that he doesn't know what he wants, he summarizes:

> Oliver: There's a worse mischief with most of us, Susan.
> What we want doesn't count. We want money and we want
> peace . . . and we want our own way. Some of us want to
> look beautiful, and some want to be good. And Clumber-
> mere gets rich without knowing why . . . and we statesmen
> puzzling the best way to pick his pocket. And you want Evan
> to come back to the middle of it all.
> Susan: He belongs here.

Oliver: If he'd come back, he or another, and make short work of the lifeless lot of us. . . .

Susan: Why didn't Joan marry him? They'd have had some happiness at least, and that would have helped.

Oliver (*a last effort*): Why doesn't life plan out into pretty patterns and happy endings. Why isn't it all made easy for you to understand?

Susan: Don't mock at me any more, Oliver.

Oliver: I'm sorry. I only do it because I'm afraid of you. [29]

And the closing cadence of the play is not a real ending:

Susan: Wouldn't you want to be raised from the dead?

Oliver: No, indeed.

Susan: You'll have to be, somehow.

Oliver: Do you wonder I'm afraid of you, Susan? (*He goes out.*) [30]

There is no prospect of anyone being 'raised from the dead', for that would mean new motives, new hopes and a new belief.

Earlier in this chapter, I used the phrase 'near-religious terminology', and it is now time to elucidate it. At the beginning of the Third Act, Strowde asks Oliver to check a quotation for him:

Strowde: Get me the Bible, will you? I want to verify. . . . I think it's first Kings, nineteen. . . .

Oliver: What's the quotation?

Strowde: Now, O Lord, take away my life, for I am not better than my fathers. Very modern and progressive and disillusioned of Elijah! Why ever should he expect to be? [31]

But that is the whole point. Strowde does expect to be, and Oliver expects to be . . . and they are not. There is an appetite for 'progress' in all Outsiders; and yet, as Strowde knows only too well, not primarily for social progress. 'Not *better* than his fathers'—that is to say, not wiser than his fathers, not less futile, being a slave to the same weaknesses, the same needs. Man is as much a slave to his immediate surroundings now as he was when he lived in tree-huts. Give him the highest, the most exciting thoughts about man's place in the universe, the meaning of history; they can all be snuffed out in a moment if he wants his dinner, or feels irritated by a child squalling on a bus. He is bound by pettiness. Strowde and Oliver are both acutely sensitive to this, *but not strong enough to do anything about it*. Human weakness. When Joan tells Strowde she cannot marry him (at the end of Act II), Strowde, left alone, murmers: 'Most merciful God . . . who makest thy creatures to suffer without understanding . . .'³² But he is not praying to God, he is only wondering at the pain he feels, his vulnerability, human weakness. And Hemingway's early work, up to the short story about the Major whose wife died, is a long meditation on human vulnerability. And meditation on human vulnerability always leads to 'religious thinking', to Hemingway's 'He must find things he cannot lose'; to a development of an ethic of renunciation and discipline. It leads to a realization that man is not a constant, unchanging being: he is one person one day, another person the next. He forgets easily, lives in the moment, seldom exerts will-power, and even when he does, gives up the effort after a short time, or forgets his original aim and turns to something else. No wonder that poets feel such despair when they seem to catch a glimpse of some intenser state of consciousness, and know with absolute certainty that *nothing* they can do can hold it fast. And this theme, implicit in Sartre, Camus, Hemingway, and even more explicit in writers like T. S. Eliot and Aldous Huxley, leads to a question, 'How can man be stronger? How can he be less of a slave of circumstances?' (Mr. Huxley's work has remained so irritatingly inconclusive because he seems to accept it as a premise for all his novels that absolutely nothing can be done about it.)

This is a question that we are not fully in a position to examine yet. First, it is important that we should understand more of the 'poet's' approach, the 'romantic' approach, and see how far this can be developed to transcend its own limitations. It might yield observations that will make the 'attempt to gain control' easier to analyse.

CHAPTER THREE

THE ROMANTIC OUTSIDER

THE ATMOSPHERE OF the Existentialist Outsider is unpleasant to breathe. There is something nauseating, anti-life, about it: these men without motive who stay in their rooms because there seems to be no reason for doing anything else. It is essentially an adult world, this world-without-values. The child's world is altogether cleaner; the air tastes of expectation. A big store at Christmas time is a new world. For the sick soul, the man outside, this 'new world' produces a feeling of horror; it is a symbol of a mechanical civilization that runs in grooves like a gramophone record, precluding freedom.

This difference between the child's world and the adult's is also one of the main differences between the world of the nineteenth century and our own. The revolutions in thought, brought about by the Victorian sages, J. S. Mill, Huxley, Darwin, Emerson, Spencer, Carlyle, Ruskin, seemed to presage endless changes in human life, and man would go forward indefinitely on 'stepping stones of his dead selves to higher things'. Before we condemn it for its short-sightedness, we survivors of two world wars and the atomic bomb, it is as well to remember that we are in the position of adults condemning children. The rationalism of the eighteenth and nineteenth centuries was not a sterile, boring state of mind; it was a period of intense and healthy optimism that didn't mind hard work and pedestrian logic because it felt free as never before; at close quarters, the Victorian sage is often found whooping and cutting capers.

In such a state of affairs, the Outsider is always the man who is not susceptible to the general enthusiasm; it may be that he is too short-sighted to see the establishment of Utopia before the end of the century. At all events, he is bound to be a child of his century if he draws his nourishment from its earth; he cannot be a nihilistic pessimist (like Camus and Sartre) in a century when the philosophers are behaving like cowboys at a rodeo. He cannot believe that it is human nature that is in the wrong, for rationalism has completely discredited such morbid dogmas as original sin. He must believe that he alone is in the wrong. Human nature cannot be sick, since the prevailing philosophy of the time declares it to be perfectible. It follows that it is the Outsider who is in some way 'not of this world', and if he dies young, like Shelley, or is a sick man, like Novalis and Schiller, or takes drugs, like Coleridge, that is all in the proper order of things. It only remains for him to set the seal of respectability on his life by claiming to be a Platonic idealist, a dreamer of dreams, and the bourgeois is quite willing to admit his right to exist. The Outsider has his proper place in the Order of Society, as the impractical dreamer.

This is the situation we find at the beginning of the last century in Europe. Goethe had invented the Romantic Outsider in his *Sorrows of Young Werther*; the type of the high, idealistic young poet, pale, but manly. In the previous century, the pining lover had been a comic figure:

> Will, when looking well can't move her
> Looking ill prevail?[1]

Young Werther brought about a change of heart. Schiller's *Robbers* and *Don Carlos* followed. (Nietzsche somewhere quotes a German military man as saying: 'If God had foreseen the *Robbers* he would not have created the world'—to such an extent does it set up the humanistic standard and discredit the divine.) There was Novalis, scientist and romantic, who created Heinrich von Ofterdingen, the poet predestined from birth for a high destiny of singing. In England, German romanticism was introduced when Coleridge translated Schiller and Byron published 'Childe Harold'. Shelley's Alastor is a young man who pines away and dies because he can find no earthly counterpart of the beautiful girl who had embraced him once in a dream. The dream reveals to Heinrich von Ofterdingen his future path.

> At a little distance rose hazy blue cliffs through whose sides shone gleaming veins of gold. All around him was a soft mellow light, and the skies above him were blue and cloudless.[2]

When, half a century later, William Morris writes of his own vision of a socialist Utopia, it expresses itself naturally in 'A Dream of John Ball'. The romantic Outsider is a 'dreamer of other worlds'. He is *not* very active—not for the same reason as Evan Strowde, but because he is essentially a dreamer, 'the idle singer of an empty day'. In this role we can trace him from Goethe's Werther to Thomas Mann's Tonio Kröger. He is the father of Barbusse's hero with his hole in the wall, and so of Roquentin and Meursault. The twentieth century simply alters the way of presenting him, feels the need to place him in his environment. The treatment of the theme becomes more clinical, more analytical. The hilltops and mountain caves disappear from the scenery props; Barbusse's Outsider comes on, with his small room in a modern city. But he is still the romantic. His main concern is still the fact that his surroundings seem incapable of fully satisfying his desires. He is afraid that the world was not created to meet the demands of the human spirit. He is troubled and frustrated today, and he is afraid he may die troubled and frustrated, with nothing but a series of only partly satisfying experiences to give him incentive to get out of bed in the morning.

We can witness the change in method of presenting the Outsider in a writer like James Joyce, who kept a foot in both traditions, romantic and social realist. His 'artist', Stephen Dedalus, begins as the type of the predestined poet:

> The noise of children at play annoyed him, and their silly voices made him feel that he was different from others. He did not want to play. He wanted to meet in the real world the unsubstantial image that his soul so constantly beheld. He did not know where to find it, or how. . . .[3]

Joyce writes of:

> The unrest which sent him wandering in the evening from garden to garden in search of Mercedes (the heroine of Dumas's *Count of Monte Cristo*). A vague dissatisfaction grew up within him as he looked on the quays and on the river and on the lowering skies, and yet he continued to wander up and down, day after day, as if he really sought someone that eluded him.

This prose, that echoes the rhythms of *Marius the Epicurean*, is deliberately hypnotic, intended to induce a dream state. It contrasts sharply with the passages of observation:

> The stout student who stood below them on the steps,
> farted briefly. Dixon turned towards him, saying in a soft
> voice:
> 'Did an angel speak?'
> Cranly turned also, and said vehemently, but without
> anger: 'Goggins, you're the flamingest dirty devil I ever met,
> do you know?'[4]

The first two passages are the prose of 'an idle singer of an
empty day'; the third has an aggressive desire to 'stand for
truth instead of imagination'. It could not have been written
before the second decade of the twentieth century. And the
two are typical of the different approaches of the realist
Outsider of the first two chapters, and the romantic Outsider.
The difference is considerable. The realist asks: Truth, what
do they mean by it? The romantic wouldn't dream of asking
such a question; his cry is: Where can I find Truth? He has
no doubt whatever that (in the words of another poet who began
as a romantic Outsider):*

> What the world's million lips are searching for
> Must be substantial somewhere. . . .

The Existentialist attitude has been replaced by a Platonic
Idealist approach; the search for the idea, the 'insubstantial
image that his souls so constantly beheld'. The Sartre of *La
Nausée* would not countenance the Joyce of *A Portrait of the
Artist as a Young Man* for a moment; Stephen's urge to 'forge in
the smithy of my soul the uncreated conscience of my race'
cannot exist at the side of the belief that 'there's no adventure'.
But if our approach is valid, the realist and the romantic
Outsider have something fundamental in common; for we are
assuming that a man becomes an Outsider when he becomes
alive to certain questions which we have called, for convenience, 'the Outsider's problems'. The purpose of the rest of
this chapter is to decide what *are* the Outsider's problems in the
terms of the romantic Outsider. For this purpose, it would be
sufficient to take any of the 'romantic' novelists or poets, and

* W. B. Yeats: 'The Shadowy Waters'.

determine from his own works what he regards as his central theme. If we decided upon Shelley or Coleridge, their bias could be defined respectively in Platonic or Kantian terms. German literature can offer many examples whose metaphysics would be more difficult to label: Schiller, Novalis, Fichte, Lessing, Holderlin; or, coming down to modern times, Thomas Mann, R. M. Rilke, Hermann Hesse. In France there is Marcel Proust, whose 'Portrait of the Artist' extends through twelve volumes, or a whole earlier generation that includes Rimbaud and Mallarmé, and even extends to curiously literary painters like Gauguin and Puvis de Chavannes. Any of these men would fit into our Outsider plan, and all have in common an approach that can be called the romantic.

In this chapter, I intend to deal with the work of Hermann Hesse; not because it has any great advantages over the work of any of the other men I have mentioned in defining the Outsider's problems, because the magnitude of Hesse's achievement is hardly recognized in English-speaking countries, where translations of most of his works are difficult to come by.*

*   *   *

Hesse's achievement divides clearly into two periods; there is that of the poetry and autobiographical novels published between 1902 and 1916, and the period of the five major novels, extending from 1919 (*Demian*) to 1945 (*The Bead Game*). The work of the earlier period makes use of the peculiarly German form, the *Bildungsroman*, the novel of education. The *Bildungsroman* sets out to describe the evolution of the 'hero's soul'; it is fictional biography that is mainly concerned with its hero's reaction to ideas, or the development of his ideas about 'life' from his experience. The *Bildungsroman* is a sort of laboratory in which the hero conducts an experiment in living. For this reason, it is a particularly useful medium for writers whose main concern is a philosophical answer to the practical question: What shall we do with our lives? Moreover, it is an interesting observation that as soon as a writer is seized with the need to treat a problem he feels seriously about in a novel, the novel automatically becomes a sort of *Bildungsroman*. The *Bildungsroman* is the natural form of serious fictional art, no

* At the time of writing, four out of five of the major novels have been out of print in England for several years, and none of the earlier novels has been translated into English.

matter how short the period of its hero's life that it treats. Shakespeare's *Hamlet* is one of the earliest *Bildungsromans* in English, because it treats the evolution of Hamlet's 'soul', his realization that killing and revenge are not simple matters of the old *lex talionis*, but something that he *feels* to be unsatisfactory as a solution of his personal problems. It will be seen at once that, within this definition, most of the books we have considered are *Bildungsromans*.

The 'novel of education' entered modern literature with Goethe's *Wilhelm Meister* (although Johnson's *Rasselas* preceded it by a quarter of a century).* Hesse admits his debt to Goethe, and the autobiographical sequence that begins with *Hermann Lauchers* in 1902 shows how great the debt was. *Unterwegs* (1916) is the last of the series. After that, there was a break of three years; in those three years great changes took place in Hesse's outlook. The war, the mass-murder, the defeat of Germany, produced a mental cataclysm that made Hesse review all his early work and find it valueless. Details of this period are lacking, but when Hesse reappeared in literature with *Demian*, the results of the upheaval, and the uncertain attempts to rebuild, are apparent; the psychology is more penetrating, the questioning of values is deeper than ever before. *Demian* is an example of the artist's miraculous power of surviving a mental earthquake that can only be compared to Strindberg's tremendous 'come-back' after his period of insanity. *Demian* and the four novels that follow it require a full analysis here.

But before proceeding to this, there is another work of the immediate post-war years that calls for comment. This is the 'testament' that grew out of the breakdown, a slim book about the same size as *Mind at the End of Its Tether* called *Blick in Chaos*.

* We owe what is probably the first modern Outsider parable to Dr. Johnson, whose *Rasselas, Prince of Abyssinia* was published in 1759. The Prince lives in a Social Utopia called the Happy Valley, where all life is controlled, ordered; where consequently everyone is condemned to an endless round of pleasure that devitalizes the few who have minds of their own and removes the last element of usefulness from the naturally worthless. The Prince is logically unable to account for his increasing boredom and irritation; he can only put his finger on it by musing: 'It has always seemed to me that man has some sixth sense, or some faculty apart from sense, that must be satisfied before he can be completely happy.' He has expressed the Outsider's problem in a sentence. In company with the astronomer Imlac (Johnson himself), Rasselas escapes from the 'Happy Valley' and goes into the world to face 'stubborn, irreducible fact'. He reaches the same conclusion as Secondborn in Shaw's *Buoyant Billions*: 'I dont want to be happy; I want to be alive and active.'

Glimpse into Chaos contains two essays on Dostoevsky, on *The Brothers Karamazov* and *The Idiot*. Hesse prophesies the collapse of belief and downfall of European morals that we have examined at close quarters in Sartre and Camus. 'It is the rejection of every strongly held moral or ethic in favour of a comprehensive *laissez-faire*.' Hesse predicted the coming of 'the Russian man', a creature of nightmare who is no longer the *Homo sapiens*, but an Existentialist monster who rejects all thought, a Mitya Karamazov without an Ivan or Alyosha to counterbalance him:

> He reaches forth beyond prohibitions, beyond natural instinct, beyond morality. He is the man who has grasped the idea of freeing himself, and on the other side, beyond the veil, beyond *principium individuationis*, of turning back again. This ideal man of the Karamazovs loves nothing and everything, does nothing and everything. He is primeval matter, monstrous soul-stuff. *He cannot live in this form*; he can only pass on.[5]

Demian begins the attempt to construct a system of values that shall not be at the mercy of the Russian man.

With its subtitle, 'The Story of a Youth', *Demian* can be thought of as Hesse's 'Portrait of the Artist as a Young Man'. In his Introduction to this story of his youth, Emil Sinclair states: 'The life of everybody is a road to himself. . . . No man has ever yet attained to self-realization, yet he strives after it, one ploddingly, another with less effort, as best he can. Each one carries the remains of his birth, slime and eggshells, with him to the end.'[6]

Chapter One begins with the statement of a dichotomy. In Emil Sinclair's childhood, he knew two worlds. In the first world, his middle-class, well-ordered home, 'were straight lines and paths that led into the future. Here were duty and guilt, evil conscience and confession, pardon and good resolutions, love and adoration, Bible texts and wisdom. To this world our future had to belong; it had to be crystal clear, beautiful and well-ordered.'

The other world is closer to the servants and workmen; there he encounters 'ghost stories and the breath of scandal. There was a gaily coloured flood of monstrous, tempting, terrible

enigmatical going-on, the slaughter-house and prison, drunken
men and scolding women, cows in birth-throes, plunging horses,
tales of burglaries, murders, suicides. . . . It was wonderful
that in our house there was peace, order and repose . . . and
wonderful that there were other things . . . sinister and
violent, *yet from which one could escape with one bound to mother.*'⁷

It is an unpleasant shock to Sinclair when he discovers that
the dark world can overflow its boundaries into his home, and
there can be no 'appeal to mother'. Through certain lies he
invents to gain the applause of some friends, he finds himself
in the power of Frank Kromer, a lout of the town, son of a
drunkard. To appease Kromer he is forced to steal money
and deceive his parents; he finds himself separated, by an act of
his own will, from the world of peace and order.

> My life at that time was a sort of insanity. I was shy, and
> lived in torment like a ghost in the midst of the well-ordered
> peace of our house.⁸

The problem is stated: order versus chaos. In the second
chapter, Hesse treats its solution. At Emil Sinclair's school there
is a boy called Max Demian, who seems in all respects to be
more 'grown-up' than the other boys. One day he gets into
conversation with Sinclair on the subject of the Bible story of
Cain and Abel, symbols of the two worlds, and suggests to
him that the Bible story is a travesty of the truth. Perhaps Cain
was not simply an evil man who killed his brother out of
envy; perhaps there was something about him, some boldness
or intelligence in his face, that made men fear him, and invent
the story of the mark of Cain to excuse their cowardice.

This version of the story troubles Sinclair; its implication is
clear: the descent into the dark world is not necessarily evil; it
may be the necessary expression of boldness and intelligence.
Demian is bold and intelligent, and rumours circulate that he
has carnal relations with girls, even with his mother. Yet it is
this Demian who frees Sinclair from the evil domination of
Frank Kromer, and who appeals to him as being above the
petty viciousness and dirty-mindedness of schoolboys. Still,
Sinclair has not enough courage to embrace the conclusions
that Demian shows him. With Kromer's domination over, he
flings himself into the peace and order of his home, and 'sings

the dear old hymns with the blissful feeling of one converted'. Only much later he realizes that it was not to his parents that he should have made confession, but to Demian. By returning to his old notion of order, he has only turned his face away from chaos; the chaos still exists.

The remainder of the book describes Sinclair's adolescence and sexual awakening. The question he has passed up repeats itself, drives home its point that you cannot escape chaos by refusing to look at it. Demian reappears on the scene while Sinclair flounders hopelessly; he introduces him to his mother, and Sinclair finds in her the answer to the question of the two worlds. She symbolizes nature, the life force, the mother figure, Lilith, in whom all opposites are resolved. The novel ends in a whirl of Shelleyan airy-fairy that is a disappointment to the unromantic reader whose attention has been held by the terseness and practical eye-to-business of Hesse's analysis. This is a fault that recurs in most of Hesse's novels, a legacy from his romantic ancestry.

In spite of this, the conclusions of *Demian* are clear. It is a question of self-realization. It is not enough to accept a concept of order and live by it; that is cowardice, and such cowardice cannot result in freedom. Chaos must be faced. Real order must be preceded by a descent into chaos. This is Hesse's conclusion. In theological terms, the fall was necessary, man had to eat of the fruit of good and evil. (Later, dealing with Nietzsche and Blake, we shall touch upon similar views: the idea that good and evil are not ultimate antinomies, but expressions of a higher force that comprehends both.) In refusing to face evil, Sinclair has gained nothing and lost a great deal; the Buddhist scripture expresses it: Those who refuse to discriminate might as well be dead.

Hesse's next novel has a delusive air of having solved great problems. *Siddhartha* was written on his return from India; it is the best written of the five novels and the most idyllic in tone. (We are reminded that it was through study of Hindu and Buddhist texts that Strindberg regained his sanity.) It suffers from the same defect as *Demian*: the reader feels that Hesse hadn't foreseen the end when he wrote the beginning.

Siddhartha is the son of a Brahmin, born in the time of the Buddha (approximately 563 to 483 B.C.). He feels the attraction to the life of the wandering monk; he leaves home while still a youth and practises rigorous disciplines that give him great control of body and mind.

Siddhartha is already beyond the problems of Barbusse's Outsider.

Still feeling that this self-control is not ultimate self-realization, he goes to listen to the preaching of the saintly Gautama, Sakyamuni, called by his disciples the Buddha. Gautama reinforces the conclusion that Siddhartha had already reached, that extreme asceticism is not an essential of self-realization, for its purpose is only to *test* the will. The Buddha teaches the 'middle way' that depends on achieving a state of contemplation, of complete separation from all the human faculties. This state achieved, the monk, having extinguished every tendency to identify himself with his body, emotions, senses or intellect, knows himself to be beyond all, and achieves freedom from 'the wheel of rebirth'.

Siddhartha accepts this, but he doubts whether following the Buddha would bring him to self-realization. (In point of fact, Gautama said as much repeatedly: 'Let each man be unto himself an island', etc.). His best friend remains as a disciple; Siddhartha goes on, still searching. He tells himself: No man can teach another to be a Buddha; you can only teach yourself. Then the question occurs: Can a man teach himself by narrowing his life and perceptions until all love of nature has been filtered off? This decides him. He puts off the robe of the holy man; in the first town he comes to he goes to court a beautiful courtesan. When she tells him that he cannot possibly become her lover unless he has some worldly success behind him, he sets his mind to make money with such acumen that he soon has a house, and the beautiful courtesan for a mistress. After a few years of this, it dawns on him that he is less near to self-realization than ever, and one day his basic misery forces itself on him so irresistibly that he tries to kill himself. He fails, but the honesty involved in facing his own unfulfilment gives him strength to renounce the house and success, and become a homeless wanderer again. This time he doesn't wander far; he joins the local ferryman (another contemplative) and again spends his days in spiritual discipline. When the courtesan dies, Siddhartha discovers that he has a son as a result of the last night they spent together; he brings the boy up, and then has to suffer the final misery of realizing that there is no real communication with other human beings, even those we love most. The son leaves home: Siddhartha accepts his loss and continues to contemplate the river. The novel draws to a close.

It must have struck the reader, even from this brief summary, that Hesse had not quite succeeded in pulling off the conjuring trick. Siddhartha leaves home full of hope; asceticism fails him, so he turns to the Buddha. The Buddha fails him, so he turns to the worldly life. That fails too, so he becomes a ferryman. The reader is waiting to be told of a successful solution, and as the novel comes towards the end, he realizes Hesse has nothing to offer. The river flows on; Siddhartha contemplates it. Hesse arrives at the conclusion that there is no ultimate success or failure; life is like the river; its attraction is the fact that it never stops flowing. There is nothing for it but to close the novel feeling rather let down.

The student of Eastern religion will object that the novel's failure is Hesse's inability to grasp the essence of Vedantism or Buddhism, that he should have tried reading Ramakrishna or the Tibetan saint Milarepa to get his facts straight before he began writing the novel. This is probably true; we can only accept what we have, a finished novel, and consider it as a part of Hesse's attempt to define his own problems.

That Hesse himself was not satisfied is proved by his next book. In *Steppenwolf* he returns to the attack, sets out all his facts, and starts from the beginning again. From the point of view of this study of the Outsider, *Steppenwolf* (1928) is Hesse's most important contribution. It is more than that; it is one of the most penetrating and exhaustive studies of the Outsider ever written.

Steppenwolf is the story of a middle-aged man. This in itself is an important advance. The romantic usually finds himself committed to pessimism in opposition to life itself by his insistence on the importance of youth (Rupert Brooke is a typical example). Steppenwolf has recognized the irrelevancy of youth; there is a self-lacerating honesty about this journal of a middle-aged man.

In all externals, Steppenwolf (the self-conferred nickname of Harry Haller) is a Barbusse Outsider. He is more cultured perhaps, less of an animal; the swaying dresses of women in the street do not trouble him. Also he is less concerned to 'stand for truth'; he allows his imagination full play, and his journal is a sort of wish-dream diary. But here again we have the man-on-his-own, living in rooms with his books and his gramophone; there is not even the necessity to go out and work, for he has a small private income. In his youth he considered himself a poet, a self-realizer. Now he is middle-aged, an ageing Emil Sinclair, and the moods of insight have stopped coming; there is only dissatisfaction, lukewarmness.

The journal opens with an account of a typical day: he reads a little, has a bath, lounges around his room, eats; and the feeling of unfulfilment increases until towards nightfall he feels like setting fire to the house or jumping out of a window. The worst of it is that he can find no excuse for this apathy; being an artist-contemplative, he should be ideally contented with this type of life. Something is missing. But what? He goes to a tavern and ruminates as he takes his evening meal; the food and wine relax him, and suddenly the mood he has despaired of having pervades him:

> A refreshing laughter rose in me. . . . It soared aloft like a soapbubble . . . and then softly burst. . . . The golden trail was blazed and I was reminded of the eternal, and of Mozart, and the stars. For an hour I could breathe once more. . . .⁹

But this is at the end of a long day, and tomorrow he will wake up and the insight will be gone; he will read a little, have a bath . . . and so on.

But on this particular evening something happens. The reader is not sure what. According to Haller, he sees a mysterious door in the wall, with the words 'Magic Theatre: Not for everybody' written over it, and a man with a sandwich board and a tray of Old Moore's Almanacs gives him a pamphlet called A Treatise on the Steppenwolf. The treatise is printed at full length in the following pages of the novel, and it is obviously Haller's own work; so it is difficult for the reader to determine when Haller is recording the truth and when he is playing a game of wish-fulfilment with himself.

The treatise is an important piece of self-analysis. It could be called 'A Treatise on the Outsider'. As Harry reads it (or writes it) certain convictions formulate themselves, about himself and about the Outsider generally. The Outsider, Haller says, is a self-divided man; being self-divided, his chief desire is to be unified. He is selfish as a man with a lifelong raging toothache would be selfish.

To explain his wretchedness, Haller has divided himself into two persons: a civilized man and a wolf-man. The civilized man loves all the things of Emil Sinclair's first world, order and cleanliness, poetry and music (especially Mozart); he takes lodgings always in houses with polished fire-irons and well-scrubbed tiles. His other half is a savage who loves the second world, the world of darkness; he prefers open spaces and lawlessness; if he wants a woman he feels that the proper way is to kill and rape her. For him, bourgeois civilization and all its inanities are a great joke.

The civilized man and the wolf-man live at enmity most of the time, and it would seem that Harry Haller is bound to spend his days divided by their squabbling. But sometimes, as in the tavern, they make peace, and then a strange state ensues; for Harry finds that a combination of the two makes him akin to the gods. In these moments of vision, he is no longer envious of the bourgeois who finds life so straightforward, for his own conflicts are present in the bourgeois, on a much smaller scale. He, as self-realizer, has deliberately cultivated his two opposing natures until the conflict threatens to tear him in two, because he knows that when he has achieved the secret of permanently reconciling them, he will live at a level of intensity unknown to the bourgeois. His suffering is not a mark of his inferiority, even though it may render him less fit for survival than the bourgeois; unreconciled, it is the sign of his greatness; reconciled, it is manifested as 'more abundant life' that makes the Outsider's superiority over other types of men unquestionable. When the Outsider becomes aware of his strength, he is unified and happy.

Haller goes even further; the Outsider is the mainstay of the bourgeois. Without him the bourgeois could not exist. The vitality of the ordinary members of society is dependent on its Outsiders. Many Outsiders unify themselves, realize themselves as poets or saints. Others remain tragically divided and unproductive, but even they supply soul-energy to society; it is their strenuousness that purifies thought and prevents the bourgeois world from foundering under its own dead-weight; they are society's spiritual dynamos. Harry Haller is one of these.

There is a yet further step in self-analysis for the Steppen-wolf: that is to recognize that he is not really divided into two simple elements, man and wolf, but has literally hundreds of conflicting I's. Every thought and impulse says 'I'. The word 'personality' hides the vagueness of the concept; it refers to no factual object, like 'body'. Human beings are not like the characters in literature, fixed, made immutable by their creator; the visible part of the human being is his dead part; it is the other part, the unconditioned Will that constitutes his being. Will precedes essence. Our bourgeois civilization is based on personality. It is our chief value. A film star has 'personality'; the salesman hoping to sell his first insurance policy tries to ooze 'personality':

The human merry-go-round sees many changes: the illusion that cost India the efforts of thousands of years to unmask is the same illusion that the West has laboured just as hard to maintain and strengthen.[10]

The treatise comes to an end with a sort of credo:

Man is not . . . of fixed and enduring form. He is . . . an experiment and a transition. He is nothing else than the narrow and perilous bridge between nature and spirit. His innermost destiny drives him on to the spirit and to God. His innermost longing draws him back to nature . . . man . . . is a bourgeois compromise.[11]

That man is not yet a finished creation but rather a challenge of the spirit; a distant possibility dreaded as much as desired; that the way towards it has only been covered for a very short distance and with terrible agonies and ecstasies even by those few for whom it is the scaffold today and the monument tomorrow.[12]

Steppenwolf knows well enough why he is unhappy and drifting, bored and tired; it is because he will not recognize his purpose and follow it with his whole being.

'He is resolved to forget that the desperate clinging to the self, and the desperate clinging to life are the surest way to eternal death.'[13] Haller knows that even when the Outsider is a universally acknowledged man of genius, it is due to 'his

immense powers of surrender and suffering, of his indifference
to the ideals of the bourgeois, and of his patience under that last
extremity of loneliness which rarifies the atmosphere of the
bourgeois world to an ice-cold ether around those who suffer
to become men, that loneliness of the garden of Gethsemane'.[14]

This Steppenwolf . . . has discovered that . . . at best he is
only at the beginning of a long pilgrimage towards this ideal
harmony. . . . No, back to nature is a false track that
leads nowhere but to suffering and despair. . . . Every
created thing, even the simplest, is already guilty, already
multiple. . . . The way to innocence, to the uncreated and to
God, leads on, not back, not back to the wolf or the child,
but ever further into guilt, ever deeper into human life. . . .
Instead of narrowing your world and simplifying your soul,
you will have at the last to take the whole world into your
soul, cost what it may.[15]

The last image of the treatise recalls an idea of Rilke's:
the Angel of the Duinese Elegies who, from his immense height,
can see and summarize human life as a whole.

Were he already among the immortals—were he already
there at the goal to which the difficult path seems to be
taking him—with what amazement he would look back over
all this coming and going, all the indecision and wild zig-
zagging of his tracks. With what a mixture of encouragement
and blame, pity and joy, he would smile at this Steppenwolf.[16]

The Outsider's 'way of salvation', then, is plainly implied.
His moments of insight into his direction and purpose must be
grasped tightly; in these moments he must formulate laws that
will enable him to move towards his goal in spite of losing sight
of it. It is unnecessary to add that these laws will apply not
only to him, but to all men, their goal being the same as his.

The treatise throws some light on Hesse's intention in
Siddhartha. We can see now that Siddhartha revolted against
the religious discipline that 'narrowed the world and simplified
his soul', but in renouncing his monk's robes, he failed to 'take
the whole world into his soul'; on the contrary, he merely

narrowed his soul to include a mistress and a house. The effort of 'widening the soul' must be controlled by a religious discipline; nothing can be achieved by ceasing to Will. All this the 'wretched Steppenwolf' knows, and would prefer not to know.

Logically, the 'Treatise on the Steppenwolf' should be the end of the book; actually, it is within the first hundred pages. Harry has only rationalized his difficulties; he has yet to undergo experiences that will make his analysis real to him. The *Bildungsroman* is only one-third completed.

After reading the treatise, he hits rock-bottom of despair; he is exhausted and frustrated, and the treatise warns him that this is all as it should be; he decides that this is the last time he allows himself to sink so low; next time he will commit suicide before he reaches that point. The thought cheers him up, and he lies down to sleep.

The treatise is the high point of the book from the reader's point of view, but Hesse still has a job to finish; he has to show us how Steppenwolf will learn to accept life again and turn away finally from the thought of cutting his throat. This comes about by a series of romantically improbable events. The man with the sandwich board has mentioned the name of a tavern; Haller goes there and meets a girl called Hermine. She takes him in hand; makes him learn ballroom-dancing and listen to modern jazz. She introduces him to the saxophone player, the sunburnt Pablo, and to the sensuously beautiful animal Maria, whom he finds in his bed when he returns home one night. Like Siddhartha, he goes through an education of the senses. In bed with Maria, he recovers his own past (as Roquentin was unable to) and finds it meaningful.

> For moments together my heart stood still between delight and sorrow to find how rich was the gallery of my life, and how thronged the soul of the wretched Steppenwolf with high eternal stars and constellations. . . . My life had become weariness. It had wandered in a maze of unhappiness that led to renunciation and nothingness; it was bitter with the salt of all human things; yet it had laid up riches, riches to be proud of. It had been, for all its wretchedness, a princely life. Let the little way to death be as it might—the kernel of this life of mine was noble. It came of high descent, and turned, not on trifles, but on the stars. . . .[17]

This experience can be called the ultimately valid core of romanticism, stripped of its externals of stagey scenery and soft music. It has become a type of religious affirmation. Unfortunately, there can be no doubt about the difficulty of separating it from the stage scenery: the overblown language, the Hoffmannesque atmosphere. Only a few pages later, Haller admits that a part of his new 'life of the senses' is smoking opium; and there is bisexuality too. (Pablo suggests a sexual orgy for three: himself, Harry and Maria; and Maria and Hermine have Lesbian relations.)

The book culminates with a dream fantasy of a fancy-dress ball in which Harry feels the barriers between himself and other people break down, ceases to feel his separateness. He kills (or dreams he kills) Hermine, and at last finds his way to the Magic Theatre, where he sees his past in retrospect and relives innocent dreams. After this scene, he has achieved the affirmation he could not make earlier in the book:

> I would sample its tortures once more and shudder once more at its senselessness. I would traverse not once more but often, the hell of my inner being. One day I would be a better hand at the game. . . .[18]

Steppenwolf ends in the same romantic dream-haze that we have noted in the previous two novels; but in this case its effect is less irritating because the reader has already, as it were, granted Haller latitude to tell what lies he chooses. Nevertheless, it is not these last scenes that impress themselves on the mind (as it should be, since they are the climax of the novel); it is the pages of self-analysis, when there is no action taking place at all. Unlike his great contemporary, Thomas Mann, Hesse has no power to bring people to life; but his ideas are far more alive than Mann's, perhaps because Mann is always the detached spectator, while Hesse is always a thinly disguised participant in his novels. The consequence is that Hesse's novels of ideas have a vitality that can only be compared to Dostoevsky; the ideas are a passion; he writes in the grip of a need to solve his own life's problems by seeing them on paper.

In *Steppenwolf* he has gone a long way towards finally resolving them. In the final dream scene, Haller glimpses the

words: Tat Tvam Asi—*That Thou Art*—* the formula from
the Upanishads that denotes that in the heart of his own being
man discovers the godhead. Intuitively, Harry knows this. The
path that leads from the Outsider's miseries to this still-centre
is a path of discipline, asceticism and complete detachment. He
shows himself aware of it in the 'Treatise on the Steppenwolf',
but he admits that it is too hard a saying for him. By the end
of the novel it would seem that he has found some of the
necessary courage to face it.

Steppenwolf is Hesse's last major study of the Outsider. The
two remaining novels call for less detailed analysis.

Narziss und Goldmund is another study in the two ways:
asceticism *versus* the world. Many critics consider it the best of
Hesse's novels; certainly it is a fine result of a quarter of a
century's novel-craft. Narziss is the young monk whose 'way'
will be the way of service to the Church. When the boy
Goldmund comes to the monastery-school as a pupil, they are
instantly attracted to one another as the two most alive beings
in the cloister. But Goldmund is no monk; he must follow the
path of Siddhartha and Steppenwolf: 'Instead of narrowing
your world . . . you will have at last to take the whole world
into your soul. . . .' On the day when Goldmund leaves the
cloister to go into the world to 'seek himself', Narziss has begun
the series of fasts and vigils that will carry him towards ascetic
world-renunciation.

The rest of the book, three-quarters of it, is concerned with
Goldmund: his love affairs (many of them!), wanderings,
hardships; he becomes a sculptor whose works are a Michelangelesque affirmation of life; he wanders through the plague
and sees universal death. The climax of his wanderings occurs
when he sees a painting on the wall of a deserted church—
a dance of death of a type to be found in many medieval
manuscripts, with skeletons dressed as priests, merchants,
beggars, lovers, and death carrying all away. He leaves it with
the knowledge: In the midst of life we are in death; and turns
his feet homeward, towards Narziss.

Narziss is now Abbot of the cloister, and is gaining political
influence: a St. Bernard or Father Joseph of Paris. Goldmund
reaches him, after a love affair which almost costs him his
neck, and enters the cloister again, not as a monk, but as a

* Chandogya Upanishad, VI, ii, 3.

lay-brother. There he spends his days carving sculptures of saints and gargoyles for the monastery; there he eventually dies, leaving behind him the sculptures that reach out towards the permanence that his life lacked, an 'unknown medieval craftsman'. He has not found self-realization, but, para-doxically, Narziss finds it for him; looking at the statues, he knows that Goldmund, without being aware of it, has dis-covered the image of the permanent and spiritual.

Hesse's last major work to date, which began to appear in 1937, and was finally published in 1945, is his finest achieve-ment. The cloying element of romanticism has disappeared almost entirely; the novel has a chastity of style and form that is a new thing in Hesse.

*The Bead Game** is set at some date in the future when the state supports an aristocratic hierarchy of intellectuals, the Castalian order. The purpose of this order is to preserve the ideals of intellect and spirit in a world of political upheavals and squabbling statesmen (the sort of function that was served by the Church in the Middle Ages). It is, in fact, the logical outcome of the Renaissance humanist ideals. It substitutes for ritualistic worship of God a ritualistic worship of knowledge called the bead game. This game, Castalia's highest form of activity, makes use of all the arts and sciences, and co-ordinates and blends them so that the total result is a sort of High Mass performed by a number of university professors.

The novel purports to be the biography of a high-priest of this bead game, Joseph Knecht (Knecht means serf; the hero embodies the ideal of service). Knecht, with the temperament of a Narziss, becomes Magister Ludi, the highest position in Castalia. But there is something subtly unsatisfactory about the life of this intellectual hierarchy; there is, for instance, their certainty that no other way of life can give such full satis-faction to man's highest needs, while Knecht can see quite clearly that it very easily gives way to intellectual sloth, smugness and self-esteem. (This is the same situation that Martin Luther found, in the Catholic Church of his day.) After writing a long letter, in which he warns the order that it is dying of emotional anaemia, Knecht resigns his post and goes into 'the world'.

* Translated into English by Mervyn Savill as *Magister Ludi*.

In the last chapter, the ex-Magister, now the tutor of a Goldmund-like boy, watches his pupil pay homage to the sun in the morning:

> ... drawing mountains, water and sky to his heart with outstretched arms, he knelt down and seemed to pay homage to the earth-mother and the wisp of mountain lake, offering as a ceremonious sacrifice to the powers his youth, freedom, and the life instinct that burned within him.[19]

Knecht realizes, watching the boy, that his pupil has revealed himself 'new and alien and completely his peer'. *This* is what Castalia knew nothing of; this is what his own life had lacked. When his pupil dives into the lake, Knecht follows him, fired, like Ibsen's Master Builder, by youth and life. The cold and the effort overcome him, and he drowns.

Still, in this last work (to date) Hesse has not drawn a clear and final conclusion from his analysis. The young Tito has revealed himself as 'completely his peer'. At the last, Hesse cannot choose between Narziss and Goldmund. We can see in retrospect why both were failures. Goldmund merely lived; he failed to 'take the whole world into his soul', although, through art he came closer to it than Sinclair or Siddhartha. Knecht merely thought; he tried, through the bead game, to take the whole world of knowledge into his soul. His ideal of service was right, but it was service to the wrong cause, as he realizes when he sees Tito performing a different sort of service in the dawn.

Considered as a whole, Hesse's achievement can hardly be matched in modern literature; it is the continually rising trajectory of an idea, the fundamental religious idea of how to 'live more abundantly'. Hesse has little imagination in the sense that Shakespeare or Tolstoy can be said to have imagination, but his ideas have a vitality that more than makes up for it. Before all, he is a novelist who used the novel to explore the problem: What should we do with our lives? The man who is interested to know *how* he should live instead of merely taking life as it comes, is automatically an Outsider. In Steppenwolf, Hesse solves the Outsider's problem to this extent: his wretchedness is the result of his incorrigible tendency to compromise, to prefer temperate, civilized, bourgeois regions. *His salvation lies in extremes*—of heat or cold, spirit or nature.

The problem then advances to the stage: which? In *Narziss und Goldmund* the hero chooses nature, but does not come anywhere near to self-realization. In *The Bead Game*, the hero chooses spirit, and he dies with a consciousness of failure too. Perhaps Hesse's failure lies in the fact that he is not sure of what he means by self-realization. Steppenwolf speaks of a sudden ecstasy, a 'timeless moment':

> Between two or three notes of the piano, the door opened suddenly to the other world. I sped through heaven and saw God at work. . . . *I affirmed all things* and to all things I gave up my heart. [Italics mine.][20]

But that is only for a quarter of an hour; Hesse nowhere speaks of the possibility of a discipline that should make all life a succession of such moments. No doubt if he were a good Christian, he would not expect anything so unreasonable; he would be contented to strive towards the Godly life and leave the rest to God. Being a romantic, Hesse refuses to accept any such half-measure; he has a deep sense of the injustice of human beings having to live on such a lukewarm level of everyday triviality; he feels that there *should* be a way of living with the intensity of the artist's creative ecstasy *all the time*. We may dismiss this as romantic wishful-thinking, but it deserves note as being one of the consistent ideals of the Outsider. In the next chapter we shall study men who could hardly be accused of being romantics, who actually made a determined effort to find such a way of living by going out and looking for it.

In the light of Hesse's contribution, the implications of the Outsiders of the first two chapters are altogether clearer. Their problem is the unreality of their lives. They become acutely conscious of it when it begins to pain them, but they are not sure of the source of the pain. The ordinary world loses its values, as it does for a man who has been ill for a very long time. Life takes on the quality of a nightmare, or a cinema sheet when the screen goes blank. These men who had been projecting their hopes and desires into what was passing on the screen suddenly realize they are in a cinema. They ask: Who are we? What are we doing here? With the delusion of the screen identity gone, the causality of its events suddenly broken, they are confronted with a terrifying freedom. In Sartre's phrase, they are 'condemned to be free'. Completely new bearings are demanded; a new analysis of this real world of the cinema has to be undertaken. In the shadow world on the screen, every problem had an answer; this may not be true of the world in the cinema. The fact that the screen world has proved to be a delusion arouses the disturbing possibility that the cinema world may be unreal too. 'When we dream that we dream, we are beginning to wake up,' Novalis says. Chuang Tzu had once said that he had dreamed he was a butterfly, and now wasn't sure if he was a man who dreamed he was a butterfly or a butterfly dreaming he was a man.

These problems follow in the wake of the Barbusse Outsider; whenever they appear, they signalize the presence of an Outsider. If we accept that they are ultimate problems of existence, to which there can be no answer, then we must regard the Outsider as the harbinger of the unanswerable problem. Before we commit ourselves to any conclusion, however, there are a great many more attempts at an answer at which we shall look.

*　　*　　*

Before leaving the romantic Outsider, there is another novelist whose treatment of the theme can be conveniently examined here. Henry James is a uniquely great novelist whose works deserve in this connexion several chapters to themselves; even more than Hesse he treated his work as a laboratory in which to investigate human life. Such a detailed analysis is impossible here, but we can trace the development of his treatment from novel to novel. James thought of himself as 'an incorrigible Outsider', and one penetrating English critic has likened him to Tennyson's Lady of Shallott, seeing life always through a magic mirror; perhaps Barbusse's 'hole in the wall' would be as good a simile.

From the beginning James's work dealt with the problem, What should we do with our lives? (The phrase is the property of H. G. Wells.) His favourite heroes and heroines are young people who, like Hesse's, 'confront life' with the questions, How must it be lived to bring the greatest self-realization?

Roderick Hudson, the hero of the first important novel, is a young sculptor who is frustrated and bored in the small-town home environment; a generous patron takes him to Rome and releases him from the necessity of drudging in an office for a living. Roderick promptly gets himself embroiled in an unhappy love affair and gradually loses his idealism and his talent. James has shown Roderick's immense expectation of life petering out as soon as he flings himself into the business of living it.

In *Portrait of a Lady* the heroine is a young woman who, again, confronts life with the question-mark. Her social success in English society leads a very eligible English Lord to propose to her; she refuses him because she feels that life is far too full of exciting possibilities to narrow it down so soon. Later, the possibilities resolve themselves in a love-marriage that is a failure, with the same prospect of future unfulfilment as in *Roderick Hudson*. She too is 'defeated by life', by her own inability to live at a constant intensity.

James is something of a defeatist where the Outsider's problems are concerned. Much later in his life he returned to the problem of self-realization. He put into the mouth of Lambert Strether, the middle-aged hero of *The Ambassadors*, a speech that begins: 'Live, live all you can; it's a mistake not to.' But Strether's own attempt to 'take the world into his soul' is miserably unsuccessful. He comes to Europe from a small American town to drag back with him a young American who likes Europe far too much to go home. Once in Paris, he is so overwhelmed by realization of what he has missed in his own narrow life that he advises the young man not to go back on any account, and announces his own intention of staying on. His course of 'self-realization' ends by scuttling the security he has left behind him in America and committing him to a very uncertain future. At this point James leaves him.

Finally, the idea behind the novel, *Wings of the Dove*, of a young woman 'in love with life' who yet knows she has only six months to live, is calculated to set the problem in a light where it could hardly fail of some solution. Yet what actually happens is that Milly Theale is betrayed by her best friend and her lover, and dies in the knowledge that she has been defeated by life as well as by death. 'At the last she hated death; she would have done anything to live.' The problem of self-realization, the Outsider's problem, is left unsolved. It would seem that James's contribution to it could be summarized in Elroy Flecker's 'The dead know only one thing: It is better to be alive'.

CHAPTER FOUR

THE ATTEMPT TO GAIN CONTROL

THE OUTSIDER PROBLEM is essentially a living problem; to write about it in terms of literature is to falsify it. Up to this point, analysis of writers has been necessary, for the writer's business is self-expression, and they have helped us towards clear and scientific definition of the Outsider's problems. But these men, Barbusse, Sartre, Hemingway, even Hesse, were not deeply and permanently concerned with the Outsider; the measure of their unconcern lies in the fact that they passed on to other subjects. The writer has an instinct that makes him select the material that will make the best show on paper, and when that has failed or been carried to a limit from which he finds it difficult to go forward, he selects a new approach. This can be seen by referring to the development of any of these writers of the previous chapters: Sartre passing from Roquentin to Communism; Hemingway from Corporal Krebs to the big-jawed, hard-fisted heroes of the later books; Barbusse from *L'Enfer* to *Le Feu* and so on to Communism. Unless a writer has unusual sincerity and unusual persistence, this is almost certain to happen to him (Mr. Eliot is the only example I can call to mind among modern writers whose development has been a consistent, unswerving line). The reason is simple: beyond a certain point, the Outsider's problems will not submit to mere thought; *they must be lived*. Very few writers treat writing (as Mr. Eliot does) as an instrument for living, not as an aim in itself.

This conclusion is not intended as a criticism of the writers I have just spoken of. A writer's conscience is his own business. We must accept what they have given us and be grateful enough to get it. But it means that, in order to pursue the Outsider's problems further, we must turn to men who *were* more concerned with living than with writing.

The three men we are to consider in this chapter had one unfortunate feature in common; they all believed, like Barbusse's hero, that 'they had nothing and they deserved nothing'. This is not a belief that puts a man at the best advantage for wrestling with a living problem. All three ended tragically; that is to say, all three *wasted* themselves and their possible development. Looking back on them, looking at a canvas by Van Gogh, or at the manuscript letters of T. E. Lawrence, or at Nijinsky's *L'Après-Midi d'un Faune* in the British Museum, we can feel the full poignancy of the fact that *these men did not understand themselves*, and consequently wasted their powers. If they had known themselves as well as we can know them, their lives need not have been tragic. The Outsider's first business is self-knowledge.

* * *

Close study of T. E. Lawrence is made difficult by the fact that no reliable, unbiased biography has yet been published. Lowell Thomas and Liddel Hart treat him simply as a soldier; Mr. Aldington's book is so hysterically biased against him that it has virtually no value except as a corrective to other books that treat him as a legendary Sir Galahad. Until an exhaustive, unprejudiced biography is published, we have nothing but the bare facts of his life, and the evidence of his own writing, to go on.

The facts of his life are briefly these:

Lawrence came of a fairly-well-to-do family; he was one of several brothers. At school he was brilliant at subjects he cared about, and had no energy to spare for the others. He always cared about history and literature. In his early teens, this developed into a passionate interest in medievalism; he read Malory and William Morris, and cycled around Oxfordshire taking rubbings of church brasses. He was always physically hardy and virile, though he never played competitive games. He cycled around in France looking at castles and cathedrals; later, ignoring the assurances of experienced travellers that it was an impossibility, he travelled through Arabia on foot and alone, examining Crusaders' castles and collecting notes for his Oxford thesis. A year later, he accompanied Leonard Woolley and the British Museum Archaeological mission to Egypt. There he picked up some Arabic, and learned a great deal more of archaeology; he still read Malory and Morris, and made plans to buy a disused windmill when he returned to England, and use its power to drive a printing press which would print books on hand-made paper; they would then be bound with vellum that would be stained with Tyrian dye.

At the outbreak of war, Lawrence was posted to Egypt as a Staff Captain in the Maps Branch of the Intelligence service. He found it boring, and when an opportunity came to take a part in the rebellion being fomented by King Hussein of Mecca against the Turkish government of Arabia, Lawrence sailed for Arabia without bothering to tell his Intelligence chiefs what he intended to do. He quickly made himself indispensable in the revolt; as the advisor of Fiesal, King Hussein's son, he steered it to success in a period of less than two years. His book *The Seven Pillars of Wisdom* is a record of those two years.

The war had given him new insights; he returned from it a wiser and in no way a happier man. We have already examined that leaking-away of the springs of motive that results from too much experience flooding an over-sensitive person, so we have no need to regard his conduct during the next seventeen years as part of a 'Lawrence enigma'. He acted as we would expect an Outsider to act. After a three-years battle in the council chamber to establish the Arab right to their own country, Lawrence joined the Tank Corps as a private, and later the R.A.F. He did no more archaeology, and refused offers of various jobs from people who wanted to help him, including the Governorship of Egypt and the Secretaryship of the Bank of England. He appears completely to have lost belief in himself, although this loss of belief did not extend to the rest of humanity (as with Evan Strowde) and he had always an exaggerated respect for certain writers and artists who certainly had not a quarter of his spiritual power.

Later, he bought a cottage at Clouds Hill in Dorset, installed many books and gramophone records, and spent most of his spare time there. After *The Seven Pillars* he did no more creative work (*The Mint* is hardly more than a journal). He was killed in a motor-cycle accident in 1935, and even at the end, with his skull and ribs smashed beyond hope of recovery, his prodigious vitality kept him living for three days when another man might have died in a few hours.

This second period of his life is the most depressing to consider, for it is not difficult to see the causes that sapped his motive power, and to see that a few insights into these causes might have showed him how to harness his enormous will-power to creative activity. It is like considering some immense machine that is made useless by a small break in the circuit. The rest of this account of Lawrence must be devoted to a study of *The Seven Pillars* and Lawrence's own diagnosis of his Outsider problems.

A letter to Edward Garnett (23 October 1922) makes this very clear. Lawrence writes:

> I have looked in poetry everywhere for satisfaction: and haven't found it. Instead I have made that collection of bonbons, chocolate eclairs of the spirit, whereas I wanted a meal. Failing poetry, I chased my fancied meal through prose, and found everywhere good little stuff, and *only a few men who had tried honestly to be greater than mankind*; and only their strainings and wrestlings really fill my stomach.
>
> I can't write poetry, so in prose I aimed at providing a meal for the fellow seekers with myself. . . .

That Lawrence lacked the healthy conceit of the man of genius is one of the root causes of his tragedy of waste.

Before passing on to this, we can mention a revealing passage on Lawrence in the volume *T. E. Lawrence by His Friends*. Eric Kennington's account of Lawrence is one of the best balanced articles in the book. A memorable paragraph tells how he showed a copy of *The Seven Pillars* to a strange, clairvoyant old schoolmaster.[1] The schoolmaster's comment was: 'Reading this book has made me suffer. The writer is infinitely the greatest man I have known, but he is terribly wrong. *He is not himself.* He has found an "I" but it is not a true "I", so I tremble to think of what may happen. *He is never alive in what he does.* There is no exchange. He is only a pipe through which life flows. He seems to have been a very good pipe, but to live truly one must be more than that.' This comment not only penetrates to the roots of Lawrence; it is an accurate characterization of the Outsider. 'He is never alive in what he does.' This is Meursault and Krebs. 'He is not himself' is even more revealing, for it suggests that the Outsider's business is to find a course of action in which he is *most himself*, that is, in which he achieves the maximum self-expression.

The Seven Pillars of Wisdom is one of the most important case-books of the Outsider that we possess. From the beginning, Lawrence's interest in ascetic religious discipline is apparent.

In an early chapter dealing with the religion of the Semitic peoples, he writes:

> The Arabs said there had been forty thousand prophets. . . .
> Their birth set them in crowded places. An unintelligible,
> passionate yearning drove them out into the desert. They
> lived there a greater or lesser time in meditation and
> physical abandonment; and thence they returned, with their
> imagined message articulate, to preach it to their old, and
> now doubting associates. The founders of the three great
> creeds fulfilled this cycle; their possible coincidence was
> proved a law by the parallel life histories of the myriad
> others, the unfortunate who failed, whom we might judge of
> no less true profession, but for whom time and disillusion
> had not heaped up dry souls to be set on fire. To thinkers of
> the town, the impulse into Nitria had been ever irresistible,
> not probably that they found God dwelling there, but
> that in solitude they heard more certainly the living word
> they brought with them. . . . Their profound reaction from
> matter led them to preach barrenness, renunciation and
> poverty.[2]

Throughout *The Seven Pillars*, Lawrence's sympathy with these prophets reveals itself. The desert becomes a symbol of purity; of escape from the human:

> The Bedouin of the desert, born and grown up in it, had
> embraced with all his soul this nakedness too harsh for
> volunteers, for the reason, felt but inarticulate, that there he
> found himself indubitably free. . . . This faith of the desert
> was impossible in the towns. It was at once too strange, too
> simple and too impalpable for common use.[3]

The chapter on religion ends with an important affirmation of the basis of Lawrence's 'religion':

> They were a people of starts, for whom the abstract was the
> strongest motive, the process of infinite courage and variety,
> and the end, nothing. They were as unstable as water, and
> like water, would perhaps finally prevail. Since the dawn of
> life, in successive waves, they had been dashing themselves

against the coasts of the flesh. Each wave was broken but, like the sea, wore away ever so little of the granite on which it failed, and some day, ages yet, *might roll unchecked over the place where the material world had been*, and God would move on the face of those waters. One such wave (and not the least) I raised, and rolled before the breath of an idea, till it reached its crest, and toppled over and fell at Damascus.⁴ [Italics mine.]

There are times, in later scenes of violence and bloodshed, when Lawrence seems to be driving home Hemingway's conclusion, Most men die like animals, not men. There are even passages when the unemotional detachment seems to be callousness, or a disguised sadistic pleasure, and this would be difficult to reconcile with the picture of Lawrence drawn by his friends. It is then that passages like the one above provide the key to Lawrence's attitude. His detachment is like Hemingway's, a desire to 'stand for truth'. But there is an element present that Hemingway lacks completely, that element of a *religious creed* that conditions his way of seeing. The violence and cruelty of the desert, and its contempt for the flesh, weigh equally in opposite balance-pans. The creed that reconciles them is the belief that the aim of life is the conquest of matter by spirit. The Arabs have the simplicity of violent opposites:

Without a creed they could be taken to the four corners of the earth (though not to heaven) by being shown the riches of the earth and the pleasures of it; but if on the road, led in this fashion, they met the prophet of an idea, who had nowhere to lay his head, and who depended for his food on charity or the birds, then they would all leave their wealth for his inspiration.⁵

What becomes undeniably apparent in reading *The Seven Pillars* is that Lawrence *did not regard himself as a soldier*. It was as the prophet of an idea that he 'raised the wave'; his power is the power of a man who can be *possessed by an idea*, and communicate his feeling to others. Again and again he repeats that the Arab war was a war of preaching, not of fighting. His frequent periods of misery and discouragement are due to a simple fact: he cannot believe in the idea that he is preaching:

If I had been an honest advisor of the Arabs, I would have advised them to go home and not risk their lives fighting for such stuff. . . .

In spite of this disbelief, the role of preacher and leader afforded Lawrence the self-expression he needed. Elsewhere he confesses:

I had one craving all my life—for the power of self-expression in some imaginative form. . . .

This war affords him an insight into himself; like Krebs, times when he did 'the one thing, the only thing'. It gives him a clear glimpse of that which is not trivial and unheroic.

His power of self-analysis is profound. He cannot see himself and his mind as a whole, but he can construct the picture in fragments, and in *The Seven Pillars*, none of the fragments is missing. His most characteristic trait is his inability to *stop thinking*. Thought imprisons him; it is an unending misery, because he knows the meaning of freedom, from such experience as this:

We started on one of those clear dawns that wake up the senses with the sun, while the intellect, tired after the thinking of the night, was yet abed. For an hour or two, on such a morning, the sounds, scents and colours of the world struck man individually and directly, *not filtered through or made typical by thought*: they seemed to exist sufficiently by themselves, and the lack of design and of carefulness in creation no longer irritated.[6]

When asked to become Feisal's advisor:

I said I hated responsibility . . . and that all my life, *objects had been gladder to me than persons, and ideas than objects*.[7]

The statements of those who knew him corroborate this. E. M. Forster wrote of him:

Though I was frank with him, he was never frank in return, nor did I resent his refusal to be so. This explains in part why he was a great leader of men; he was able to reject intimacy without impairing affection.[8]

Essentially, Lawrence was not interested in human beings:

The lower creation I avoided, as a reflection upon our failure to attain real intellectuality. If they forced themselves on me, I hated them. To put my hand on a living thing was defilement, and it made me tremble if they touched me or took too great an interest in me. . . . The opposite would have been my choice if my head had not been tyrannous. I . . . lamented myself most when I saw a soldier with a girl, or a man fondling a dog, because my wish was to be as superficial and as perfected, and my jailer held me back.[9]

And speaking of the Arabs:

Before me lay a vista of responsibility and command that disgusted my thought-riddled nature. I felt mean, to fill the place of a man of action, for my standards of value were a wilful reaction against theirs, and I despised their happiness. Always my soul hungered for less than it had, since my senses, sluggish beyond the senses of most men, needed the immediacy of contact to achieve perception. . . .[10]

He transfers his own characteristics to the Arabs, crediting them with his own love of emptiness, or he generalizes to include himself:

We westerners of this complex age, monks in our body's cells. . . .[11]

But it was Lawrence alone who was a 'monk in his body's cell', a man who could never achieve the 'immediacy of perception' because *he could never stop thinking*. He was a 'pipe through which life flowed':

It was a hard task for me to straddle feeling and action.

For such a person, the world is an unbelievably colourless place, without vivid perception of sights and tastes to remove the attention from human beings and their inanities. The result is a state of unending mental strain:

> It was only weakness which delayed me from mind-suicide
> —some slow task to choke at length this furnace in my brain:
> I had developed ideas of other men . . . but had never
> created a thing of my own, *since I could not approve creation.*[12]
> [Italics mine.]

This disapproval of creation is of the same nature as Oliver Gauntlett's 'The ignorant, the deceived, the superficial, were the happy among us', and consequently, the creative among them. It is dislike of human beings, 'the mob', 'chattering, snivelling, scolding'.[13]

We can see that Lawrence combines the central characteristics of Roquentin and the Barbusse Outsider. Roquentin had said: 'I was like the others—I said with them, the ocean *is* green, that white speck up there *is* a seagull, but I didn't feel that it existed.' Lawrence's inability to escape his 'thought riddled nature' has the same effect upon him; *everything is unreal.* And like Barbusse's hero, he cannot be happy in society, because he 'sees too deep and too much'. The desert war provided Lawrence with the same kind of peep-show into human suffering that Barbusse's hero found in his hotel room. These experiences were necessary to him, as they were necessary to the Barbusse Outsider, because their violence left no room in his mind for the irrelevancies of a civilization based on compromise. Violence helped to dissipate the unreality. Whatever happened, Lawrence could have no truck with compromise: he describes his winning over of an Arab tribe that refused to join them on a raiding expedition:

> . . . We put it to them . . . how life in the mass was sensual
> only, to be lived and loved in its extremity. There could be
> no rest houses for revolt, no dividend of joy paid out. Its
> spirit was accretive, to endure as far as the senses would
> endure, and to use each such advance as a base for further
> adventure, deeper privation, sharper pain. Sense could not
> reach forward or backward. A felt emotion was a conquered
> emotion, an experience gone dead, which we buried by
> expressing it.

To be of the desert was, as they knew, a doom to wage

unending war with an enemy who was not of this world, nor life, nor anything, but hope itself; and failure seemed God's freedom to mankind. We might only exercise this our freedom by not doing what it lay within our power to do, for then life would belong to us, and we would have *mastered it by holding it cheap.* Death would be the best of all our works, the last free loyalty within our grasp, our final leisure, and of these two poles, death and life, or less finally, leisure and subsistence, we should shun subsistence (the very stuff of life) in all save its faintest degree, and cling close to leisure. Thereby we would serve to promote the not-doing rather than the doing. Some men there might be, uncreative, whose leisure is barren; but the activity of these would have been material only. To bring forth immaterial things, things partaking of spirit, not of flesh, we must be jealous of spending time or trouble upon physical demands, since in most men, the soul ages long before the body. Mankind has been no gainer by its drudges.[14] [Italics mine.]

The importance of this passage cannot be overestimated. It shows Lawrence taking his stand in an extreme of Asiatic world-contempt, the antithesis of the modern Western spirit. Steppenwolf's contempt for the bourgeois ideal reaches its logical end: anti-humanistic world-negation.

In another matter, Lawrence reinforces Steppenwolf's conclusions: Haller's recognition that he has not two, but many conflicting I's.

Now I found myself dividing into parts. . . . The spent body toiled on doggedly and took no heed, quite rightly, for the divided selves said nothing I was not capable of thinking in cold blood . . . they were all my natives. Telesius, taught by some such experience, split up the soul. Had he gone on to the furthest limit of exhaustion, he would have seen his conceived regiment of thoughts and acts and feelings ranked around him as separate creatures, eyeing, like vultures, the passing in their midst of the common thing that gave them life.[15]

This capacity of Lawrence's to bear physical pain is of central importance in understanding him. His clear-sighted intellect could not conceive of moral freedom without physical freedom too; pain was an invaluable instrument in experiments to determine the extent of his moral freedom. His nihilism was fortified when he found himself unable to bear extremes, when, for instance, beaten by Turkish soldiers, the pain mastered his will not to cry out. Yet his conclusions point towards ultimate moral freedom:

> During [our revolt] we often saw men push themselves or be driven to a cruel extreme of endurance, yet never was there an intimation of physical break. Collapse arose always from a moral weakness eating into the body, which of itself, without traitors from within, had no power over the Will.
>
> While we rode we were disbodied, unconscious of flesh or feeling, and when, at an interval, this excitement faded and we did see our bodies, it was with some hostility, a contemptuous sense that they reached their highest purpose, not as vehicles of the spirit, but, when dissolved, their elements served to manure a field.[16]

The will is supreme, but, as for Schopenhauer, it can exercise its ultimate freedom only by willing negation. Yet the belief in its fundamental importance gives us the key to Lawrence's life; he had never ceased to experiment to test the power of his will:

> Such liberties [abstaining from food and sleep] came from years of control (contempt of use might well be the lesson of our manhood) and they fitted me peculiarly for our work; but in me they came, half by training, half by trying . . . not effortlessly, as with the Arabs. Yet in compensation stood my energy of motive. Their less taut wills flagged before mine flagged, and by comparison made me seem tough and active.

There is, admittedly, a sort of contradiction involved in the two paragraphs quoted above. The Emersonian parenthesis, 'Contempt of use might well be the lesson of our manhood', follows logically from his earlier statement that 'his senses . . . needed the immediacy of contact to achieve perception'. His asceticism is an attempt to 'cleanse the doors of perception' (in Blake's phrase). Yet this does not fit in with the earlier paragraph and its complete denial of the body. One line of thought leads to the conception that the body reaches its highest purpose with perfect 'immediacy of perception achieved', which is the conclusion of the mysticism of Boehme and Blake. The other leads to complete contempt, a cleansing of the senses that ultimately leads to throwing the senses away too.

Obviously, Lawrence's metaphysics does not form a self-complete system, and where it shows contradictions, it does so because he never worked systematically at self-analysis. This particular contradiction is inherent in mysticism—the saint who sees all existence as holy, and the saint who is completely withdrawn from existence—and if Lawrence had ever empirically resolved it, the last fifteen years of his life might have been much easier to understand. The 'mind suicide' of joining the R.A.F., and thereby involving himself with 'the ignorant, the deceived, the superficial', might have been rejected in favour of some less frustrating form of asceticism. Lawrence deliberately complicated the difficulty of self-realization by refusing to believe that he had any self to realize. He stated: 'Indeed, the truth was I did not like the "myself" I could see and hear',[17] but had no notion of how to proceed to unearth the self he *didn't* dislike, the self he was aware of on that 'clear dawn that woke up the senses with the sun, while the intellect . . . was yet abed'. Lawrence has all of the powers of a man who is capable of making tremendous efforts of will; he fails because he has no purpose towards which to direct the will. His failure is due to his inability to analyse the vague urges that stir in him, and bring them into the light of consciousness.

It is a curious fact that Granville-Barker sent Lawrence one of the first copies of *The Secret Life*, which he acknowledged reading in a letter of 7 February, 1924. There is no evidence that Lawrence saw a reflection of his own spiritual state in Evan Strowde or Oliver Gauntlett; he praises the play as being one of the best pictures of real politicians ever drawn! This is the disconcerting thing about Lawrence after the war; he seems to have given up the struggle. There is something about the abnegation of will of his R.A.F. years that is terribly like that paralysis of motive in the insanity of Nijinsky or Nietzsche. Steppanwolf has said, 'There is no way back . . . the

way lies on, ever further into guilt, ever deeper into human life.'
But often a point of strain is reached where the Outsider cannot
go on; the complications are too much. He asks for nothing but
rest. Lawrence reached that point, and perhaps, in some ways,
Steppenwolf's ideal of cutting his throat would have been a
more satisfactory conclusion than the 'mind suicide' of the
R.A.F. But there were still some things that had the power of
exciting Lawrence to direct sensation, in spite of the 'thought-
riddled nature', and one of these was speed. It was speed that
eventually killed him, for he swerved his motor-bike to avoid
two errand boys at the top of a hill, and crashed into a hedge
at seventy miles an hour.

*   *   *

Lawrence's work has introduced new implications into our
study of 'the Outsider's problems', and these can be seen most
clearly by reviewing the ground covered so far. Lawrence has
characteristics in common with all the Outsiders we have
considered, and in him we can see the point to which some of
them were tending.

From Barbusse, we can see that *the Outsider's problem is the
problem of denial of self-expression*. This gave rise to the question
of whether the Outsider is therefore a merely sociological
problem. The introduction, in Wells's pamphlet, of a definitely
un-sociological aspect, led us naturally to Roquentin, where it
was seen that the problem is, in fact, metaphysical.

Camus and Hemingway have emphasized its *practical*
nature. It is a living problem; the problem of *pattern or purpose*
in life. The Outsider is he who cannot accept life as it is, who
cannot consider his own existence or anyone else's *necessary*.
He sees 'too deep and too much'. It is still a question of self-
expression.

In *The Secret Life* we see the Outsider cut off from other
people by an intelligence that ruthlessly destroys their values,
and prevents him from self-expression through his inability to
substitute new values. His problem is Ecclesiastes' *'Vanitatum
vanitas'*; nothing is worth doing.

The romantic Outsider has broadened the approach by
showing that it is not necessarily the problem of disillusioned
men. On a different level, the romantic lives it in his striving to
give flesh to the romantic ideal. Hesse's conclusion was: more

self-analysis, 'to traverse again the hell of the inner being'. The Outsider must know himself more. This involves Roquentin's way and Meursault's way; the way of metaphysical analysis and the way of acceptance of physical life. But the ultimate failure of both Goldmund and the Magister Ludi, the ways of flesh and spirit, leave us still faced with Strowde's: Nothing is worth doing, no way is better than another.

It is Lawrence who has finally indicated the way out of this impasse. The others have accepted it as a problem in one variable, as it were. A 'way' is to be sought. The question 'A way *for whom*' would be answered by Roquentin or Strowde: 'A way for me, obviously.' Lawrence has made the great step forward: 'You are not what you think you are.' Instead of saying: Nothing is worth doing, you should say, '*I* am not worth doing anything.' Oliver Gauntlett's question of *where* the enemy is, has been answered by Lawrence: 'You think he *is* you.' Oliver's real war is a war against oneself. Lawrence has made the vital distinction in one sentence: 'Indeed, I did not like the "myself" I could see and hear.' 'He is not himself', Kennington's schoolmaster had said. Lawrence does not divide himself up into two parts like Haller and then say 'Man hates wolf'. It was a whole complex of body and mind and emotions that Lawrence hated, his ideas about himself that made a constant suffocating-blanket around his vital impulses.

This is a situation that is by no means unfamiliar to saints and mystics; Lawrence's misfortune is in having so far found no biographer qualified to deal with his spiritual conflicts. The popular ideas of a 'Lawrence enigma' have culminated in Mr. Aldington's attempt to explain Lawrence in terms of Freud's inadequate psychology. But the 'Lawrence enigma' was cleared up by Lawrence himself in *The Seven Pillars*. Man is not a unity; he is many. But for anything to be worth doing, he must become a unity. The divided kingdom must be unified. The deluded vision of personality that our Western civilization fosters and glorifies, increases the inward division; Lawrence recognized it as the enemy. The war against it is therefore inevitably a revolt against Western civilization.

Lawrence's achievement takes us even further. The war is not to be fought by mere reason. Reason leaves the personality comfortable on its own ground. The will's power is immense when backed by moral purpose. Reason's only role is to establish moral purpose by self-analysis. Once the enemy is defined, the will can operate, and the limit of its power over the body is only the limit of moral purpose to back it.

If our reasoning is correct, the Outsider's problem is not new; Lawrence points out that the history of prophets of all time follow a pattern: born in a civilization, they reject its standards of material well-being and retreat into the desert. When they return, it is to preach world rejection: intensity of spirit versus physical security. The Outsider's miseries are the prophet's teething pains. He retreats into his room, like a spider in a dark corner; he lives alone, wishes to avoid people. 'To the thinkers of the desert, the impulse into Nitria had proved ever irresistible.' He thinks, he analyses, he 'descends into himself': 'Not that probably they found God dwelling there, but that in solitude they heard more certainly the living word they brought with them.' Gradually the message emerges. It need not be a positive massage; why should it, when the impulse that drives to it is negative—disgust?

The prophet is a man of greater spiritual integrity than his neighbours; their laxness revolts him, and he feels impelled to tell them so. In his embryonic form, as the Outsider, he does not know himself well enough to understand the driving force behind his feelings. That is why his chief concern is with thinking, not with doing. In the Outsiders we shall deal with in the rest of this book, we shall watch the emergence of the distinctly prophetic element in the Outsider.

* * *

Consideration of Hemingway introduced the Outsider's obsession with pain and death. One of the finest passages in his novel *For Whom the Bell Tolls* is the episode of El Sordo's last fight on the hilltop. As the Republicans, led by El Sordo, watch the coming of the planes that will bomb them, the boy Ignacio begins to repeat an aphorism of the Communist heroine Passionaria, then switches into prayer: Hail Mary, full of grace. . . . With the roar of the planes in his ears, he can only remember: Now and at the hour of our death, Amen. A few minutes later, everyone on the hilltop is dead; Hemingway's evocation of the suddenness and brutality of their deaths is oppressively convincing. Dramatically, the episode is perhaps even finer than the end of *A Farewell to Arms*. The two extremes are swept together: religion, deeper-ingrained in man than any political creeds; and death. It is death that seems to have the last word.

For a certain type of Outsider, this problem is the only real problem. Basically, it is the same problem as Roquentin's 'nausea'; instead of 'humanity *versus* naked existence' it expresses itself 'as aspiration to life *versus* death'. Its effect is the same: negation of the will to live. It goes without saying that no half-way houses will serve instead of an answer, no belief in spiritism or an after-life or reincarnation; it must be the one and only answer, and no '*credo ut intelligam*' involved.

But we have already stated that no amount of thinking can lead to a final answer. It looks as if we have arrived at another impasse; but if we follow the course of the argument backwards, we discover that the impasse occurs when we identify the two concepts 'understanding' and 'reason'. '*Credo ut intelligam*', to believe in order to understand, does not cut off the Outsider completely from using his reason. But it demands that he use *other means beside reason.* The remainder of this chapter will make this point clear; we must consider the lives of two men who were in no sense philosophers. The first of these Outsiders was a painter, the other a dancer.

*　　　*　　　*

Vincent Van Gogh was born in Holland in 1853, the son of a Protestant pastor. He began to paint when he was twenty-nine. Eight years later, he shot himself in the stomach with a revolver, and died, at Auvers in Provence, in August, 1889. All his life he had lived on the edge of nervous crises, and during the last two years, he was for periods actually insane.

Of all painters, Van Gogh is perhaps the greatest letter-writer; it would not be an exaggeration to say that he owes his universal acclaim since his death to the letters (and popular biographies constructed from them) more than to the paintings themselves. In spite of this, their value as self-revelation is not to be compared with the introspective documents we have studied so far; he was a painter; words gave him no release. His interest for us lies in the incidents of his life, and in his painting. He is the first Outsider to be considered in this book who was not a writer and not an analytical thinker.

Van Gogh was never an easy person to live with; fits of

nervous depression made his temper uncertain. He left home when he was sixteen to work in an art gallery in La Haye, and four years later he came to work in London. There he had an unhappy love affair that increased his tendency to brood. He returned to his father's home, and the atmosphere soon became overcharged with irritation and intolerance. A year later, he again returned to London to make another attempt to persuade the girl to marry him, and again failed. Obviously, he was not one to take life lightly; miseries and disappointments cut deep.

In the following year he was in Paris, and had crises of mysticism. He read and commented on the Bible. But the unsatisfaction refused to let him alone; he gave up his job and returned to London; there he had an experience of the slum quarter that stirred a deep feeling of pity. The religious enthusiasm grew, and he made his decision: to become a pastor, like his father. A year later, he was among the miners of the Borinage, in Belgium, preaching, giving away his money and clothes until he was poorer than the miners. But even this was a failure; the miners were poor, but it was a mistake to suppose that their experience of hardship would make them sympathetic to the voluntary poverty of a saint. Van Gogh was as much a stranger among them as he had been among his bourgeois relations in Holland. Finally, someone notified his superiors of his 'eccentricities', and he was recalled.

There exists a painting from the last year of his life called 'Memory of the North'. A red winter sun sinks behind masses of sludgy green-grey cloud; all the sky is full of dirty, twisted scraps of cloud, tinted with the sun. In the foreground, small grimy houses, trees and bushes, repeat the twisting, red-tinted lines of the sky. The whole picture is overcast with a sulphurous light. We see the North as Van Gogh saw it in the year of his 'mission'.

He decided to study drawing; for a while, this satisfied him. Then, in the following year, there was another unhappy love affair. This time the defeat was so bitter that he contemplated suicide. From this period we have a typical story of the 'wild man' aspect of his nature that made people he lived with nervous and suspicious. He had called on the girl's family— she was his cousin—to make a last attempt to persuade her to marry him. He was told that she was not at home, but could see, at the dinner table, her place still partly laid, as she had left it when his arrival was announced. He held out his hand towards the candle and asked: 'Let me see her for as long as I can hold my hand in this flame.' Someone snatched the candle away. Eventually he got his own way and was allowed to see his cousin. It came to nothing. That was the last time he saw her.

A year later, he took up painting seriously. He had also taken in a woman of the streets who was pregnant, thereby scandalizing all his friends, who abandoned him as lost. Even this affair was a failure. But now he had the painting to counter-balance his nervous tensions. As each crisis was overcome, the painting became stronger, more certain. In Paris, he absorbed the influence of the Impressionists, and the canvases became lighter. His brother Theo supplied him with money to live on while he painted; but even Theo, his most constant ally, found the 'wild man' a strain to live with. Finally, constant nervous tension had its effect on Vincent's health, and he left Paris for the South in 1888. Gauguin joined him there, but, like every-one else, found him too explosive and highly strung to live with; the rupture occurred when Vincent attacked him with a razor and then, later, cut off his own ear and presented it in a matchbox to a prostitute at the local brothel. Periods of insanity followed; he was removed to the hospital, but continued to paint.

His style had developed in these last two years. His canvases were no longer realistic landscapes and interiors influenced by Millet and the Dutch school. The colours and lines are bolder, and in some of them, a strange technique of distortion makes it appear that trees, cornfields, houses are all burning upwards like flames. In contrast to these 'brainstorm' canvases, others are calm, relaxed, full of light and silence. He painted many portraits in the South—almost anyone he could persuade to sit for him—and many still-lifes. Some of the portraits show an odd feeling for decorative values which brings to mind Japanese prints; the still-lifes, on the contrary, often have a dynamic quality of the sort we find in a Michelangelo drawing. (The best known of these is the 'Yellow Chair', of which Gauguin exclaimed delightedly: 'No one ever painted a chair like that before!')

Vincent removed from the hospital at Arles to a private

sanatorium kept by a Dr. Gachet, Theo still continuing to send money. But Theo had more responsibilities now; he had married and his wife was expecting a baby. Beside this, he was quarrelling with the proprietors of his art gallery, who disliked Theo's taste in the new 'young painters'. Vincent began to feel that his life was simply a burden on the world; he was terrified of complete insanity. His last canvas is the 'Cornfield with Crows': the sky blue-black with a coming storm; a road that runs in from the left of the canvas, and shoots away through the middle of the ripe corn like a fast stream. There is a curious atmosphere of strain and foreboding. A few days after painting it he returned to the same place and shot himself with a revolver. But he bungled it, missing the heart; he buttoned the coat over the wound and walked back to his room. Two days later he died; his last words to Theo were: 'Misery will never end.' At the end of his last letter to Theo occur the words: 'Well, as to my work, I've risked my life for it, and my reason has half foundered. . . .'

Van Gogh's life recalls to mind Hesse's words in *Demian*: 'Everyone's life is a road to himself, to self-realization. . . .' In Van Gogh's case, 'self-realization' meant simply self-expression. For us, he is primarily a painter; but we should remember that he lived for nearly four decades, and that it was only in the last eight years of his life that he thought of himself as a painter. Thirty years is a long time to live without a direction. Most people have a fairly definite idea of what they are and where they belong, before they are twenty. Van Gogh was aware of himself as a dynamo of energy and will-power before he was seventeen; but he had no idea of *what to drive* with his energy. In many ways he reminds us of the young George Fox, with his tormented feeling of having a purpose, yet not being conscious of it. 'I was a man of sorrows in those days.' (We shall examine Fox's claim to be classed as an Outsider in Chapter VIII of this book.)

The one thing that is certain of the young Van Gogh is the intensity of his religious feeling; and by this, I do not mean intensity of *devotional* feeling, but simply a sense of *purpose*. This is in no way different from the feeling that made Lawrence regard himself as a preacher rather than as a soldier. If carefully analysed, it can only be resolved into the idea that there is a higher power than man in the universe, and man reaches

his highest purpose in serving it. At the same time, it is necessary to bear in mind Hesse's recognition that, strictly speaking,
there is no such thing as man; 'Man is a bourgeois compromise.' The primitive religious notion of man's relation to his
creator collapses under the Outsider's criticism. The Outsider's
wretchedness lies in his inability to find a new faith; he tends to
regard his condition of unbelief as the result of a Fall.

This is the essential Van Gogh; not a painter, but an Outsider, for whom life is an acute and painful question that
demands solution before he begins living. His earliest experiences teach him that life is an eternal Pro and Contra.
His sensitivity makes him unusually aware of the Contra,
of his own misery and the world's. All his faculties are exerted in
a search for the Pro, for instinctive, absolute Yea-saying. Like
all artists, he has moments when he seems to be in complete
accord with the universe and himself, when, like Meursault,
he feels that the universe and himself are of the same nature;
then all life seems purposive, and his own miseries purposive.
The rest of the time is a struggle to regain that insight. *If*
there is an order in the universe, if he can sometimes perceive
that order and feel himself completely in accord with it, then it
must be seeable, touchable, so that it could be regained by some
discipline. Art is only one form of such a discipline.

Unfortunately, the problem is complicated by quite irrelevant human needs that claim the attention: for companionship
and understanding, for a feeling of participation in the social
life of humanity. And of course, for a roof over one's head, and
food and drink. The artist tries to give attention to these, but
it is difficult when there are so much more important things to
think about; and it is all made more difficult by the hostility
of other people who every day arouse the question, Could it
be that I'm wrong? Sometimes the strain makes the Outsider-
artist think of suicide, but before he gets to that point, the
universe is suddenly making sense again, and he has a glimpse
of purpose. Moreover, that sense of accord is not the warm,
vague harmony of a sleeping baby, but a blazing of all the
senses, and a realization of a condition of consciousness unknown to the ordinary bourgeois. He realizes that this was
what he left out of account in making up his mental balance-
sheet of Pro and Contra in the universe. The Christian might
call it a sense of the Fatherhood of God; a Hindu would

probably prefer to call it a sense of the Motherhood of God, and his symbolism would be more congenial to the artist, who can only find comparison for the feeling in a child's confidence in its mother. In any case, these are only symbols of a state that is too little known to human beings for their descriptions of it to be accurate.

When we turn to Van Gogh's canvases, we find attempts to express this sense in another medium than language. Writers on mysticism may sneer at such attempts as completely inadequate, but this is to miss the really important point that, inadequate as it is, these attempts completely transcend most of their critics' knowledge of reality, and express an insight that very few human beings catch a glimpse of once in a lifetime. In approaching the work of such a man as Van Gogh, an attitude of completely uncritical acceptance (such as most of us feel towards the dogmas of higher mathematics) may be more rewarding than the intellectual-critical approach. What we are most aware of in Van Gogh is that the 'thought-riddled nature' has been very decisively kicked-out, and the result achieved is Lawrence's 'immediacy of sense perception'. The Pro and Contra have disappeared; with the senses awakened, it becomes nonsense to talk about human misery. Certainly there is misery, but it doesn't matter. Nothing matters that any human being ever thought; only this. The canvases try to express it with light and form: fields of corn with colour that almost hurts the eyes, a starry night with the sky looking like water full of cross-currents, and the stars no longer pinpoints, but rings and circles of light; cypresses like green flames. This interior vision transfigured a chair, an old boot, a few onions as El Greco's illuminated the Virgin.

For Vincent the battle was never conclusively won; the day after he had painted a chair 'as no one else ever painted it', he bickered with Gauguin and wrote an irritable letter to Theo; at other times it was simply that there was no hope of his painting ever contributing to his support, and the painting suddenly seemed hopeless and bad. His last words to Theo are the words of a man who feels that defeat is inevitable, that life is a baited trap; who kills himself to escape the necessity of taking the bait again. The last canvas is more than a landscape tinged by a mood of depression and fatigue; it is a summary of life as he knew it; his judgement is: No.

But other canvases are more direct affirmations than any other painter has ever achieved (El Greco perhaps excepted), expressions of spirit for which the words 'nature mysticism' are completely inadequate. Wordsworth was a nature mystic, and the rather complacent rationalism of 'The Excursion' is his natural mode of expression: Jehovah and the heavenly hosts 'he passes unalarmed', but nature, delightful nature, etc. . . . (William Blake, who was a nature mystic in a profounder sense, made one of his explosively irritable notes beside this passage in his copy of 'The Excursion'.) The real nature mystic, Jacob Boehme, Thomas Traherne, is as concerned with 'God in the soul' as with God in nature: consequently, no one ever speaks of them as nature mystics. This is also true of Van Gogh.

Nature reflects what he sees inside him. When he sees nothing, the canvases are realistic studies that might be curiously brilliant photographs. At other times, they express a vision that is inexpressible in words because it runs in a different direction; words are horizontal; this is vertical. The point of intersection of the two planes can only be called Is-ness (to borrow a phrase from Eckhart). Compare Van Gogh's copy of the prison yard with Doré's original; Van Gogh's is more 'visionary', there is more light; at the same time it is *more real* than Doré's. Van Gogh's chair *is* more than other chairs; his sunflowers *are* more than other sunflowers. Roquentin's words, 'I was like the others. . . . I didn't feel it existed', are fantastically inapplicable to Van Gogh. When he saw a tree full of leaves, it existed so much for him that he could not paint it as a tree (as Constable would) or give the general impression of a tree with colours (as Monet and the Impressionists did); it explodes into life and looks more like a tree burning with Bengal fires. This is no literary trick (any fool could paint a tree to look like a flame); it is a way of seeing; it is built into his vision, and the proof of its sincerity lies in watching the development of the vision through his painting.

Or compare his canvas called 'Landscape near Auvers' with Cézanne's canvas of the same name (any of them); the difference is more than a difference of technique; it is a completely different way of seeing. Cézanne *rendered* painstakingly, as Henry James rendered his pictures of European society, with innumerable small brush strokes. The final result has an orderliness that springs out of *discipline*. From Cézanne's painting, we learn a great deal about the surface of the object painted and its distance from the eye, and a great deal about the *will* of the man who was determined to render it fully. We learn nothing of Cézanne's emotion. This is precisely what we do learn from Van Gogh's canvases, and the emotion is important; it is not just a sentimental gushing about nature, but an emotion that could only correspond to some recognized awareness of the nature of life itself. Cézanne's painting is strictly painting, and its value is immense; but Van Gogh's painting has the Outsider's characteristic: it is laboratory refuse of a man who treated his own life as an experiment in living; it faithfully records moods and development of vision in the manner of a *Bildungsroman*.

To experts on art, this way of treating Van Gogh must seem completely without bearing on his importance *as a painter*. This is true; for the purposes of this study, he is not a painter; he is an Outsider who happened to choose painting as his medium.

When we consider him primarily as an Outsider, his importance in defining 'the Outsider's problems' is at once apparent. He has in common with T. E. Lawrence an unfortunate lack of conscious direction where his own unusual powers are concerned. He consistently underestimates himself and overestimates other people. This has its repercussions on his work every time he comes into contact with other people. In old age, Goethe built a mental wall around himself, and other people could not reach him with either praise or blame; if Van Gogh and Lawrence had done the same, their lives might have taken a completely different course.

This is the negative side of Van Gogh's contribution; the positive side suggests an important direction of thought. Together with Lawrence, he has introduced into the Outsider's problem the *concept of discipline*. But with him, it is no longer a discipline of the intellect; his powers of will were directed towards a development *of the emotions*. Now we have before us the fact that both he and T. E. Lawrence failed, and one of the reasons for this failure has been indicated in the previous paragraph: that failure of self-knowledge that produced something like an inferiority complex. But the sources of this failure are different in the two men, and we can express the difference by saying that Van Gogh *felt* too much just as Lawrence thought too much. One felt without thinking; the other thought without feeling.

Before examining the implications of this conclusion and its bearing on the Outsider generally, there is a third element to be considered. Both men began by a purely physical type of discipline: physical hardship, starvation, etc. Their earliest efforts at discipline were attempts to gain control of the body.

Any attempts to draw general conclusions from the Outsider's 'attempt to gain control' must be only partially satisfying until we can supplement them with the case-history of an Outsider who was primarily concerned with discipline of the body. We must go on to consider such a man before generalizing further about Van Gogh and Lawrence. There are many saints and fakirs who would serve as examples, but these would not conform to the conditions we have observed so far, that the Outsider should 'start from scratch' as far as his religion is concerned. The Outsider must not *start from* religion, he must start from grounds all can understand and accept: the world and human life. This narrows the field considerably; but luckily, there is an example to hand, the case of the ballet dancer Vaslav Nijinsky; and the various books about him, notably his wife's biography and Anatole Bourman's *Tragedy of Nijinsky* (the latter not entirely reliable), supply the necessary facts about his life. And most important, there is the *Diary* of Nijinsky, published in 1937, that gives us insight into Nijinsky's state of mind immediately before his mental collapse. These are more than sufficient for our purposes.

*　　　*　　　*

The element of tragedy seems to have been present in Nijinsky's life from the beginning. His family was always poor; his father was a dancer who travelled all over Russia, and seems to have left the support of the family to his wife.

Vaslav Nijinsky was born in Kiev in 1890. A year before his birth, his mother had received a painful shock to her system when bandits attacked the inn where she was staying; their violence and cruelty horrified her so that she lost the power of speech for three days.[18]

Vaslav was a delicate and sensitive child, passionately attached to his mother. While he was very young, his brother

Stanislav fell from a third-floor window; as a result of the concussion of the brain, he was an idiot for the rest of his life. Vaslav's father, who had been unfaithful to his wife for several years, deserted her after the accident, and left her to provide for the family of three children.

When Vaslav was nine, he was accepted into the Imperial school of dancing in St. Petersburg. This meant that his support was taken over by the Tsar, and he was trained to dance by men who had been famous dancers. His training lasted until he was eighteen, when he automatically became a member of the Mariinsky Theatre. His talent was so well known that he began immediately to dance leading roles opposite the prima ballerina. Before he was twenty, Nijinsky was famous in Petersburg.

About this time he met Sergei Diaghileff, and the meeting was a turning-point in his life.

Diaghileff was a rich amateur of art whose energies and organizing ability were so great that he was not content to be merely a patron and onlooker of dancers; he had to organize a ballet company, with his own musicians, choreographers, painters and dancers. With no artistic talent himself, he succeeded in associating his name with most of the major artists of Europe between 1907 and 1930: Stravinsky, Benois, Bakst, Pavlova, Karsavina, Fokine, Debussy, Ravel, Picasso, Chirico, Massine, De Falla, Cocteau . . . many of whom produced their best work in response to his cheque-book. Personally, Diaghileff was unattractive; his role of hard-headed business-man among artists made him unscrupulous; his belief in his mission as artistic saviour made him self-centred; with these qualities he combined some of the characteristics of the worst type of homosexual—sensuality, vanity and complete lack of intellectual driving force.

His first interest in Nijinsky was sexual: Nijinsky speaks of their meeting in his *Diary*: 'I disliked him because of his too assured voice but I went with him to seek my luck [to Diaghileff's hotel room]. . . . At once I allowed him to make love to me. . . . I hated him, but pretended to like him because I knew that my mother and I would die of starvation otherwise.'[19]

The last statement may be an exaggeration, but it is certain that Nijinsky felt the need to contribute to his family's support; since he had become a member of the Mariinsky, their expenses had rocketed; they had moved into an expensive flat that they could not really afford; Nijinsky's position required this; to add to this, his brother had become violently insane, and had to be removed to an institution, where the family had to continue to support him. Diaghileff knew that Nijinsky's wages from the Mariinsky were not enough to support the family; he offered him a position in his own newly formed ballet company. Nijinsky obtained leave from the Mariinsky and opened with the first Russian Ballet season in Paris in the spring of 1910.

The season made both Diaghileff and Nijinsky world-famous. Critics named Nijinsky *'le dieu de la danse'*; they acclaimed him the greatest male dancer the world has ever seen. The Russian Ballet followed up its success with seasons in all the capitals of Europe. Upon his return to St. Petersburg, Nijinsky plotted with Diaghileff to break his contract with the Mariinsky. In 1912 and 1913, Nijinsky produced choreographies for Debussy's *L'Après-Midi d'un Faune* and Stravinsky's *Sacre du Printemps*; in the first the scandal was caused by Nijinsky's choreography, in the second, by Stravinsky's score; but both added to the commercial success of the Russian Ballet.

Nijinsky found the overheated emotional atmosphere of the Diaghileff *ménage* a strain; Nijinsky had a deep-rooted religious tendency that made the unending theatre atmosphere of art and sensuality unsatisfying to him. He quarrelled with Diaghileff several times; he was getting tired of the 'artist and lover' business. In these quarrels, Stravinsky always supported Diaghileff; Nijinsky, after all, was only a brainless child-prodigy, while Diaghileff was the Connoisseur, the Artist with a capital A.

In 1913, Nijinsky took the opportunity of a sea voyage away from Diaghileff to get married; he proposed to a young dancer who was obviously in love with him; they were married in Buenos Aires. Diaghileff sent a telegram dismissing him from the Russian Ballet.

The five years that followed were years of strain and confusion. Nijinsky's wife was a Hungarian, and Hungary was at war with Russia. They went to live in Budapest, at her home, and the next year was full of petty spite, of relatives who tried to force her to divorce Nijinsky, family plotting and quarrels. In the years following his marriage, Nijinsky was badgered by the Outsider's greatest enemy, human triviality. There was a ballet season in New York, with Nijinsky's own company and a new Nijinsky ballet, and endless difficulties and annoyances to be overcome. Nijinsky had no business ability; his temperament was almost completely introverted, contemplative (various observers have spoken of him as having the face of a Tibetan Llama, of 'a Buddha in meditation', of an Egyptian statue); these endless, unimportant demands by the outside world were an immense strain. In this state of strain, the war began to weigh heavily on him; he was haunted by visions of dead soldiers.

In December, 1917, the family (they now had a child) moved to St. Moritz; and the last stage began. Nijinsky worked on the choreography of a new ballet, and read a great deal; he and his wife went for long walks or went for sleigh rides, or ski-ing. But the inactivity began to tell on Nijinsky; he needed something to do. He began to write a Diary, a sort of rambling exposition of his ideas on things in general, and perfected a technique of drawing with curves and arcs. He had made friends with a Tolstoyan, and now began to speak of the idea of giving up dancing and retiring somewhere in Russia, on a little farm, or perhaps to a monastery. His wife was impatient, and had little sympathy with the ideas that were now absorbing her husband. But Nijinsky thought a great deal about Tolstoy, and about Dostoevsky and Nietzsche. One Sunday, a young servant informed Madam Nijinsky that her husband had been standing in the middle of the village street, wearing his cross outside his shirt, and asking passers-by if they had been to church; as a child, the young man had known Nietzsche, and he added, 'Mr. Nietzsche used to behave like that just before he was taken away.' Madame Nijinsky consulted a psychiatrist. There were other disturbing signs; his study was full of drawings coloured in red and black 'like a bloodstained mortuary cover'. 'They are dead soldiers' faces,' he told his wife. 'It is the war. . . .'

On two occasions he was violent with her; then, she notes, 'he seemed like a stranger'. Finally, there was the incident of the 'marriage with God'. He had been asked to dance; in front of a crowded audience, he stood and stared for nearly half an hour. 'The audience behaved as if hypnotized', his wife records. Finally he told them: 'I will dance you the war, with its suffering and death . . . the war which you did nothing to prevent, so for which you are also responsible.' 'His gestures were all monumental. The public . . . seemed to be petrified.' He danced them a sort of choreographic counterpart of Picasso's 'Guernica'.[20]

The end was not long in coming. A few weeks later, a psychiatrist in Zürich told her: 'You must try to be brave. . . . Your husband is incurably insane.'

The same day, her parents arrived in Zürich; when they heard that Nijinsky had been pronounced insane, they waited until his wife had left the hotel, then called the police to remove 'the madman'. Their rough treatment brought on a catatonic attack, and Nijinsky never recovered from its consequences. He retreated into a world of his own, and nothing was interesting enough to bring him out; for years afterwards, in various sanatoriums, he stared into space, never replying to questions, taking no interest in what went on around him. His need to retreat into himself had been denied too long; in disgust and fatigue, he retreated permanently, disowning all responsibilities. On Good Friday, 1950, he died at last in a London institution, still in a mental twilight.

The *Diary of Vaslav Nijinsky*, published in English in 1937, provides us with the insight we need to judge what went on in his mind in those last days at St. Moritz. It is a strange document, typical in its jerkiness and vagueness, of a mind approaching insanity. There are signs of various delusions: for instance, in the opening sentences:

> People will say that Nijinsky pretends to be mad on account of his bad deeds. Bad deeds are terrible and I do not want to commit any. I made mistakes before because I did not understand God. . . .[21]

It is impossible to say what 'bad deeds' Nijinsky had in mind, or what mistakes he made; we have no record of anything discreditable in his adult life; he seems to have been harmless and very sincere, with a sort of Prince Myshkin-like simplicity about him. A few pages later, he records: 'I feel a piercing stare from behind', which, his wife explains in a footnote, was one of his visual hallucinations.[22] He begins to tell a story: 'I invited some friends on a sleigh ride to Maloja . . .', but a few sentences later he has forgotten about it and is talking about something else. This sort of evidence of insanity, fixed ideas, incoherency, etc., would incline most readers to give up reading the *Diary* after the first few pages. But, as we persist, a curious kind of sanity begins to make itself felt underneath this surface of aimlessness.

I do not want the death of the senses. I want people to understand. I cannot cry and shed tears over what I write, but I cry within me.[23]

I will tell the whole truth, and others will continue what I have begun. I am like Zola, but I want to speak, and not write novels. Novels prevent one from understanding feeling.[24]

I am in a trance, the trance of love. I want to say so much and cannot find the words. . . . I write in a trance, and that trance is called *wisdom*. Every man is a reasonable being. I do not want unreasonable beings, and therefore I want everyone to be in a trance of feelings.[25]

The whole life of my wife and of all mankind is death. . . .[26]

I want . . . to heal my wife, but I cannot be healed. I do not want to be healed. I am not afraid of anything except the death of wisdom. I want the death of the mind. My wife will not go mad if I kill her mind. The mind is stupidity, but wisdom is God.[27]

These passages are chosen almost at random from the early part of the book, yet a kind of reason can be discerned running from one to the other. Nijinsky has his own terminology: there are 'feeling', 'wisdom', 'God', and these are roughly synonymous; and then there are 'mind', 'death', 'stupidity'. The important sentence for understanding of Nijinsky's way of seeing 'mankind' is that comment: 'The whole life of my wife and of all mankind is death.' He records, in passing a lighted hotel after a night walk: 'I felt tears, understanding that life in places like this is like death. Mankind makes merry and God mourns. It is not the fault of mankind.'[28]

Again, what we are witnessing is the Outsider, with his intenser and deeper insight, feeling a Jansenist disgust with mankind. They are shallow; they are 'thinkers' who feel no need to retreat into themselves; consequently, they have no idea of their own real identities, nor of their possibilities:

'I am God in a body. Everyone has this feeling, but no one uses it.'[29] and later: 'God is fire in the head.'[30]

It is a permanent sorrow to Nijinsky that his wife, for whom he feels so much affection, is just another shallow 'thinker', another butterfly on the surface of life. After the sentence about his wife's way of life being death, he adds, 'I was shocked, and thought how lovely it would be if my wife were to listen to me.' But no one will listen to him, just as years before, in the Russian Ballet, Diaghileff and Stravinsky treated him as a brainless child. This is what worries Nijinsky. He is a natural contemplative, used to withdrawing deep into himself, gathering his energies into a tight coil, then unleashing them in self-expression. But these people—they know nothing of self expression, nothing of what lies inside them. Nijinsky knows: 'I am God in a body', he knows because it is a realization that has come to him many times while dancing, the self-transcendence, the Outsider's glimpse of a 'power within him'. He has seen that power, and he knows: 'I am God, I am God, I am God.'

Dancing is his natural form of self-expression, but outside dancing, he meets all the Outsider's usual problems. Like Barbusse's hero, he has wandered around the Paris streets staring at the women who pass, but once, when he picked up a prostitute who 'taught him everything', he was suddenly sure that this was not what he needed: 'I was shocked and told her it was a pity to do things like that. She told me that if she didn't do it she would die of hunger. . . .'[31]

And always, there is the tearing, excoriating demand, of pity. This is the worst of Nijinsky's problems. He loves his wife, he pities her unhappiness, yet he knows that her life is death. Misery and death are moulded into the very stuff of the world. He had known them as a child when the family almost starved. He had known them even in the school of dancing, for he had been present in the 1905 revolution in Petersburg, when the soldiers had slashed down unarmed civilians with swords, or crushed their skulls with knouts; after the reign of terror, Nijinsky and his schoolfellows had walked along rows of bloodied corpses in the morgues, looking into the faces of the women to try to identify the sister of Babitch, a beautiful girl of seventeen with whom they were all secretly in love; she was never seen again. In the revolution of 1917, Nijinsky's brother had been accidentally killed when the madhouses were thrown open by the Bolsheviks. Of Nijinsky's schoolfellows, one was killed in a duel, another shot by a jealous husband, another committed suicide. . . . Deaths, miseries, privations, these were of the common stuff of life, and Nijinsky knew as well as Van Gogh: 'Misery will never end.'

In the scales of the gigantic balance-pan in Nijinsky's brain, the world's misery bulked heavy on one side. But the other? First, there was dancing, the rhythmic, violent Dionysian upsurge of the vital energies; while he could dance regularly, every day, and restore contact with the vital, instinctive parts of his own being, Nijinsky could not go insane. Sanity lay in creation. Then there was the deep religious sense; Nijinsky had been brought up a Roman Catholic; a feeling of the universal fatherhood of God was as fundamental in him as the urge to create. Perhaps the most striking thing about the Diary is the use of the name of God. 'God' occurs five times on the first page, and, on a average, about the same number of times on every page of the book. There are certain pages in the Diary when its repetition would seem to justify the conclusion that Nijinsky was obsessed with the idea of becoming God, but it would be equally true to say that he was obsessed with the idea of becoming Christlike. He observes:

> I look like him, only he has a calm gaze, and my eyes look around me. I am a man of motion, not of immobility.[32]

And this is the centre of the problem. Denied motion, the strain begins. The static personality is a prison:

'I want to be God, and therefore I try to change myself. I want to dance, to draw, to play the piano, to write verses, to love everybody. That is the object of my life.'[33]

In the Diary, denial of self-expression has reached a point where it produces an atmosphere of physical suffocation:

'I like hunchbacks and other freaks. I am myself a freak who has feelings and sensitiveness, and I can dance like a hunchback. I am an artist who likes all shapes and all beauty.'[34]

Denial of self-expression is the death of the soul; without creation, the balance is gone. The scale dips on the side of misery and suffering:

I believe I suffered more than Christ. I love life and I want to live, to cry but cannot—I feel such a pain in my soul—a pain which frightens me. My soul is ill. My soul, not my mind. The doctors do not understand my illness. . . . Everybody who reads these lines will suffer. . . . My body is not ill, it is my soul that is ill.[35]

Nijinsky understood himself well enough to know what he needed to keep sane. But what he did not know was how much suffering and frustration his mind could stand; the pain frightened him. His statement, 'I am a man of motion, not of immobility', is the key to his breakdown, and at the same time, the key to his relation to Van Gogh and Lawrence. It would not be true to say of either of these, that they were 'men of motion', for the development of the intellect or the emotions makes for immobility, for contemplation. Nijinsky knew this could not be his way. With astounding penetration he analyses his creative urges: '*I am feeling through flesh, and not through the intellect.*'

He is always intensely aware of his physical being. Now compare with Lawrence and Van Gogh; Lawrence's problem is that 'he is never alive in what he does', he never *feels* what he thinks. He could write: 'I am insight through mind, not through feeling.' Van Gogh could write: 'I am insight through feeling, not through mind.' It is Nijinsky who can say: 'I am insight through *flesh*, not through either mind or feeling.'

I am aware that these terms lack precision: intellect is capable of a white heat of feeling as well as body or emotions. The vagueness can be overcome by keeping in mind the following concrete illustrations: In respect of intellect, the absorption of a Newton or an Einstein in some mathematical problem: in respect of emotion, the intensity of Wagner's *Tristan und Isolde*; in respect of body, the ecstasy of an ancient Greek festival of Dionysus, or the Egyptian phallic God Menu, when wine and dancing bring about a temporary loss of identity of individual worshippers in the identity of the god. With this last in mind, we can understand the meaning of phrases in the *Diary* like 'I am God, I am God, I am God',[36] without falling into the misunderstanding of the provincial newspaper that stated in its obituary: 'Nijinsky's madness took the form of a delusion that he was God.' Nijinsky's body obeyed his creative impulses as Van Gogh's brush and

Lawrence's pen obeyed theirs. The body can be made drunk
with its own vitality far more easily than the intellect or the
emotions with theirs. Many men have experienced the feeling
'I am God' in a sexual orgasm; few have experienced it from
listening to music or looking at painting; fewer still from any
intellectual activity.

William James has observed that 'the power of alcohol over
mankind is unquestionably due to its power to stimulate the
mystical faculties of human nature, usually crushed to earth by
the cold facts and dry criticisms of the sober hour'. 'Mystical
faculties' here refers to that flood-tide of inner warmth and
vital energy that human beings regard as the most desirable
state to live in. The sober hour carries continuous demands on
the energy; sense-impressions, thoughts, uncertainties, suck
away the vital powers minute by minute. Alcohol seems to
paralyse these leeches of the energies; the vital warmth is left
to accumulate and form a sort of inner reservoir. This concentration of the energies is undoubtedly one of the most
important conditions of the state the saints call '*Innigkeit*',
inwardness. The saint achieves inwardness by a deliberate
policing of the vital energies. He comes to recognize the
energy-stealing emotions, all the emotions that do not make for
inwardness, and he sets out to exterminate them in himself.
As he moves towards his objective, he increases steadily his
supply of surplus vital power, and so increases his powers of
foresight and hind-sight, the sense of other times and other
places; there is a breaking-free of the body's sense of imprisonment in time and a rising warmth of life-energy that is
spoken of in the Gospel as 'to have life more abundantly'.

Nijinsky, Lawrence, Van Gogh, each had his own form of
discipline towards this end. Each one had, as it were, discovered in some moment of insight a source from which these
supplies of 'more abundant life' flowed, and each concentrated
on a discipline that would make the source accessible. Lawrence
was a thinker who had found imaginative relief in his study of
the past. Van Gogh's religious temperament needed to accumulate *sense impressions*; his striving towards a sense of
'otherness' took the form of a sort of pictorial memory of other
imes and other places: a memory that was, after all, in-
omplete, since he could not capture the scent of the almond
ee or the hot July wind, or the tension in the air of a rising

storm on his canvas. But Nijinsky's kingdom was the body. People who saw him dance have testified to his amazing ability to *become* the part he was acting, whether the Negro in *Scheherezade*, the puppet in *Petrouchka*, or the Prince in *Giselle*. His discipline gave him the power to dismiss his identity at will, or to expand some parts and contract others to give an illusion of a completely new personality. It was this power that, at times, became a mystical intensity of abnegation in his dancing, that occasionally gave him glimpses into the ecstasy of the saint.

And herein lies the cause of his breakdown. Such a man is spiritually and artistically far above the level of the '*homme moyen sensuel*'; even above a man who was more than averagely sensual, like Diaghileff. And if he happens to lack the common-place power of verbal self-expression, and the self-assurance that most men pick up in their dealings with the 'world', his position among other men is made completely false. He has no *reason* to credit himself with unusual spiritual maturity, and still less for refusing to credit other men with it, when their self-assurance impresses on him his own inferiority in respect of intelligence and logic. If he happens to be young and inexperienced (Nijinsky was only twenty-nine when he went insane), he has practically no defence against the world.

Diaghileff's protectorship was intolerable; this is hardly surprising. But unfortunately, Nijinsky's marriage left him no better off. For his wife he was a mixture of god and child; she understood the child part only too well, the god part, not at all. It was the same with Nijinsky's colleagues. He was '*le dieu de la danse*', but from most critical accounts, he was a bungling choreographer whose ballets either defied performance or left the audience mystified. His *Rite of Spring* contains complex dancing parts which the dancers of his day declared to be un-danceable much as the violinists in Beethoven's day had declared passages in the last quartets to be unplayable. He had taken Debussy's *Prélude à L'Après-Midi d'un Faune*, and con-structed to the sensuous, fleshly, drowsy music a choreography that was hard and angular. The ballet looked like a series of 'flats', a Greek vase design; in Nijinsky's hands it lost the qualities that Diaghileff could so well understand—warmth, humanity, sensuality; it had substituted hardness, heaviness, angularity, violence. Hulme's comment on Byzantine art might be applied to it:

> . . . the emotion you get from it is not a pleasure in the reproduction of natural or human life. The disgust with the trivial and accidental characteristics of living shapes, the searching after an austerity, a *perfection* and rigidity that vital things can never have, lead here to the use of forms that can almost be called geometrical.[37]

Hulme went on to state his conclusions from this angular art:

> Man is subordinate to certain absolute values; there is no delight in the human form leading to its natural reproduction; it is always distorted to fit *the more abstract forms which convey intense religious emotion*.[38]

Nijinsky's *Diary* shows us his capacity for 'intense religious emotion', and its style is correspondingly hard and angular. In the same way, his conception of the ballet was more than an attempt to follow Jacques Dalcroze's theory that each note in the music should have a corresponding movement from the dancer; it was the effort of the Outsider to find expression for emotions that wanted to emerge like bullets from a machine-gun. With Nijinsky, the Outsider's strain reached bursting-point, and his mind plunged into darkness.

The Diary of Vaslav Nijinsky reaches a limit of sincerity beyond any of the documents we have referred to in this study. There are other modern works that express the same sense that civilized life is a form of living death: notably the poetry of T. S. Eliot and the novels of Franz Kafka; but there is an element of prophetic denunciation in both, the attitude of healthy men rebuking their sick neighbours. We possess no other record of the Outsider's problems that was written by a man about to be defeated and permanently smashed by those problems. Nijinsky's *Diary* is the most unpleasant document we shall have to refer to in this book.

In this chapter, we have examined three distinct types of Outsider, and three distinct kinds of discipline designed to combat their 'Outsiderishness': discipline over the intellect, discipline over the feelings, discipline over the body. We have seen that none of these forms of discipline is complete in itself. Van Gogh and Nijinsky went insane; Lawrence's mental suicide is really the equivalent of Nijinsky's insanity: both men gave up the struggle and turned their faces away from the problems. Nijinsky's madness was as *voluntary* as Lawrence's enlistment in the R.A.F.

The most interesting observation to be made from comparison of the three concerns their degree of 'lostness'. Nijinsky lived so close to his instincts that it took a great deal of complexity and confusion to wrench him away from his inner certainties and make him reason about those certainties. Lawrence, on the contrary, reasoned all the time, and never knew the ground of his instincts as Nijinsky did. Yet, here is the point: Lawrence *could*, with an immense effort, have thrown himself into comprehension of Nijinsky's state of mind; he could, if you like, have *become* a Nijinsky in all essentials. Nijinsky could never have become a Lawrence; the effort needed to develop the reasoning powers would have separated him from his instinctive certainties long before he would be capable of writing a *Seven Pillars*. In other words, Lawrence was paradoxically the most 'lost' of the three, the most destroyed by self-doubt and yet the least lost. Nijinsky was the least lost because his instincts made a better compass than Lawrence's intellect, and yet the most lost as far as his possible development went. If the ideal combination were a compound of Lawrence's powerful intellect, Van Gogh's mystical nature-love and Nijinsky's realization of his body's potentialities, then it would be better, as it were, to start from Lawrence and add the other two to him, than to start from Van Gogh or Nijinsky and try to develop them up to Lawrence's level. This is not to say that Lawrence was a greater 'artist' or what have you than Nijinsky or Van Gogh; I am not at the moment concerned with them as artists, but as Outsiders. As far as the Outsider is concerned, it is more important to have a powerful intellect than a highly developed capacity to 'feel'.

But the most important assumption that is tacit in this chapter is that the Outsider's chief desire is *to cease to be an Outsider*. He cannot cease to be an Outsider simply to become an ordinary bourgeois; that would be a way back, 'back into the wolf or the child', and Harry Haller has already stated that this way is impracticable, is no true solution of the Outsider's problems. His problem is therefore *how to go forward*. Lawrence, Van Gogh, Nijinsky, all went back. All three were defeated, and our examination has told us something of why they were defeated. In the next chapters, we shall have to follow the hints picked up from these three men, and see how far other Outsiders have succeeded where they failed.

We can see now that we must examine all attempts at solution carefully, in case they are not really solutions. There is a way forward and a way back. Either way resolves the Outsider's problems. And the Outsider can follow both ways at once; a part of him can go forward and press a discipline to its conclusion, another part accept a compromise like Lawrence's mental suicide. In such a case, the man will claim to have found a valid solution of the Outsider's problems, and in examining his solution, we shall have to apply the distinctions we have developed in this chapter—the three disciplines—and find if his solution would have fitted the Nijinsky type of Outsider as well as the Van Gogh or Lawrence type. If we detect a ring of truth in Hesse's dictum that no man has ever yet attained to self-realization, we shall be predisposed to believe that no man has ever solved the Outsider's problems fully.

What *is* certain is that the Outsider's problems have begun to resolve themselves into terms of Ultimate Yes and Ultimate No; for the intellectual Outsider, the Existentialist form: being or nothingness? for the emotional Outsider: Eternal love or eternal indifference? and for the Nijinsky type of Outsider, the man of action, the physical Outsider, it is a question of life or death, the body's final defeat or triumph, whether the final truth is 'I am God' or an ultimate horror of physical corruption. The last words of Nijinsky's *Diary* are an affirmation:

> My little girl is singing: 'Ah ah ah ah.' I do not understand its meaning, but I feel what she wants to say. She wants to say that everything . . . is not horror, but joy.[39]

The Outsider's problem is to balance this against Van Gogh's last words: Misery will never end. It is a question no longer of philosophy, but of religion.

CHAPTER FIVE

THE PAIN THRESHOLD

THE TITLE OF THIS chapter is an expression coined by
William James in his *Varieties of Religious Experience*. This is
how he defines it:

> Recent psychology . . . speaks of the threshold of a man's
> consciousness in general to indicate the amount of noise,
> pressure, or other outer stimulus which it takes to arouse his
> attention at all. One with a high threshold will doze through
> an amount of racket by which one with a low threshold would
> be immediately waked. . . . And so we might speak of a
> 'pain threshold', a 'fear threshold', a 'misery threshold',
> and find it quickly overpassed by the consciousness of some
> individuals, but lying too high in others to be often reached
> by their consciousness. The sanguine and healthy minded
> habitually live on the sunny side of their misery line; the
> depressed and melancholy live beyond it, in darkness and
> apprehension.[1]

James goes on to ask:

> Does it not appear as if one who lived habitually on one
> side of the pain threshold might need a different sort of
> religion from one who habitually lived on the other?

This is the problem towards which our consideration of the
Outsider has been imperceptibly leading us. Our findings point
more and more to the conclusion that the Outsider is *not* a
freak, but is only more sensitive than the 'sanguine and
healthy-minded' type of man; Steppenwolf makes no bones
about it, but declares that he is a higher type of man altogether.
If by religion we mean a *way of life* that resolves man's spiritual
tensions, the Outsider will refuse to admit that the 'sanguine
and healthy-minded' man has a religion at all; unless a man
lives by a belief, the Outsider objects, then it is no more material

to him than whether he believes that Mount Everest or Mount Meru is the highest mountain in the world. The Outsider begins with certain inner tensions; we have asked ourselves the question: 'How can these tensions be resolved?' and, in the course of our investigation, we have discovered that the healthy-minded man's confident answer, 'Send him to a psychiatrist', does not fit the case at all. The next stage is to say: 'Very well, let us treat it as a mathematical problem.' Let us, in other words, ask the healthy-minded man: *If* your pain threshold lay as low as this, how would you resolve these tensions? The Outsider we are to consider in this chapter will illustrate a determined and objective approach to this question, but before we pass on to him, it would perhaps be as well to enlarge on the tensions, or rather the problems that cause them; in this way we shall have a broader idea of what the Outsider means by 'Ultimate No'.

Obviously, we are back at Pessimism, and we could conveniently begin by mentioning the Shakespearean type:

> As flies to foolish boys are we to the gods;
> They kill us for their sport. . . .

It is the problem of the uncertainty of life, of how man can set up any aim or belief when he is not certain whether he will 'breathe out the very breath he now breathes in'. A lesser-known example than Gloucester's lines is the Duke's speech from Beddoes's *Death's Jest Book*:

> The look of the world's a lie, a face made up
> O'er graves and fiery depths, and nothing's true
> But what is horrible. If man could see
> The perils and diseases that he elbows
> Each day he walks a mile, which catch at him,
> Which fall behind and graze him as he passes,
> Then would he know that life's a single pilgrim
> Fighting unarmed among a thousand soldiers.[2]

It is worth mentioning here that Beddoes's negation ended, like Van Gogh's, in suicide. His plays breathe a sort of romantic death-worship that probably owes something to Novalis and Tieck; they remind us of Keats's:

> Now more than ever it seems rich to die,
> To cease upon the midnight with no pain. . . .[3]

In this connexion, too, we might mention many writers of the nineteenth century, especially of its last three decades; and the poets Yeats called 'the tragic generation': Lionel Johnson, Dowson, Verlaine, Corbière, men who are the tail-end of nineteenth-century romanticism; and their immediate fore-bears, Baudelaire, Mallarmé, Lautréamont and the Italian Leopardi. James Thomson's 'City of Dreadful Night' deserves more space than we can afford to give it here, as being a sort of nineteenth-century forerunner of T. S. Eliot's 'Waste Land', with its insistence on the illusory nature of the world:

> For life is but a dream whose shapes return
> Some frequently, some seldom, some by night
>   . . . we learn
> While many change, and many vanish quite
> In their recurrence with recurrent changes,
> A certain seeming order; where this ranges
> We count things real; such is the memory's might.[4]

Which invites comparison with:

> Unreal city
> Under the brown fog of a winter dawn . . .[5]

De Lisle Adam's *Axel* belongs to the same period, and its hero would almost have served as a symbol of the Outsider as well as Barbusse's hole-in-corner man: he, the young Count Axel, lives in his lonely castle on the Rhine, and studies the Kabbala and Hermetic philosophy in his oak-panelled study; in irritation at the vulgarity of his 'man of the world' cousin, the Commander, he runs him through with his sword. In the last Act, he and the beautiful runaway nun Sarah stand clasped in each other's arms in the vault of the castle, and vow to kill themselves rather than attempt the inevitably stupid and disappointing business of living out their love for each other. 'As for living, our servants can do that for us.'

They follow the Strowde-Joan Westbury dilemma to its logical conclusion, and kill themselves. Strowde and Joan are not so different from Axel and Sarah; they are only less tormented by 'lack of pattern and purpose in nature'; they commit mental suicide, like Lawrence.

But most of these poets of the late nineteenth century were only 'half in love with easeful death'; the other half clung very firmly to life and complained about its futility. None of them, not even Thomson, goes as far as Wells in *Mind at the End of Its Tether*. But follow their pessimism further, press it to the limits of complete sincerity, and the result is a completely life-denying nihilism that is actually a danger to life. When Van Gogh's 'Misery will never end' is combined with Evan Strowde's 'Nothing is worth doing', the result is a kind of spiritual syphilis that can hardly stop short of death or insanity. Conrad's story *Heart of Darkness* deals with a man who has brought himself to this point; he dies murmuring: 'The horror, the horror.' Conrad's narrator comments: '. . . I wasn't arguing with a lunatic either. . . . His intelligence was perfectly clear; concentrated . . . upon himself with a horrible intensity, yet clear. . . . But his soul was mad. Being alone in the Wilderness, it had looked within itself, and . . . it had gone mad: he had summed up; he had judged; "the Horror". He was a remarkable man.'[6]

'The horror' was the constant theme of the Russian Leonid Andreyev; his story 'Lazarus' presses the theme of the fundamental horror of life to a point where it is difficult to imagine any other writer following him. Hawthorne's 'Ethan Brand' might be mentioned as another treatment of the same theme that probably sprang out of Hawthorne's own experiences of religious doubt. Hawthorne's Outsider flings himself into a furnace to escape his vision of futility.

The subject is unpleasant to dwell on, and further enumeration of treatments of the theme will serve no purpose here, so we can conclude our survey of 'life-denial' by quoting an example taken from James's *Varieties of Religious Experience*. James is writing of his own experience of nervous collapse (although he does not actually say so in the book):*

Whilst in a state of philosophic pessimism, and general depression of spirits about my prospects, I went one evening

* My authority for this statement is Professor F. O. Mathieson, in his book *Henry James, the Major Phase*. Professor Mathieson gives no source for his information, but simply quotes the experience as 'James's own'.

into a dressing-room in the twilight . . . when suddenly there came upon me, without any warning, just as if it came out of the darkness, a horrible fear of my own existence. Simultaneously, there arose in my mind the image of an epileptic patient I had seen in the asylum, a black-haired youth with greenish skin, entirely idiotic, who used to sit all day . . . moving nothing but his black eyes, and looking absolutely non-human. This image and my fear entered into a species of combination with each other. *That shape am I*, I felt, potentially. Nothing I possess can defend me from that fate if the hour should strike for me as it struck for him. There was such a horror of him, and such a perception of my own merely momentary discrepancy from him, that it was as if something hitherto solid in my breast gave way, and I became a mass of quivering fear. After this, the universe was changed for me altogether. I awoke morning after morning with a horrible dread at the pit of my stomach, and with a sense of the insecurity of life that I never knew before.[7]

It is interesting to note that Henry James, Sr., the father of William and of Henry the novelist, had a similar experience, which he records in his book *Society, the Redeemed Form of Man*:[8]

One day towards the close of May, having eaten a comfortable dinner, I remained sitting at the table after the family had dispersed, idly gazing into the embers of the grate, thinking of nothing and feeling only the exhilaration incident to a good digestion, when suddenly—in a lightning flash, as it were—'fear came upon me, and trembling made all my bones to shake'. To all appearances it was a perfectly insane and abject terror without ostensible cause, and only to be accounted for, to my perplexed imagination, by some damned shape, squatting invisible to me within the precincts of the room, and raying out from his fetid personality influences fatal to life. The thing had not lasted ten seconds before I felt myself a wreck, that is, reduced from a state of firm, vigorous, joyful manhood to one of almost helpless infancy. I felt the greatest desire to shout for help to my wife . . . but by an immense effort I controlled these frenzied impulses and determined not to budge. . . . until I had recovered my self-possession. This purpose I held to for a good hour . . . beat upon meanwhile by an ever-growing tempest of doubt, anxiety and despair. . . .

The parallels between the cases of father and son are immediately striking; for both, the panic fear 'came upon them' without any warning; both of them felt themselves cut off from all appeal to other people by it. James Sr. always referred to his experience as his 'vastation'—the word suggests the suddenness and inexplicable nature of the vision—but readers will recognize that the 'vastation', in one form or another, is an experience common to most Outsiders. The difference to be noted between the two experiences of father and son is this: that the father could only speak of a *feeling* of collapse; the son was able to fix it in an object, the black-haired idiot, and explain it objectively. And it is from William James's account that we can observe the reality and the authenticity of the causes of the 'vastation'. 'That shape am I, potentially' is objectively true. Elsewhere in *The Varieties of Religious Experience* James cites the example of a tiger leaping out of the jungle and carrying off a man 'in the twinkling of an eye', and various other cases to enforce his point that evil, physical pain and death cannot be dismissed by neo-Platonists as 'inessential'; the neo-Platonist, having explained his view that 'all is for the best in this best of possible worlds' is just as likely to be knocked down by a bus at Marble Arch as the deepest-dyed pessimist. It is this *irrelevancy* of a man's beliefs to the fate that can overtake him that supplies the most primitive ground for Existentialism, and means that a belief in some sort of providence or destiny is the essential prerequisite of all religion and most philosophy. If William James had lived to see the two World Wars, he could have cited far more impressive examples that 'life's a single pilgrim': nothing in 'the Sick Soul' chapter of *The Varieties of Religious Experience* equals in horror the account by John Hersey of the effect of the first ato·ı bomb on Hiroshima, or the account by a young Armenian girl of the Turkish deportation and massacre of Armenians in the First World War: '. . . the deadly horror which the melancholiac feels is the literally right reaction to the situation'.

Now the interesting fact that arises out of these considerations is that awareness of these unpleasant experiences usually leads to some sort of *religious* solution to the question they excite. In Buddhism, for instance, the legend tells how the young Gautama Sakyamuni saw the three signs—an old man, a sick man, a dead man—and how his reaction was the same as James's: 'That shape am I, potentially', and a frantic search for a *way out* that led him to renounce everything. The fundamental notion of religion is *freedom*. Such moments of horror as James describes are a feeling: '*I have no freedom whatever*'. In Hindu and Buddhist scriptures, the word 'bondage' is the equivalent of the word 'sin' in the Christian, or at least bondage is regarded as an absolute and inevitable consequence of sin. The necessary basis for religion is the belief that freedom *can* be attained. James's vision, with its implication of absolute, final and irrevocable bondage *can be called the essence of evil*.

We can have no difficulty in recognizing the fact that the Outsider and freedom are always associated together. The Outsider's problem *is* the problem of freedom. His preoccupation with Ultimate Yes and Ultimate No is really a preoccupation with absolute freedom or absolute bondage. Furthermore, we have only to glance back over a few examples from earlier chapters, Roquentin, Steppenwolf, Van Gogh, to see that a man becomes an Outsider when he begins to chafe under the recognition that he is not free. While he is the ordinary, once-born human being, like Camus's Meursault, *he is not free but does not realize it.* That is not to say his ignorance makes no difference; it does. Meursault's life is *unreal*, and he is aware of this, vaguely and subconsciously, all the time. But when he has his glimpse of reality facing death, it is to know that all his past life has been unreal.

The implications of this train of thought are so manifold that we had better pause and get them clear before pressing on with our survey of pessimism in literature. At the end of the last chapter, we stated our conclusion that the Outsider always aims at ceasing to be an Outsider, and we enumerated three distinct types of discipline towards that end. The question that then presents itself is: *Towards what?* If he doesn't want to be an Outsider, and he doesn't want to be an ordinary well-adjusted social being, what the devil *does* he want to become?

Now we have complicated the question a little more by our analysis of freedom. The Outsider wants to be free; he doesn't want to become a healthy-minded, once-born person because he declares such a person is not free. He is an Outsider because he wants to be free. And what characterizes the 'bondage' of the once-born? Unreality, the Outsider replies. So we can at least say that, whatever the Outsider wants to become, that new condition of being will be characterized by a perception of reality. And reality?—what can the Outsider tell us about that? That is more difficult. We have got two distinct sets of answers. Let us try posing the question to various Outsiders, and compare their answers: So, our question: What is Reality?

Barbusse: Knowledge of the depths of human nature.

Wells: The Cinema sheet; man's utter nothingness.

Roquentin: Naked existence that paralyses and negates the human mind.

Meursault: Glory. The Universe's magnificent indifference. No matter what these stupid and half-real human beings do, the reality is serene and unchanging.

This is a fuller answer than the other three; we can follow it up by asking Meursault: And what of the human soul?

Meursault: Its ground is the same as that of the universe. Man escapes his triviality by approaching his own fundamental indifference to everyday life.

Hemingway too would give us some such answer. Ask him what he means by 'reality':

Krebs: The moment when you do 'the one thing, the only thing', when you know you're not merely a trivial, superficial counter on the social chessboard.

Strowde: Ineffable. Unlivable. The man who has seen it is spoilt for everyday life.

And now for the 'practical Outsiders'.

T. E. Lawrence: Unknowable. My glimpses of it caused me nothing but trouble because they ruined me for everyday triviality without telling me where I could find another way of living. After it, my life became a meaningless farce.

Van Gogh: Promethean misery. Prometheus was the first Outsider.

Nijinsky: God, at one extreme. Misery at the other. The universe is an eternal tension stretched between God and misery.

We have two types of answer, two extremes of yes and no; Roquentin's Existence that negates man; Nijinsky's Existence that affirms man.

Again, Roquentin's answer began as a reaction to the *salauds*. A *salaud* is one who thinks his existence is necessary. And Van Gogh, Nijinsky, Lawrence? Van Gogh: No, not when he killed himself; but when he painted: Yes, most certainly. Lawrence: No, not when he committed mind suicide, but when he was driven by the idea of a mission: Yes, certainly. Nijinsky? The answer is in the *Diary*: I am God. Again, yes. So these three men were *salauds* in their highest moments! This is a hard conclusion, and we only have to think of Nijinsky, Lawrence, Van Gogh, in connexion with the town's benefactors in the portrait gallery at Le Havre to know that such an idea is nonsense. There is a mistake somewhere, and we haven't to look far to find it. There are two ways of solving the Outsider's problems, the forward and the backward route. To believe your existence is necessary if you are one of these people in the portrait gallery is blasphemy; to believe it necessary after some immense spiritual labour like Lawrence's or Van Gogh's is only common sense. The Existentialist objects: That is mere sophistry. Van Gogh is greater than the Havre ex-Mayor only in degree, not in kind. Absolutely speaking, his existence is no more necessary.

It is a difficult question. For what have we: that Van Gogh created great paintings when he believed his existence to have some *raison d'être*, and shot himself when he ceased to have it?

Here it is Nijinsky who provides the answer. Could he ever have been overwhelmed by Roquentin's nausea? No, the idea is unthinkable; he lived too close to his instincts to wander into such a *thinker's dilemma*. He didn't *think* his existence necessary with the complacent, conscious certainty of a public benefactor; he *felt* it—and sometimes didn't feel it—with the inwardness of the saint. And the same applies to Van Gogh. As

to Lawrence, his case history is Roquentin's; he *thought* himself
into disbelieving in the spiritual power that drove him. Nijinsky
would never have been so foolish.

Another curious parallel arises. Now we have contrasted
Nijinsky's instinctive self-belief with the town councillor's
conscious complacency, we are reminded of a similar distinction in certain Christian writers: in Bunyan, for instance, who
writes of the life of the town councillor, the good citizen, etc.,
and calls him Mr. Badman; Bunyan's Christian awakes with
a jarring shock, like Roquentin, to the realization, My existence was Not Necessary. . . . What must I do to be saved?
Sartre has explained that Camus is not really an Existentialist,
but a descendant of the eighteenth-century moralists, but our
parallel makes it appear as if Sartre is the real descendent of
the moralists. And in fact Sartre would probably agree that
some such revelation as Roquentin's nausea lies at the bottom
of Bunyan's, What must I do to be saved? He would point out,
however, that intellectual honesty prevents either himself or
Roquentin from accepting the Blood of the Saviour as atonement for his own futility.

This opens a new range of questions to us: If it is possible that
Bunyan and Sartre have a common basis, where do their roads
towards a solution diverge? Is it—is it thinkable that certain
Christian saints were concerned about the same metaphysical
problems that Sartre has produced, with the air of a conjurer
flourishing a rabbit, as the latest development of twentieth-
century thought? The idea is a long way ahead of the present
stage of our examination, and it is time we returned to the
thread of the argument. Later, we must come back to it.

Before we digressed to consider the Outsiders' different
conceptions of reality, we were considering Camus's Meursault,
and the fact that he is not free, but does not know it. The
Outsider wants freedom. He does not consider that the ordinary
once-born human being *is* free. The fact remains that the
Outsider *is* the rarity among human beings—which places him
rather in the position of the soldier who claims he is the only
one in step in the platoon. What about all the millions of men
and women in our modern cities; are they really all the
Outsider claims they are: futile, unreal, unutterably lost
without knowing it?

James asked himself the same question at the end of the

lecture we have drawn on already in this chapter: once born
or twice born? Healthy-minded or Outsider?

> In our own attitude, not yet abandoned, of impartial
> onlookers, what are we bound to say of this quarrel? It
> seems to me that we are bound to say that morbid minded-
> ness ranges over the wider scale of experience, and that its
> survey is the one that overlaps. The method of averting one's
> attention from evil, and simply living in the light of the good,
> is splendid as long as it will work. . . . But it breaks down
> impotently as soon as melancholy comes; and even though
> one be quite free from melancholy oneself, there is no doubt
> that healthy-mindedness is inadequate as a philosophical
> doctrine. . . .[9]

Inadequate, but not wholly wrong, James implies. The
Outsider is more sweeping about it, and says without hesitation: shallow, stupid and short-sighted. The Outsiders we have
listened to in the course of this book have been more articulate
than the 'morbid-minded' souls James chose, and they have
established their position with considerable dialectical skill.
But this position is incomplete, and the Outsider would be the
first to admit it. They have given adequate reasons for disliking
the 'once-born' bourgeois and proving that such a creature is in
no way superior to the Man Outside. But the bourgeois has
every right to ask a sarcastic, What then? How much better
off is your Outsider? Isn't this act of showing us a row of
morbid-minded degenerates (with all respect to Van Gogh, of
course) and proving that they are types of the 'higher man',
tantamount to asking us to throw out our dirty water before we
get any clean?

This is incontrovertible. The Outsider must make his position
look more positive before we can seriously consider any claim
as to his superiority over the man in the street. And at the
present stage of our analysis, it is anything but positive. For
what have we?—the assurance of several men that evil is
universal and must be faced. Well, we don't mind this; Hesse's
Emil Sinclair made a convincing case of it. But now we have a
number of writers who inform us that evil is so universal, so
unsusceptible to adaptation into a 'higher scheme of good',
that the act of facing it honestly will bring the mind to the

point of insanity. What are we to say to this? What if the 'brutal thunderclap of halt' takes the form of the choice, Dishonesty or insanity? What use is honesty to an insane mind? Which of us would not choose dishonesty?

But if we choose dishonesty, what happens to our philosophers' desire to get at fact?

This is a difficult question; we could not do better than leave it in the hands of an Outsider whose trained mind brought him to face precisely that problem: to the 'pagan Existentialist' philosopher, Frederick Nietzsche.

But before we pass on to speak of him, there are two other modern expressions of 'literary pessimism' that may broaden our grasp of the subject; we have, in fact, already referred to both in other connexions: Franz Kafka and T. S. Eliot. Kafka's story 'The Fasting Showman' is the climax of his work,[10] his clearest statement of the Outsider's position. It deals with a professional ascetic, a man who starves himself on fairgrounds for money. In the days of the fasting showman's popularity, it had always been his wish to go on fasting indefinitely, for he was never at the limit of his endurance when compelled to break his fast. When public interest in his feats of abstention wanes, he is finally assigned a cage in an unimportant corner of the fair-ground; there he sits amid his straw, forgotten, able at last to fast for as long as he likes. He is so completely forgotten that, one day, someone notices his cage and asks why a perfectly good cage is left empty; they look inside, and find the fasting showman dying, almost completely fleshless. As he dies, he whispers his secret in the ear of an overseer: it was not that he had any tremendous will-power to abstain from food; there was simply *no food he ever liked*.

Here again, we have a perfect symbol for the Outsider, that would have served us as well as Barbusse for a starting-point. Lack of *appetite for life*, that is his problem. All human acts carry the same stigma of futility; what else should he do but sit in his straw and die?

The development of T. S. Eliot brought him to expressing the same point; the most striking lines in his poetry are his symbols of futility; in his first volume, *Prufrock* (1917):

I have measured out my life with coffee spoons.

In 'Gerontion' (1920):

> Vacant shuttles
> Weave the wind. I have no ghosts.
> An old man in a draughty house
> Under a windy knob.

In the 'Waste Land' (1922):

> I see crowds of people walking around in a ring.

and:

> On Margate sands I can connect
> Nothing with nothing
> The broken fingernails of dirty hands.

Culminating in 'The Hollow Men', with its vision of utter negation, a despair as complete as that of William James's vastation: complete denial of freedom and even its possibility:

> This is the way the world ends
> This is the way the world ends
> This is the way the world ends
> Not with a bang but a whimper.

This being the point to which our analysis has brought us at present, it is interesting to note the way Eliot developed. He has left no stage in his religious evolution undocumented, and we can follow the process stage by stage in his poetry. 'Ash Wednesday' (1933) begins with a repetition of the position of 'The Hollow Men':

> Because I do not hope to turn again
> Because I do not hope
> Because I do not hope to turn. . . .

Then follows a statement of the position we are already familiar with: middle-aging despair, loss of faith, and the inability to stop thinking:

> I pray that I may forget
> Those matters that with myself I too much discuss
> Too much explain. . . .

Endless thinking to no purpose, as with T. E. Lawrence, has brought the poet to a point where he prays:

> Teach us to care and not to care
> Teach us to sit still.

But the metaphysical point upon which Eliot bases his movement of retreat from the impasse is stated in the fourth poem:

> Will the veiled sister pray
> For the children at the gate
> Who will not go away and cannot pray?

> Will the veiled sister between the slender
> Yew trees pray for those who offend her
> And are terrified and cannot surrender. . . .

This is the Outsider's extremity. He does not prefer *not to* believe; he doesn't like feeling that futility gets the last word in the universe; his human nature would like to find something it can answer to with complete assent. But his honesty prevents his accepting a solution that he cannot reason about. His next question is naturally: Supposing a solution *does* exist somewhere, undreamed of by me, inconceivable to me, can I yet hope that *it might one day force itself upon me* without my committing myself to a preliminary gesture of faith which (in point of fact) I cannot make?

The poet finds that he can answer this question with a 'yes'. His position is understandable. He begins with Reason, which, as it were, makes him self-sufficient (as it made the Victorians) and he subjects all to the test of reason. Ultimately, his reason informs him: you are *not* self-sufficient; you are futile, floating in a void. This is unanswerable. What is he to do? Demolish his own premises? 'Since I am futile, my reason must be futile too, in which case, its conclusions are lies anyway.' That is too much. He must commit himself to the idea: There may be something which is not futile, but it is completely beyond me, incomprehensible to me. And what if there isn't anything 'beyond' . . . no, he *cannot* say 'I believe'. Hence the question:

Will the veiled sister between the slender
Yew trees pray for those who offend her
And are terrified and cannot surrender?

With these lines, Eliot was over his stile, out of the Outsider's position. It was not a long step to realizing that this experience of terror on the edge of nothingness was not an unfamiliar experience to many of the saints, Christian and otherwise, and that therefore religion need not be synonymous with a belief in fairy-stories. Admittedly, this is still a long way from actually *joining* a Church, for it is one thing to admit that some of the Church's doctrines are intellectually tenable; quite another to offer full assent to the tremendous compromises which the Church is forced to accept in order to make a religion in which millions of Insiders will be comfortable, as well as the occasional Outsider.

In going on to speak of Eliot's development in 'Ash Wednesday', I have made a point which is not especially relevant in this chapter; I have done this for the convenience of not having to split up the story of Eliot's development. Still, readers who feel dubious about the connexion of the last two paragraphs with what has gone before can dismiss them as unproved; we shall have to return to the subject later from a completely different angle, and for the moment it is not important.

For the moment, we are concerned with the question, Ultimate Yes or Ultimate No, and compelled to admit that most of our analyses so far point to the answer, Ultimate No. Vaslav Nijinsky would object that this is because we treat Reason as if it were capable of affording a key all on its own. Well, that is the philosopher's business. But a philosopher who did not do so . . . he would be not quite 'a philosopher', perhaps? Would such a person be able to offer any helpful suggestions about the Outsider? This is the question we are to keep in mind while examining the contribution of Friedrich Nietzsche.

*   *   *

Nietzsche was born at Roecken in Saxony in 1844. His father, like Van Gogh's, was a Protestant clergyman. Recently published documents show that Nietzsche was intensely religious as a child, and that during his adolescence he considered entering a monastery.[11] We shall attempt to show that the impulses that drove to his life's work—his devaluation of all values—were at bottom, religious impulses. The later attack on Christendom, for instance, sprang from a feeling that Christendom was *not religious enough*. But unlike Kierkegaard, who attacked Christendom for the same reasons, Nietzsche did not support the idea of Christianity. His dislike of it went to the length of proclaiming its errors to be fundamental, worthy to be pitched-out lock, stock and barrel. Yet all his life Nietzsche preached his ideas with the fervour of a prophet, and a prophet cannot be an irreligious man. He asserted that Christians generally are intellectually dishonest and morally lazy, and that these grave deficiencies are partly accountable to what the Christian believes. Nietzsche had an alternative system of belief, which we must examine in due course. What is important is the fact that he began as a fervent Christian. In a letter written when he was twenty-one and militantly atheistic, he tells his friend Von Gersdorff:

'If Christianity means belief in a historical person or event, I have nothing to do with it. But if it means the need for salvation, then I can treasure it.'

And this is the reason why Nietzsche must be recognized as a religious man; above everything else, he was aware of the need for what he called 'salvation'. We may disagree with him; we may even agree with a Jesuit theologian that his heresies were 'poisonous and detestable', but we cannot doubt the sincerity of his need for 'salvation'.

Nietzsche was a romantic; he belongs to the same tradition as Schiller, Novalis, Hoffmann. As a boy and adolescent he read a great deal, took lonely walks, wrote poetry, thought about himself and his possible destiny; at thirteen he wrote an introspective autobiography; a year later he records his intention of dedicating his life to the service of God. Among his friends he was nicknamed 'the little pastor'. But his conception of religion was always elastic; a tradition tells how he and his sister once built a makeshift altar on the site of an old pagan sacrificial altar in a churchyard, and then paced gravely around it, intoning 'Odin hear us' into the rising smoke.

At fourteen Nietzsche was sent to the famous Landschule at

Pforta; this was the school that had produced Novalis, Fichte, the Schlegels. There, without his sister to share his thoughts, Nietzsche dramatized himself as the romantic hero. A later aphorism asserts: 'All great men are play actors of their own ideal.'* Nietzsche's ideal was compounded from Byron's *Manfred*, Schiller's *Robbers* and Novalis's *Heinrich*. He learned from Novalis that every man is potentially hero and genius; that only inertia keeps men mediocre. The lesson sank deep; when he read Emerson's essays at sixteen he was elated to find Novalis and his own intuitions confirmed in the pronouncements on 'Self-reliance' and 'The Oversoul'. From Emerson he absorbed an element of Stoicism that never left him till the end. Once, listening to a conversation among schoolboys about Mucius Scaevola, Nietzsche set a heap of lighted matches on fire on the palm of his hand to demonstrate that it could be done. New influences on his mind were undermining his Lutheran training. He bought the piano score of Wagner's *Tristan und Isolde* and learnt it by heart. He helped to found a society of intellectuals called 'Germania', and wrote essays for its magazine. The essay on 'Fate and History' that he published in *Germania* stated: 'Vast upheavals will happen in the future, as soon as men realize that the structure of Christianity is only based on *assumptions*. . . . *I have tried to deny everything*. . . .'

Certainly his innate religiousness became at this period (to quote his *Gaya Scienza*) 'a will to truth at all costs, a youthful madness in the love of truth'. And what is equally certain from his own utterances is that he found himself close to the edge of William James's condition of moral horror, complete negation, like looking into an abyss. James quotes an example which is worth requoting for the insight it gives us into Nietzsche's mind at this time; it concerns the French philosopher Jouffroy, and it illustrates the way in which the questioning mind can systematically weed out all affections and beliefs that seem groundless, until it is left in a vacuum that terrifies the human soul. Jouffroy writes:[12]

I shall never forget that night of September in which the veil that concealed from me my own incredulity was torn. I hear again my steps in the narrow, naked chamber where, long after the hour of sleep had come, I had the habit of

* *Beyond Good and Evil*, IV, 97.

walking up and down. . . . Anxiously I followed my thoughts as they descended from layer to layer towards the foundation of my consciousness, scattering one by one all the illusions that until then had screened its windings from my view, making them at every moment more clearly visible.

Vainly I clung to these last beliefs as a shipwrecked sailor clings to the fragments of his vessel, vainly, frightened at the unknown void into which I was about to float. I turned with them towards my childhood, my family, my country, all that was dear and sacred to me; the inflexible current of my thought was too strong—parents, family, memory, beliefs—it forced me to let go of everything. The investigation went on more obstinate and more severe as it drew near its term, and it did not stop until the end was reached. I knew then that in the depth of my mind, nothing was left that stood erect. This moment was a frightful one, and when towards morning, I threw myself exhausted on my bed, I seemed to feel my earlier life, so smiling and so full, go out like a fire, and before me another life opened, sombre and unpeopled, where in future I must live alone, alone with my fatal thought that had exiled me there, and which I was tempted to curse. The days that followed this were the saddest days of my life.

Such an experience is not strange to thinkers; James quotes John Stuart Mill's case, which has much in common with this, and in the next chapter we shall examine early experiences of Tolstoy that resemble it closely. Nietzsche experienced it. More than one of his books tell us about it obliquely; we shall also touch on those in due course. Particularly there is a passage in *The Joyful Wisdom* that speaks of 'pain . . . that compels us philosophers to descend into our ultimate depths and divest ourselves of all trust and all good nature wherein we have formerly installed our humanity. I doubt whether such pain improves us, but I know it *deepens* us.'[13] Nietzsche was used to being alone. He regarded it as part of the destiny of the man of genius. His hero, Schopenhauer, convinced him of it when he was barely twenty, and although he came later to reject Schopenhauer, he never rebelled against his destiny of aloneness.

Nietzsche read Schopenhauer at Leipzig University in 1865.

It was Schopenhauer who had informed a friend, when he was still in his teens: 'Life is a sorry affair, and I am determined to spend it in reflecting on it.' We have an account of Nietzsche's first reading of the 'gloomy philosopher' that affords us a moving glimpse of the 'artist as a young man':

> In young people, if they have a tendency to melancholy, ill humours and annoyances of a personal kind take on a general character. At the time, I was hanging in the air with a number of painful experiences and disappointments, without help, without fundamental beliefs. In the happy seclusion of my rooms I was able to gather myself together.... One day I happened to find this book in old Rohn's second-hand book shop . . . picked it up and turned over the pages. I don't know what demon whispered to me, 'Take this book home with you.' . . . At home, I threw myself into the corner of the sofa, and began to let that forceful, gloomy genius work upon me. Here, where every line cried renunciation, denial, resignation, here I saw a mirror in which I observed the world, life and my own soul in frightful grandeur. Here there gazed at me the full, unbiased eye of Art, here I saw sickness and healing, exile and refuge, heaven and hell. The need to know oneself, even to gnaw at oneself, laid a powerful hold on me. . . . There remain the uneasy, melancholic pages of my diary for that time . . . with their desperate looking-upwards . . . for the reshaping of the whole kernel of man. Even bodily penances were not lacking. For example, for 14 days on end, I forced myself to go to bed at 2 o'clock and get up at 6 o'clock. A nervous irritability overcame me....[14]

We see that, as with Lawrence, intellectual awakening and physical penance go together. But more important is the change in Nietzsche's way of regarding himself. Depressed, wretched, with a feeling of imprisonment in his brain and body, his earlier enthusiasm for Greek philosophy offered him no mirror to see his own face. Schopenhauer's philosophy did. It confirmed what he felt about the nature of the world and his place in it. Schopenhauer gave Nietzsche that *detachment from himself* which is the first condition of self-knowledge.

There are two vital experiences in Nietzsche's life that I shall refer to several times, and which I may as well quote here

together (although they are separated by several years); both
are characteristic of Nietzsche in the way that the candle-flame
episode was characteristic of Van Gogh. The first is related in a
letter of 1865 to his friend Von Gersdorff:

> Yesterday an oppressive storm hung over the sky, and I
> hurried to a neighbouring hill called Leutch. . . . At the top
> I found a hut, where a man was killing two kids while his son
> watched him. The storm broke with a tremendous crash,
> discharging thunder and hail, and I had an indescribable
> sense of well-being and zest. . . . *Lightning and tempest are
> different worlds, free powers, without morality.* Pure Will, without
> the confusions of intellect—how happy, how free.[18]

The experience seems simple enough, and yet its effect on
his way of thinking was far-reaching. Normally the sight of
blood would have been unpleasant to him; now, the exhilaration of the storm combined somehow with the smell of blood,
the flash of the knife, the fascinated child looking on; and the
result was the sudden intuition of pure Will, free of the troubles
and perplexities of intellect: an intuition which was release
from the 'thought-riddled nature' which had so far been his
chief trouble.

The second episode happened some years later, during the
Franco-Prussian War, when Nietzsche was serving as an
orderly in the ambulance corps. He told it to his sister in later
life, when she asked him once about the origin of his idea of the
Will to Power.

For weeks Nietzsche had attended the sick and wounded on
the battlefields until the sight of blood and gangrened limbs
had swallowed up his horror into a numbness of fatigue. One
evening, after a hard day's work with the wounded, he was
entering a small town near Strasbourg, on foot and alone. He
heard the sound of approaching hoofbeats and stood back under
the wall to allow the regiment to pass. First the cavalry rode by
at top speed, and then behind them marched the foot soldiers.
It was Nietzsche's old regiment. As he stood and watched them
passing, these men going to battle, perhaps to death, the
conviction came again that 'the strongest and highest will to
life does not lie in the puny struggle to exist, but in the Will to
war, the Will to Power. . . .'

Both experiences must be examined carefully and without prejudice. In a sense they were 'mystical experiences'. Normally Nietzsche was imprisoned in the 'thought-riddled nature'. These experiences point to an exaltation of Life. In Blake's phrase: Energy is eternal delight. 'Free powers without morality', 'pure Will'. Such phrases are the foundation of Nietzsche's philosophy, a memory of a mystical experience in which an unhealthy student saw a vision of complete health, free of his body's limitations, free of the stupidity of personality and thought. This was Nietzsche's profoundest knowledge. It is introduced into the first pages of his first book, *The Birth of Tragedy*, written when Nietzsche was a young professor at Basle University:

> ... the blissful ecstasy that arises from the innermost depths of man, ay, of nature, at this same collapse of the *principium individuationis*, and we shall gain an insight into the Dionysian, which is brought into closest ken, perhaps, by the analogy of *drunkenness*. It is either under the influence of the narcotic draught, of which the hymns of all primitive men and peoples tell us, or by the powerful approach of Spring penetrating all nature with joy, that those Dionysian emotions awake, in which the subject vanishes to complete forgetfulness.[16]

Nietzsche *knew* this emotion; it became the acid test by which he judged everything. According to Nietzsche, Socrates never knew it; therefore (he shocked the academic world by announcing) Socrates represents the decay of Greek culture; its apex had been the earlier worship of Bacchus, the god of raw, up-surging vitality. He applied the same test to most of the philosophers and literary men of his day; none of them survived it except Schopenhauer (and the day would come when even Schopenhauer would get kicked after the rest). And so, at the age of twenty-eight, Nietzsche stood alone, except for the two men for whom he still felt respect: Schopenhauer and Wagner. Three men against the world ... but what men!

Nietzsche had known Wagner personally since 1868; he had met him in Leipzig before he was appointed professor at Basle when Wagner was fifty-nine, Nietzsche twenty-four. At Basle, Nietzsche was able to follow up the acquaintance, which soon developed into a warm friendship. Wagner was living at

Tribschen, on the Lake of Lucerne, working on the composition of *The Ring*; his companion there was Cosima von Bülow, daughter of Franz Liszt, who had deserted her husband to live with Wagner. In their unconventional household, Nietzsche felt at home at last; he and Wagner frequently sat up talking until the early hours of the morning. It was here that Wagner read Nietzsche his essay, 'On the State and Religion', with its doctrine that religion and patriotism are indispensable as 'opiums of the people'; that only the King stands above it all, with the courage to suffer, to reject the common delusions, sustained by art 'that makes life appear like a game and withdraws us from the common fate'. (Only ten years later, Dostoevsky was to project the same idea into *The Brothers Karamazov*, substituting for the King his Grand Inquisitor.)

Nietzsche felt Wagner was a brother spirit; Wagner thought of Nietzsche as a brilliant young disciple. Both were wrong. The day would come when Nietzsche would write a pamphlet exalting Bizet above Wagner, and Wagner would write a pamphlet to prove that Nietzsche was a Jew. Those who, like myself, read Nietzsche unstintedly and listen to Wagner whenever they get the chance, may wonder why two such men had to fall out and denounce each other. The answer is that Nietzsche was a tireless poet-philosopher who never ceased to want to transcend himself, while Wagner (in 1868) was a very successful musician who was perfectly satisfied with himself as he was. The self-surmounter* can never put up with the man who has ceased to be dissatisfied with himself. One day Nietzsche would hear *Die Meistersinger* and be aware of nothing but self-satisfaction in the violins and French horns. And the prophet Wagner would feel bitter about the apostacy of his one-time disciple.

But in 1868 the two were on the best of terms; their capacity for enthusiasm obscured their basic unlikeness. Nietzsche added a chapter to his *Birth of Tragedy* to hail Wagner as the new artistic Messiah, and Wagner returned the compliment by declaring the book one of the finest he had ever read.

Nietzsche's academic colleagues were less complimentary; they expected Nietzsche to write like a professor, and when he wrote like a prophet they all rounded on him and called him a conceited upstart. Nietzsche was unlucky; it would have taken

---

* *Übergänger*, literally 'over-goer' or 'self-surmounter'.

him another ten years establishing himself as a professor before such weighty *ex cathedra* pronouncements could be taken seriously. As a young man of genius, he could hardly be expected to realize this. But it is a pity he didn't, for the failure to size up the situation would eventually cost him his sanity. The life-long persecution had begun. He would be driven further into his manner of dogmatic self-assertion by the opposition of diehards who considered him half-insane, until the chapters of his last book would be headed: 'Why am I so Wise?', 'Why am I so Clever?', 'Why I Write such Excellent Books'.

The remainder of Nietzsche's life can be divided into three periods. *The Birth of Tragedy* exalted life above thought: 'Down with thought—long live life!' The books of the next ten years reversed the ideal: 'Down with life—long live thought!' Socrates is reinstated; truth becomes the only important aim. Then, at the time when ill-health forced him to retire from University duties, another change began with *The Joyful Wisdom* and *Thus Spake Zarathustra*, and again 'energy is eternal delight'. And so it was to the end.

The end came in 1899 (the same year as Van Gogh's collapse). He began writing strange letters, signing them 'Caesar' and 'The King of Naples' and, more significantly, 'the crucified one'. His last letter to Cosima Wagner read: 'Ariadne, I love thee. Dionysus.' It was complete mental collapse. Nietzsche was insane until his death, ten years later.

It is almost impossible to do justice to the range of Nietzsche's thought in a study of this length. He wrote no single major work that could be called 'the essence of Nietzsche'. There is a pugilistic air about his books that he himself recognized when he subtitled one of them: 'How to Philosophize with a Hammer.' They are not component parts of a system; they are rather parts of a continual self-revelation of Nietzsche the man. Fully to understand Nietzsche, it would be necessary for the reader to be acquainted with at least half a dozen of them besides *Zarathustra*, with, say, *The Birth of Tragedy, Human All Too Human, Beyond Good and Evil, The Genealogy of Morals, Ecce Homo* (the autobiography) *The Will to Power* (a rather doubtful collection of notes arranged after Nietzsche's death by his sister—Nietzsche's *'Pensées'*). In this chapter I shall not attempt a summary of these books; that would be difficult enough even with unlimited space, and besides, it is not necessary for our purposes. The questions that concern us now are: How far did Nietzsche express his problems as an Outsider, and how far did he solve them? The first question can be answered immediately: he expressed the Outsider problems more fully than anyone we have yet considered. The second will require an examination of his life.

Critics and doctors have been divided on the cause of his insanity. Modern research supports the view that his collapse was brought on by venereal disease contracted in his student days from a prostitute. (A fictionalized version of this story is given in Thomas Mann's novel based on Nietzsche's life, *Doktor Faustus*.) Such a physical cause would be as relevant to the collapse as the inherited nervous tension of Nijinsky or the irritability of Van Gogh. But the deeper cause is to be sought in the problems he faced.

He was always alone. He never married, never had a mistress, never (as far as we know) even had sexual relations with any woman except a prostitute.* Few people liked and supported him; his admirers during his life can be counted on the fingers of one hand; and even they sometimes turned against him. Above all, there was ill-health (a legacy from his Army period); his sedentary way of life encouraged headaches, indigestion, mental and physical exhaustion; he was so myopic as to be almost blind at times. These things acted as brakes on his creativity. The intellect climbed to great heights in his periods of good health and well-being; but, just as with Van Gogh, the pettinesses were waiting to irritate and exhaust him when he came down. His self-esteem received some hard kicks. When he sent a friend to propose to a young lady for him, she rejected him and married the friend. (The young lady was Lou Salomé, who was later to become the close friend of that other great Nietzschean poet, Rainer Rilke.) His sanest and best-argued books provoked Germany's guardians of culture to accuse him of extravagant self-worship or insanity. Thoughts that seemed to him gigantic, world-shaking, were received without interest. The continued optimism of his letters is an amazing feat:

* Although a posthumously discovered 'autobiography' published in America under the title *My Sister and I* (1950) would seem to indicate otherwise. But as far as I know, its authenticity has not yet been established by Nietzsche scholars.

Well my dear friend, the sun of August shines on us, the year slips on, calm and peace spread over the mountains and forests. I have seen thoughts rising on my horizon the like of which I have never seen before. . . . I must live a few years longer. I feel a presentiment that the life I lead is a life of supreme peril. *I am one of those machines that sometimes explode.* The intensity of my emotion makes me tremble and burst out laughing. Several times I have been unable to leave my room for the ridiculous reason that my eyes were swollen —and why? Each time I have wept too much on my walks the day before—not sentimental tears, but actual tears of joy. I sang and cried out foolish things. I was full of a new vision in which I forestalled all other men.[17] [Italics mine.]

The sentence I have italicized recalls Van Gogh's: 'Well, as to my work, I have risked my life for it, and my reason has half foundered.' But the last part brings to mind another deeply religious man; 'tears of joy', *'pleurs de joie'*: it is the phrase that Pascal used in that strange testament, found sewn into the lining of his coat after his death, to describe the vision that came to him after long illness and suffering:

feu
Dieu d'Abraham, dieu de Jacob, dieu d'Isaac
Non des philosophes et savants. . . .

Pure will, free of the perplexities of intellect. . . .

For Nietzsche also it came after long suffering; he writes of *The Joyful Wisdom*:

It seems to be written in the language of a thawing wind. . . . Gratitude continually flows, as if the most un-expected thing had happened—the gratitude of a convales-cent—for convalescence was that most unexpected thing. The whole book is nothing but a long revel after long priva-tion and impotence, the frolicking of returning energy, *of newly awakened belief in a tomorrow after tomorrow.* . . .[18]

The 'long privation and impotence' had been the period that had produced the Socratic books, *Thoughts Out of Season*,

The Dawn of Day, Human All Too Human. Now he declares new scepticism, and it is the scepticism of an intellectual who discovers that he has neglected the body and the emotions:

> The unconscious disguising of physiological requirements under the cloaking of the objective, the ideal, the purely spiritual. . . . I have asked myself whether philosophy hitherto has not been merely an interpreting of the body *and a misunderstanding of the body.*[19]

He speaks of that questioning of everything (of which I quoted Jouffroy's example):

> . . . one emerges from such dangerous exercises in self-mastery as another being . . . with a will to question more than ever. . . . Confidence in life has gone; life itself has become a problem. One doesn't necessarily become a hypochondriac because of this. Even love is still possible—only one loves differently. It is the love of a woman of whom one is doubtful.[20]

This is Nietzsche's version of the twice-born state. And he goes on to express his disillusion with the Socratic spirit:

> . . . as artists, we are learning to *forget and not know.* . . . We are not likely to be found again in the tracks of those Egyptian youths who at night make the temples unsafe, embrace statues,* and would fain unveil, uncover and put in clear light, everything which for good reasons is kept concealed. No, we have got disgusted with this bad-taste, this will-to-truth, to 'truth at all costs', this youthful madness in the love of truth; we are now too experienced for that; we no longer believe that truth remains truth if the evil is withdrawn from it.[21]

And in the first Aphorism of Book IV, 'Sanctus Januarius', Nietzsche summarizes:

---

* This striking image reappears in W. B. Yeats poem 'The Statues'. Yeats was a confirmed admirer of Nietzsche, and it seems probable that this passage was his source. It is interesting to see the use Yeats makes of it in his difficult poem.

I still live, I still think; I must still live, for I must still think. *I wish to be at all times hereafter only a Yea-sayer.*

Henceforward, this is to be the keynote of Nietzsche's philosophy; he questions unceasingly; he dismisses all previous Western philosophers as fools and blockheads whose 'systems' reveal at every turn their puny, human-all-too-human limitations. Kant, with his *ersatz* morality, is a special target, Hegel another. These men exalted thought as if it could be separated from life and instated in a superior order. Consequently, they de-valued life, failed to recognize that thought is only an instrument to 'more abundant life'. Man's way is the way of affirmation, Yea-saying, praise. These mere thinkers were poisoners, cheapeners of life ('professors of what another man has suffered', Kierkegaard called them). The greatest act man is capable of is to 'praise in spite of', to become aware of the worst forms of the Eternal No and to make the gigantic effort of digesting them and *still* finding life positive.

Little by little, Nietzsche was learning to say Yes. This was the problem that occupied him on his long walks: Ultimate Yes or Ultimate No? He had left Basle a very sick man, sick of life, sick of fools, sick of opposition and re-gathering his strength only to waste it again; and sick of Friedrich Nietzsche and his dreams that were out of gear with the universe. He was getting tired of the everlasting pendulum that swung between Yes and No, of happiness that made him think misery unimportant, and misery that made happiness seem a delusion. He wanted to know for certain. He looked into himself and faced the fact that he could not say Yes or No. He asked himself: Is this true of the nature of life itself, or *could* a man exist who could say finally: I accept everything? His imagination set to work on the problem, to conceive a man great enough to affirm. Not the Hero—no hero could ever command a philosopher's complete admiration. But the prophet, the saint, the man of genius, the man of action; or, perhaps, a combination of all four?

And two great concepts were born together: the Superman and Eternal Recurrence. Yea-saying depends on the will to live. But the will to live depends upon nothing except the man himself; it can be deepened, broadened by meditation, by constant mental struggle, by an act of faith that commits itself *to affirming life at all costs*. Experience is conceived as an Enemy, not to be conquered by turning away from it ('as to living, our servants will do that for us') but only by an *act of assimilation*. Experience conceived as an enemy, the question then becomes: Master or slave, master of experience or slave to it? And experience itself is of such vast possible extent that to imagine a man capable of assimilating it all is to imagine man swelling like a balloon. *He could no longer be man*. But Nietzsche was not so intoxicated with the idea of a Super-prophet Super-hero as to set it up like a stone deity. He kept his feet on the earth by weighting them with an infinitely heavy weight, the idea of Eternal Recurrence. By this he insured himself against idealism, against the weightless idealism of Hegel or Leibniz that tied up the Universe in a System and declared: All is for the best in this best of possible worlds. Eternal Recurrence makes Existentialism absolute, or (if this sounds too complicated to make sense) it is the ultimate Act of Faith. Eternal Recurrence and the Superman are not conflicting conceptions; on the contrary, they are so closely connected that they may not on any account be separated. Eternal Recurrence is the condition that keeps the Superman an Existential conception, for *the Superman is an Existential and not an ideal conception*.* (This, of course, is the hurdle on which

---

* In this chapter, I have assumed a knowledge of the bases of Nietzsche's philosophy; the sort of outline that could be picked up from the introduction to any popular edition of *Also Sprach Zarathustra*. But for the benefit of readers for whom the idea of Eternal Recurrence is a stumbling-block to understanding of Nietzsche's thought, the following parallels might help to simplify it: first, Shaw in the Third Act of *Man and Superman*: Don Juan is speaking:

'. . . Granted that the great Life Force has hit on the device of the clock-maker's pendulum, and uses the earth for its bob; granted that the history of each oscillation, that seems so novel to us the actors, is but the history of the last oscillation repeated; nay more, that in the unthinkable infinitude of time the sun throws off the earth and catches it again as a circus rider throws up a ball, and that our agelong epochs are but the moments between the toss and the catch, has the collossal mechanism no purpose?'

As to the nature of the 'moment of vision' in which Nietszche conceived Eternal Recurrence, we can only make vague guesses. It would seem to have been a moment of supreme *detachment*, an Existentialist revelation of the *unconnectedness* of external nature and the internal 'ego': something of the same sort as seems to underly *Mind at the End of Its Tether*.

'The manner in which the "I Ching" tends to look upon reality seems to dis-favour our causalistic procedures. The moment under actual observation appears to the ancient Chinese view more of a chance hit than a clearly defined result of Concurring causal chain processes. The matter of interest seems to be the con-figuration formed by chance events in the moment of observation, and not at all the hypothetical reasons that seemingly account for the coincidence.'

This last quotation will be better understood if read in its context, Jung's Introduction to Wilhelm's translation of the *I Ching*. It will also make clear that way of dissociating the subject from objective Nature (an Existentialist proceeding which is thoroughly typical of ancient Chinese thought) which is the key to Nietzsche's idea of Eternal Recurrence.

hundreds of Nietzsche-critics have broken their shins, even that great Nietzschean Nicholas Berdyaev. Mencius said once: 'Those who follow that part of themselves which is great are great men; those who follow that part of themselves which is little are little men.' This is a religious, not a humanistic conception, and it is the starting-point of the idea of the Superman.

Before I go on to speak of *Thus Spake Zarathustra*, I should say a few words concerning misunderstanding of the Superman idea. The usual complaint is that Eternal Recurrence is an entirely negative concept, and that the Superman is a humanistic monster. Berdyaev, for instance, writes: 'Men of real genius . . . do not look upon themselves as Supermen for whom all things are lawful . . . on the contrary, they do great things for the world by subordinating themselves to that which they put above man. . . . Dostoevsky showed the folly of claiming to be a Superman, a lying idea that is the death of man.' Anyone who can understand that the Buddhist idea of Nirvana is not simply negative, and that the Buddha himself who (like the Superman) 'looks down on suffering humanity like a hillman on the plains' is not an atheistic monster, will instantly see how this view misses the point. Nietzsche was not an atheist, any more than the Buddha was.* Anyone who reads the Night Song and the Dance Song in *Zarathustra* will recognize that they spring out of the same emotion as the Vedic or Gathic hymns or the Psalms of David. The idea of the Superman is a response to the need for salvation in precisely the same way that Buddhism was a response to the 'three signs'. Berdyaev's criticism (in common with many modern commentators) assumes that the Superman is something *personal*, like *Rule, Britannia* or *Deutschland uber Alles*, an 'opium of the people'.

Now, the difference between a religious concept and a superstition (an 'opiate') is that one corresponds to psychological reality and the other doesn't; and by 'psychological reality' I mean an Outsider's reality. The Outsider's problems (I hope everyone would by now agree with me) are real problems, not neurotic delusions. They are not, of course, the sort of problems that everyone confronts every day, and probably the average plumber or stockbroker never confronts

---

* Professor Radakrishnan has powerfully argued this point in his edition of the *Principal Upanishads*. See also the appendix by Ranindranath Tagore.

them once in a lifetime. But the most practical-minded stockbroker would agree that the question, Where does the universe end? is not meaningless, and that the man who attaches some importance to it need not be a neurotic dupe. But if the man answered his own question: The universe is balanced on the back of a bull, which is balanced on the back of an elephant, etc., the stockbroker might be justified in condemning this as an outrage to common sense. In doing so, he would be endorsing the Outsider's view that metaphysics (i.e. a complete answer to the Outsider's problems) should be no more than *glorified common sense*, just as higher mathematics is only glorified arithmetic. And he would involve himself in an admission that to achieve glorified common sense, one would need to develop the 'glorified' sensitivity that leads to a perception of the problems that we call Outsider's problems. *All religious teaching is a plea for such development.*

In order to understand Nietzsche, we must first of all understand the way he approached the Outsider's problems, try to place ourselves 'inside' him to see as he saw. It is not enough to make this attempt with a volume of *Also Sprach Zarathustra* in one hand and a modern biography of Nietzsche in the other (most of the books on him that I know are either misinformed, or unfair: the major exception being Daniel Halévy's biography); what is required is a thorough knowledge of the Outsider as a type. Such a knowledge is the only real 'key' to Nietzsche.

In many ways, we shall be in a better position for understanding Nietzsche when we have examined Blake in a later chapter. Blake is very definitely a 'religious Outsider', and we shall need Dostoevsky to expand the Outsider's religious solution before we can appreciate the astounding psychological subtlety of Blake's approach. But we can say at this point that Blake, in common with another great English mystic, Traherne, achieved a 'Yea-saying' vision that brings Van Gogh's blazing canvases to mind. Blake's vision expressed itself in phrases like: 'Energy is eternal delight', 'Everything that lives is Holy, life delights in life'. Nietzsche wrote in his *Autobiography*: 'I am a disciple of the philosopher Dionysus, and I would prefer even to be a satyr than a saint.' If we remember what Nietzsche has written of Dionysus in *The Birth of Tragedy*, what his two experiences of 'pure will, free of the troubles of intellect' meant to him, we shall understand how fundamentally similar Nietzsche's vision was to Blake's.

The convalescence that began with *The Joyful Wisdom* brought Nietzsche back to that early intuition of the 'will to power'. When the idea of Eternal Recurrence came to him as he walked by the lake of Silvaplana, he wrote on a slip of paper: 'Six thousand feet above men and Time.' This is characteristic. At such moments he felt that he alone of all men had achieved such complete detachment from the circling of days, the wheel of activity. And later, at Rappallo, the idea of Zarathustra 'waylaid him' (to use his own phrase). Immediately he was seized up in creative violence; Zarathustra was the nearest he would ever come to being an artist-pure-and-simple. For Nietzsche, the essence of what he detested about Christian sainthood was contained in the words of the medieval churchman who said: 'We should marvel at nothing in Nature except the redeeming death of Christ.' But Nietzsche's saint would be a man who would marvel at everything in Nature, who would live in a continually healthy ecstasy of praise for being alive.* In Book One of *Also Sprach Zarathustra*, the old hermit greets him: 'Yea, I know thee that thou art Zarathustra. Clear is his eye, nor lurketh any loathing about his mouth. Goeth he not his way like a dancer?' And this is Zarathustra, the prophet of great health, who began his 'mission' like Lawrence's desert prophets, by leaving the crowds and retiring into solitude for ten years. Like the Biblical prophets, Zarathustra comes down to denounce idolatry. There are two idols that he finds being worshipped: the idealistic systems worshipped by the professors, and the anthropomorphic monster set up by the Church. Blake and Kierkegaard selected the same two points for attack; Blake wrote in 'Vala':

Then man ascended mourning into the splendours of his palace
Above him rose a Shadow from his weary intellect. . . .
Man fell prostrate upon his face before the watery shadow

---

* Nietzsche's most important analysis of asceticism, the third essay of his *Genealogy of Morals*, attacks it uncompromisingly, but this can be compared with an earlier statement, Nietzsche's comment on Dühring's book, *The Value of Life*. Dühring asserted: 'Asceticism is unhealthy, and the sequel of an error.' Nietzsche answered: 'No. Asceticism is an instinct that the most noble, the strongest among men have felt. It is a fact; it must be taken into account if the value of life is to be appreciated.' His own attitude was always consistent with this; he never attacked without carefully weighing the pros and cons.

Saying: 'O Lord, whence is this change? Thou knowest I am nothing.' . . .[22]

At first sight this seems to be mere humanism, as if Blake were saying: Man invented the idea of God. But it isn't; it is only this particular God that man invented—the bargainer for righteousness, the puppet-maker. And Zarathustra, the prophet of life, the nature mystic, declares: '. . . this I teach to men: No more to bury the head in the sand of heavenly things, but freely to carry it, a head of earth, giving meaning to the earth.'

This is the beginning of Nietzsche's positive philosophy. It might, admittedly, be a stepping-off point for almost any kind of materialism, for Marxism or Spencerian rationalism. But Nietzsche's religious intuitions carried him far beyond any 'rational materialism'. The idea of Zarathustra began as a reaction against Nietzsche's own soul-sickness; it was his attempt to give body to the idea of *great health*. Zarathustra was not a Superman; he was only a man who had succeeded in throwing off the sickness that poisons all other men. Like Hesse, he sees men as sick, corrupt, sinful, and he preaches the need for recognition of man's sickness if he is to escape from it:

> Verily, a polluted stream is man. One must be an ocean to receive a polluted stream without becoming unclean.
>
> I teach you the Superman. He is the ocean; in him can your contempt be overwhelmed.
>
> What is the greatest thing you can experience? It is the hour of great contempt. The hour in which even your happiness is loathesome to you, and your reason and your virtue likewise.
>
> The hour in which you say: What is my happiness worth? It is poverty and uncleanness and despicable ease. Yet my happiness should justify being itself. . . .
>
> Not your sin but your sufficiency cries unto heaven, your niggardliness even in sin cries unto heaven. . . .[23]

Our previous experience of Outsiders can have left us in no doubt as to what Zarathustra is talking about. He is describing the Outsider's experience of collapse of values, self-contempt; and *he is telling his audience that they ought all to become Outsiders.*

He condemns the middle way, the bourgeois way, and implies that it is better to be a great sinner than a bourgeois. Zarathustra is a preacher of extremes.

But what has he to offer, what is the 'heaven' of his new religion? The answer, we have already seen, is the Superman:

> Where is the lightning to lick you with its tongues? Where is the frenzy with which you must be infected?
> Behold, I teach you the Superman; he is the lightning, he is this frenzy. . . .[24]

Again, Nietzsche is obviously thinking in terms of his two 'vastations'. 'Lightning and tempest are different worlds, free powers without morality . . .' 'Pure Will, without the troubles of intellect. . . .' He does not think of the Superman as some tall, bronzed-skinned god; rather he begins from his own highest vision, and keeps that to the forefront of his mind. He does not want to set up another idol (and the literature of the anaemic life-force worshippers who sprang up as disciples of Nietzsche in the first two decades of our century, proves what a real danger he anticipated). In *Ecce Home* he states this unambiguously:

> The very last thing I should promise to accomplish would be to improve mankind. . . . To overthrow idols (idols is the name I give to all ideals) is much more like my business. *In proportion as an ideal has been falsely worshipped, reality has been robbed of its value, its meaning and its truthfulness.* . . . Hitherto the *lie* of the ideal has been the curse of reality; by means of it, the very source of mankind's instincts has become mendacious and false; so that the very values have come to be worshipped that are the exact *opposite* of the one that would assure man's prosperity, his future and his great right to a future. . . .[25]

This is the essence of Nietzsche's Existentialism; from it, Existentialism is seen to be the gospel of the will. It does not deny the ideal, provided the ideal comes second and the will first. But if their roles get reversed; if the will to more abundant life is made the slave of the ideal (or if it becomes non-existent, as in most professors and professional philosophers), then

Nietzsche will have no more of it; he calls for it to be scrapped and thrown into the dustbin, after all the other ideals that have served their purpose.

But Zarathustra soon learnt that it is no use preaching the Outsider gospel to the people:

'When Zarathustra had thus spoken, one of the people cried: We have heard enough about this tightrope-walker (the Superman); now let us *see* him. And all the people laughed at Zarathustra. . . .'[26]

And Nietzsche goes on to elaborate the parable. Zarathustra has described man as a rope stretched between the Ape and the Superman (here, of course, is the origin of Hesse's phrase: 'Man is a bourgeois compromise'). As the people in the market-place watch, a tightrope-walker comes out of his tower and starts across the rope stretched above the market-place. Suddenly a clown emerges from the tower, runs on to the rope and leaps over the tightrope-walker, who loses his balance and plunges into the market-place. It is Zarathustra who bends over the dying man and quiets his fear of hell by telling him: 'There is no devil and no hell; your soul will be dead even sooner than your body.' Then Zarathustra takes up the body and carries it away to inter it.

It was no accident that Zarathustra had spoken to the people of the Last Man shortly before the tightrope-walker fell to his death.

Alas, the day comes of the most contemptible man who can no longer condemn himself. . . .
Then the earth will have grown small, and upon it shall hop the Last Man who makes all things small; his kind is inexterminable, like the ground flea. The last man lives longest.[27]

The clown had hopped—like a flea—over the tightrope-walker. The Outsider is destroyed by human pettiness, human triviality and stupidity. It is Van Gogh and Nijinsky over again. And Zarathustra muses:

Man's life is a strange matter and full of unreason; a buffoon may be fatal to it.

Nietzsche, too, would fall off the tightrope. It would happen only seven years after he had written *Zarathustra*. Close reading of *Zarathustra* will give us a very clear insight into the causes of the breakdown. For Nietzsche had known what it meant to stand completely alone; to feel that he was the only healthy man in a sick universe, to feel that he had been destined by some force greater than himself to stand as a witness and, if necessary, to die completely alone. There is a passage in Rilke, in *Malte Laurids Brigge*, that catches the essence of the Nietzschean Outsider; it is a passage that should not be omitted from any study of the Outsider. Alone in his room, in a foreign city, the young poet asks himself:

It is possible that nothing important or real has yet been seen or known or said? Is it possible that mankind has had thousands of years in which to observe, reflect, record, and allowed these millennia to slip by like the recess interval at school in which one eats a sandwich and an apple?

Yes, it is possible.

Is it possible that, despite our discoveries and progress . . . we still remain on the surface of life? . . .

Yes, it is possible.

Is it possible that the whole history of the world has been misunderstood? . . .

Yes, it is possible.

Is it possible that these people know with perfect accuracy a past that has never existed? Is it possible that all the realities are nothing to them, that their life runs on, un-connected with anything, like a watch in an empty room?

Yes, it is possible. . . .

But if all this is possible—if it has even no more than a semblance of possibility—then surely . . . something must be done. The first-comer . . . must begin to do some of the neglected things . . . there is no one else at hand.[28]

And Zarathustra expresses Nietzsche's own experience of these Outsider thoughts in 'The Way of the Creator':

'He who seeks may go astray. All solitude is sin,' says the herd. And long were you yourself of the herd.

The voice of the herd still lingers in you, and when you

shall say: 'I no longer have a common conscience with
them', it shall be a grief and pain to you.

You call yourself free? I would hear of your master-
thought, not of your escape from the yoke.

Are you a man that should escape from the yoke? Many
have cast off all their values when they cast off their servitude.

Free from what? How does that concern Zarathustra?
Let your eye answer me frankly: Free *for* what?[29]

... a day will come when loneliness shall weary you, when
your pride shall writhe and your courage gnash its teeth.
In that day you shall cry: I am alone.

A day will come when you shall see your high things no
more, and your low things all too near; you shall fear your
exaltation as if it were a phantom. In that day you will cry:
All is false.

There are emotions that seek to slay the solitary; if they
don't succeed they must perish themselves. Are you able to
be a murderer?[30]

Only a year before he had written this, Nietzsche had written
in his Sanctus Januarius: 'I wish to be at all times hereafter
only a Yea-sayer.' In *Zarathustra* we learn something of the
difficulties encountered by a man who is determined only to
praise:

> Thus in a good hour once spake my purity: 'All beings
> shall be divine for me.'
> Then you came with filthy phantoms. Alas, whither fled
> the good hour?
> Once I vowed to renounce all disgust. Then you changed
> those nearest to me into ulcers. ... What happened then to
> my noblest vow?[31]

Nietzsche himself, we can say without unfairness, lacked the
elements of a Superman; or at all events, let us say, he lacked the
initial power of self-discipline to overcome these emotions
aroused by human stupidity. So, of course, did Van Gogh and
Lawrence and Nijinsky, and the heroes of Sartre and Barbusse
and Camus. Hemingway's heroes escaped the stupidity by
going in for high excitement: big game hunting and bullfighting
and war. That solved no problems. It all comes back (to borrow

a phrase from Shaw) to the 'appetite for fruitful activity and a high quality of life'. It is the problem of our second chapter, the World without Values. For the Outsider, the world into which he has been born is always a world without values. Compared to his own appetite for a purpose and a direction, the way most men live is not living at all; it is drifting. This is the Outsider's wretchedness, for all men have a herd instinct that leads them to believe that what the majority does must be right. Unless he can evolve a set of values that will correspond to his own higher intensity of purpose, he may as well throw himself under a bus, for he will always be an outcast and a misfit.

But once this purpose is found, the difficulties are half over. Let the Outsider accept without further hesitation: I am different from other men because I have been destined to something greater; let him see himself in the role of pre-destined poet, predestined prophet or world-betterer, and a half of the Outsider's problems have been solved. What he is saying is, in effect, this: In most men, the instinct of brother-hood with other men is stronger—the herd instinct; in *me*, a sense of brotherhood with something other than man is strongest, and demands priority. When the Outsider comes to look at other men closely and sympathetically, the hard and fast distinctions break down; he cannot say: I am a poet and they are not, for he soon comes to recognize that no one is entirely a business-man, just as no poet is entirely a poet. He can only say: the sense of purpose that makes me a poet is stronger than theirs. His needle swings to magnetic pole without hesitation; theirs wavers around all the points of the compass and only points north when they come particularly close to the pole, when under the influence of drink or patriotism or sentimentality. I speak of these last three conditions without disparagement; all forms of stimulation of man's sense of purpose are equally valid and, if applied for long enough, would have the effect of making a man into an Outsider. 'If the fool would persist in his folly he would become wise', Blake wrote.

All of these conclusions become obvious after a study of Nietzsche. For Nietzsche has taken certain steps which throw more light on the Outsider's obscure way to salvation. To begin with, Nietzsche reached our conclusions of Chapter IV: intellectual discipline is not enough. Zarathustra is primarily an intellectual, like his creator. He is also a poet and nature mystic, like Van Gogh. He is also a lover of the physical, like Nijinsky: he never ceases to liken himself to a dancer and to speak of dancing as the most vital form of self-expression. In him we can find the same reaction against thin-blooded intellectualism as in Blake or Walt Whitman. Zarathustra also 'sings the body electric'. 'Body I am throughout and nothing but body, and soul is only a word for something in the body'; Blake had written: 'Man has no body distinct from his soul, for that called body is a portion of the soul discerned by the five senses.' The two statements sound contradictory, but they are both a response to the same perception, that body itself is vital and good.

But Nietzsche considered that his perception clashed with the Christian idea, that the body is the 'frail and unimportant tenement of the soul'. The doctrine of introversion that underlay most ascetic Christianity in the Middle Ages (and still governs a great deal of monastic life) holds that Man originally was completely free; the Fall made him a slave of outward things; his salvation, therefore, lies in turning the attention inward, away from outside things. Blake, who was always more interested in Christ than in historic Christianity, found no body-contempt in Christ and could therefore declare himself a Christian without misgivings; Nietzsche was always more aware of Luther than Christ; Luther undoubtedly *was* a contemner of the body; Nietzsche called 'himself an Anti-Christ when he more probably meant an Anti-Luther. Nietzsche's temperament was less devotional, more intellectual, than Blake's; there is a fundamental similarity all the same, and it would be more accurate to regard Nietzsche as a Blakeian Christian than as an irreligious pagan. Always provided, of course, we know what we mean by a Blakeian Christian (unfortunately, it is beyond the scope of this book to study Blake's conception of Christianity).

Nietzsche understood the Outsider far better than anyone we have spoken of so far. Lawrence and Van Gogh were men working in the dark; Nietzsche wasn't.

Not the height, but the drop, is terrible.
That precipice in which the glance falls down while the hand gropes up. . . .
My Will clings to man; with chains I bind myself to man,

because I am drawn upwards towards the Superman; thither tends my *other* Will.[32]

For Nietzsche had taken the next great step; he had escaped from Evan Strowde's world without motive; he had grasped with both hands his destiny as a prophet. He grasped it, even though it meant standing completely alone. At first he believed it was a 'will to truth at all costs' that drove him. Later he plumbed his purpose to its depths; not simply a will to truth— that is not enough—but a will to life, to consciousness, to infusion of spirit into dead matter.

That was not the end of the problem. It might have been, if our civilization were two thousand years younger. What Nietzsche wanted to do was to start a new religion. Like Rilke's Malte, he felt that he was the only man who realized the necessity, and consequently that he alone should begin the tremendous work. But he wasn't sure how to begin. He had been trained as a philologist. He might have been better off if he had been trained as a priest or a novelist. Newman, for instance, was fundamentally very like Nietzsche, and he was lucky enough to find his way into an existing institution; *that* was the sensible thing to do, since retiring into the wilderness is not a practical expedient for a modern European. At the same time, we must admit that Nietzsche's influence has been far greater than Newman's, simply because Newman *did* choose to express himself inside the Church. Nietzsche's heroism is relatively greater; his suffering was greater; his tragedy affects us as Newman's obscurer tragedy does not.

Yet the really terrible element in Nietzsche's life is the *waste*. Under the right circumstances, Nietzsche would have had the strength to bring about a spiritual revival; instead he died insane, like a big gun with some trifling mechanical fault that explodes and kills all the crew. With all the power in his hands, with a psychological insight into himself that makes even Lawrence seem by comparison an amateur in introspection, Nietzsche cracked up. Why did he crack up? How could he have avoided it? Something was wrong. The new religion was never born. Nietzsche was misunderstood, more by the neurotics who claimed to be Nietzscheans than by his enemies. It is an immense problem. Since Nietzsche's death, two major prophets of Nietzschean rank have attacked it again: Shaw and Gurdjieff

(I shall glance briefly at their contributions to the Outsider's solution, in the last chapter of this book). Neither can be said to have solved it, although both have taken it on to new ground, and achieved some intellectually exciting results. Mr. Eliot has solved it for himself by his 'back to tradition' doctrine. This is also an aspect that will be easier to approach when we speak of T. E. Hulme in the last chapter.

At this point, we can summarize Nietzsche's contribution. He has solved the body-emotions-intellect equation, and arrived at the same conclusion we arrived at in Chapter IV. He has shown that he feels the Outsider to be a prophet in disguise—disguised even from himself—whose salvation lies in discovering his deepest purpose, and then throwing himself into it. He has no tendency towards a Sartre doctrine of commitment—that any purpose will do provided it is altruistic. If we tried to express the prophet's purpose in its simplest graspable form, we could say that it was a desire to shout 'Wake up!' in everybody's ear. But wake up to what? Wake up from what? Are all men asleep then?

Obviously, what we lack now is a penetrating psychological estimate of the human situation. All this has only a limited meaning until we can say: This is what man is, this is what he is intended to do.

In this chapter, I have not tried to survey the full extent of Nietzsche's attempted answer to these questions; I have not even quoted the books in which he deals most seriously with Outsider problems (*Beyond Good and Evil*, *The Genealogy of Morals*, *The Will to Power*). To a certain extent, the next two chapters will make this superfluous. Besides, it is not a philosopher's problem; Nietzsche himself discovered: Intellect is not enough. Yet he remained a philosopher who continued to attack the problems with a philosopher's tools: the language of criticism, the ordering of thoughts into paragraphs and chapters. But Zarathustra made it clear in which direction the answer lay; it is towards the artist-psychologist, the intuitional thinker. There are very few such men in the world's literature; the great artists are not thinkers, the great thinkers are seldom artists. One of the few nations that have produced great men who combined the two faculties is Russia; and it is to Russia's two greatest novelists that we must turn now for further treatment of the Outsider.

CHAPTER SIX

THE QUESTION OF IDENTITY

THE OUTSIDER IS NOT sure who he is. 'He has found an "I", but it is not his true "I".' His main business is to find his way back to himself.

This is not so easy. In fact, strictly speaking, we have not touched on the problem yet. We have only analysed the Outsider's 'lostness'. Even 'the attempt to gain control' was a failure that only provided more insight into the Outsider's complicated clockwork. 'To find a way back to himself': that is how we have provisionally defined his aim. But it is not a simple affair, as certain successful modern novelists have made it appear in their fictionalized treatment of Outsiders ('best-sellers' about the life of Van Gogh, Gauguin, etc.). It calls for detailed psychological analysis; for an exactitude of language for which there is no precedent in modern literature (if we except the poetry of Mr. Eliot, especially the 'Four Quartets', and certain passages in Joyce's *Ulysses*). It is a subject which is full of pitfalls for the understanding. And writing about it drives home the fact that our language has become a tired and inefficient thing in the hands of journalists and writers who have nothing to say.

Now language is the natural medium for self-analysis; the idea of 'a way back to himself' cannot be expressed in any other medium. But it cannot have escaped the reader's attention that all our analysis so far has aimed at defining what the Outsider means by 'himself', and that we have barely touched on the question of '*the way*'. To a certain degree, of course, one question follows another, but the point I wish to make here is the fact that the 'way' is not a matter for *words*, but a matter for action. At a certain point, the Outsider asks Bunyan's question, 'What must I *do* to be saved?' If his answer is Evan Strowde's: 'Nothing is worth doing', then there is no help for it, he had better cut his throat or commit mind-suicide. Fortunately, Strowde's answer is not a logical bottleneck; we can still attack the question from another angle and ask: saved from *what*? And this reduces the problem to a more graspable form; in fact to our Ultimate Yes or Ultimate No. For 'saved from what' immediately involves the further question: What is the *worst* you can be saved from? in short, what is the worst form of Ultimate No? We have mentioned some appalling examples: Hiroshima, the Armenian Massacre—and there are pages in *The Seven Pillars of Wisdom* that are terrible enough to put a sensitive person off his dinner. But after all, they are not ultimate forms of evil; they are old stuff, quite familiar in history. You can read several examples in the Assyrian Room at the British Museum: how Assur Nasir Pal II 'burned their young men and maidens in a fire' and committed other cruelties that are too revolting to quote, but that, after all, can quite easily be paralleled by Belsen and Buchenwald after another three thousand years of civilization have elapsed. No, these evils are oppressive, but they do not hang over us with a sense of being inescapable.

It is when we consider the 'vastations' of the Jameses, father and son, that we come closer to the problem of real evil. This evil comes nearer home; *it attacks the mind*, not the body. Assur Nasir Pal and the men he tortured to death could alike be reduced to 'a quivering mass of fear' by it. Hitler would be as defenceless against it as the Jews of the Warsaw Ghetto. In such an appalling light, men are no longer real beings; they are reduced to a common level of unreality:

> Think of us, not as lost, violent souls
> But only as the hollow men, the stuffed men.

> If the hour should strike for me as it struck for him,
> nothing I possess could save me. . . .

This is a terrible conclusion to accept. As human beings, we cannot accept it. We must repeat the question: Is there no way out?

* * *

Our method in approaching this problem must be the same as usual: to take concrete examples. Again, we might look to William James for a direction. Religious cases are 'out'; this narrows the choice of 'sick souls'. But among other cases, James quotes Tolstoy's *Confession*, and this seems to be an excellent starting-point, for Tolstoy at least *began* as a free-thinker, after the fashion of the 30's of the last century. Moreover, Tolstoy resembles Nietzsche and Kierkegaard in that he reached religious conclusions while finding it impossible to support the orthodox Church—another feature common to Outsiders.

A Confession tells how, in his fiftieth year, Tolstoy (by that time the famous author of *War and Peace* and *Anna Karenina*) began to be troubled by the questions: 'What is life? Why should I live? Why should I do anything? Is there any meaning in life that can overcome inevitable death?'

It is interesting to note that Tolstoy says, and evidently believes, that these questions had never seriously troubled him before; in spite of which, fifteen years earlier, we have him putting into the mouth of Peter Bezhukov in *War and Peace* the words: 'What is bad? What is good? . . . What does one live for? What am I? What is life and What is death?', etc.[1] There are obviously *degrees* of awareness of Outsider problems, and the force of the later occasion made Tolstoy dismiss the earlier. But we must also note the fact that, the harder the problems strike, the more they disable the man. Tolstoy is an example of the phenomenon I mentioned in Chapter IV, partial solution of the problems and partial remaining in the old, once-born state. Again, in *War and Peace*, in the firing-squad scene, Peter observes that the soldiers *are not aware of the nature of what they are doing*.[2] The problem of death, and of meaning in life, is completely dissociated from human cruelty and 'man's inhumanity to man'. Assur Nasir Pal and Hitler hardly enter into it. It is the observation of Walter Pater's Florian* that all living creatures are involved in 'a vast web of cruelty', no matter how gentle and humane they may be. Evil is Outside.

Tolstoy's experiences began like Roquentin's: 'Five years ago something very strange began to happen to me. At first I experienced moments of perplexity and arrest of life, as though I did not know how to live or what to do. . . . Then these moments of perplexity recurred oftener and oftener . . .'[3]

Finally, attacks of 'the nausea'. 'I felt that what I had been standing on had broken down, and that I had nothing left under my feet. What I had lived on no longer existed, and I had nothing left to live on.'[4]

'There's no adventure': there is no need to press the parallel. Tolstoy has found a parable that brings home to the full

* *Child in the House.*

the Outsider's attitude to other men: he cites an Eastern fable
of a man who clings to a shrub on the side of a pit to escape an
enraged beast at the top and a dragon at the bottom. Two mice
gnaw at the roots of his shrub. Yet while hanging, waiting for
death, he notices some drops of honey on the leaves of the
shrub, and reaches out and licks them.[5] This is man, suspended
between the possibilities of violent accidental death and
inevitable natural death, diseases accelerating them, yet still
eating, drinking, laughing at Fernandel in the cinema. This is
the man who calls the Outsider morbid because he lacks
appetite for the honey!

At this point, we can turn from Tolstoy's *Confession* to a
fictional account he wrote of the crisis in the short story,
'Memoirs of a Madman'. This will make the case even clearer.
The hero of this short story explains that he has just been
examined by a board to be certified insane. He was not
certified, but only because he restrained himself and did not
give himself away. He goes on to tell how he went 'mad'. As
a child, he had once had an 'attack' when he heard the story
of the Crucifixion: the cruelty made a deep impression: 'I
sobbed and sobbed and began knocking my head against the
wall.'

There follows on account of his growing-up, his teens and
'sexual impurities' (the later Tolstoy had an obsession about
sexual impurity that Kierkegaard or Nietzsche would have
found funny). Then the Civil Service, marriage and managing
his estates; finally, he becomes a Justice of the Peace. He is
now entering middle age.

Then the first attack comes. He is on a journey to buy a
far-distant estate when he wakes up in the carriage 'with a
feeling that there was something terrifying'. It is like Henry
James Sr.'s attack, striking into the middle of contentment
and health. Its effect is rather like Roquentin's nausea; it
fixes itself on certain objects, a wart on the cheek of an inn-
keeper, the corners of a whitewashed room.

In the night, the terror comes again, and he thinks: 'Why
have I come here? Where am I taking myself? ... I am running
away from something dreadful and cannot escape it. *I am always
with myself, and it is I who am my tormentor.* ... Neither the Penza
or any other property will add anything or take anything from
me: and it is myself I am weary of and find intolerable and a

torment. I want to fall asleep and forget myself and cannot. I cannot get away from myself.'⁶ [Italics mine.]

Here, in one passage, we can hear echoes of T. E. Lawrence ('. . . I did not like the "myself" I could see and hear'), Roquentin, Nijinsky, William James ('nothing I possess can save me . . .').

The story details several of these attacks. The idea of death troubles him, and the meaninglessness of life.

What is life for? To die? To kill myself at once? No, I am afraid. To wait for death till it comes? I fear that even more. Then I must live. *But what for?* In order to die? And I could not escape from that circle. I took up the book, read, and forgot myself for a moment, but then again, the same question and the same horror. I lay down and closed my eyes. It was worse still.⁷

He tries prayer, prayer in the doubting sense, as in 'Ash Wednesday'. 'If Thou dost exist, reveal to me why and what I am.' No result.

The ending of the story is rather disconcerting. On a hunting expedition he gets lost in the forest, and is again attacked by 'the horror'. But he is closer to an *intuitive* understanding of the way out. At home again, he begins to pray for forgiveness of his sins. A few days later, when a nearby estate is for sale on terms that would give great advantage to the landlord and none to the peasants, he realizes that 'all men are sons of the same father' and decides not to buy it. Later, at the church door he gives away all his money to beggars, and walks home with the peasants, talking of religion. (Again the curious parallel with Nijinsky.)

After this, we assume, his relatives try to have him certified.

Now up to a point we can follow what happens to the 'madman' because we have seen it happening to other Outsiders. But all this praying, studying the Old Testament? The story was written when Tolstoy was seventy, but its conclusion does not seem a great advance on Peter Bezukhov's solution, written when he was half that age, of becoming a Freemason and adopting actively the doctrine of the brotherhood of all men. Yet Tolstoy was no fool. There must be something valid in the conclusion, something that follows from the Outsider's premises.

Before we press the question, there is another treatment by Tolstoy of the same theme that will give us more to go on. At the beginning of *A Confession*, he speaks of the increasing frequency of the attacks:

'There occurred that which happens to everyone sickening with a mortal internal disease. At first trivial signs of indisposition occur ... then these signs reappear more and more often and merge into one uninterupted period of suffering. .... The suffering increases, and before the sick man can look round ... it is death.'[8]

Tolstoy's *Death of Ivan Ilytch* follows this plan. It shows the once-born petty official, Ivan Ilytch, as he advances to become a Justice of the Peace ('judge not that ye be not judged' was one of Tolstoy's favourite sermon texts), with home, children, admiring colleagues, a club, etc. Then, the first 'slight indisposition'. The cancer begins to eat into his being, and as the realization that he is going to die breaks upon him, he begins to ask himself: 'What if my whole life has really been wrong?' A realization, foreshadowing that of Roquentin, of the meaningless of his life, of all other people's, dawns on him. But *how* should he have lived? he asks himself. There he can find no answer. There were moments, but they were just flashes, impulses he suppressed or forgot. And his wife and children, they don't care for him really, and if they did it wouldn't matter. All his life he has lived with other people; now he is dying alone. But a sudden impulse of charity towards his wife—he has come to hate her insincerity and shallowness—suddenly illumines the darkness, and gives him a glimpse of *selflessness*. And in a flash, the fear of death has gone:

> In place of death there was light ...
> 'It is finished' somebody said near him.
> He heard the words and repeated them in his soul·
> 'Death is finished.'[9]

The words that released him from his wretchedness were: 'Forgive me.'

We now have four versions of religious awakening from Tolstoy. *All of them begin by the person's becoming an Outsider.* They are to be divided into two types: Peter Bezukhov, the 'madman' and Tolstoy himself all suffered from 'attacks', like

Roquentin. Ivan Ilytch lived an 'unreal life' and only realized its unreality when facing death, like Meursault. In all four cases, the main symptom was self-hatred, a desire to escape oneself. In all four cases, the escape is achieved by seizing on the essence of Christianity as *selflessness*. The aim is to escape oneself. Other people are a means to this end: but the end is still to escape oneself. If the end became to love other people and practical charity, its result could easily be a new form of self-love.

It will be seen at once that there is not such a wide divergence between this view and Nietzsche's teaching in *Zarathustra*. Zarathustra says 'What is the greatest thing a man can experience? It is the hour of great [self-] contempt.' The *means* are different for Nietzsche, but the end is the same.

Tolstoy cannot take us a great deal further where the Outsider's problems are concerned. He can take us a great distance, but if we stick to our original intention, not to plunge into any religious conclusion, then we had better stop short of Tolstoyan Christianity. Admittedly, it is a rational Christianity, that finds the meaning of Christ's message in His life and teachings, not in His 'atoning death'. But it also wanders to limits that can throw no light on the subject of this study, into a sort of Manicheism, for instance, where the spirit world is good and of God and the material world is evil and of the devil. In the Middle Ages, Manicheans carried their belief to its logical conclusion, and condemned even reproduction of the species; the sex-act itself was evil (as with Tolstoy); when someone was dying, they helped him on his way by starvation, assuring him that he was leaving all evil behind him with the flesh. Tolstoy pulls up short of this extremity, but his later beliefs as to what was sinful and what not suggest a religion of Talmudic law and dogma that can hardly be reached from our Existentialist premises of Chapter I.

* * *

Who am I?—This is the Outsider's final problem. Well, who precisely is he? 'Man is a bourgeois compromise', a half-way house. But a half-way house towards what? The superman? We have seen that the superman is not a gigantic piece of Nietzschean crankery, but a valid poetic concept that develops from the same urges as the saint and spiritual reformer. But

'the great man is a play-actor of his own ideals', and you cannot
act well unless you have a clear idea of the part you are going
to play. So when Tolstoy's madman wakes up in his carriage
with a nightmare sense of horror, and the question What am I?
then the road towards the superman, or the saint or the
artist of genius, is temporarily blocked up. The question of
Identity lies across it.

An interesting point, this; for what is identity? These men
travelling down to the City in the morning, reading their
newspapers or staring at advertisements above the opposite
seats, they have no doubt of who they are. Inscribe on the
placard in place of the advertisement for corn-plasters, Eliot's
lines:

> We are the hollow men
> We are the stuffed men
> Leaning together

and they would read it with the same mild interest with which
they read the rhymed advertisement for razor blades, wondering what on earth the manufacturers will be up to next. Some
of them even carry identity cards—force of habit—that would
tell you precisely who they are and where they live.

They have *aims*, these men, some of them very distant aims:
a new car in three years, a house at Surbiton in five; but an aim
is not an ideal. They are not play-actors. They change their
shirts every day, but never their conception of themselves.
Newman confessed that, when he looked at the world, he
couldn't see the slightest evidence for the existence of God.[10]
We, who may have known Vaslav Nijinsky's instinctive
certainty in some intuition—listening to music, perhaps—
can understand that the idea of God is associated with the
dynamic, 'spirit breaking on the coasts of matter', and understand what Newman meant, looking at this sea of static
personality.

These men are in prison: that is the Outsider's verdict. They
are quite contented in prison—caged animals who have never
known freedom; but it *is* prison all the same. And the Outsider? He is in prison too: nearly every Outsider in this book
has told us so in a different language; *but he knows it*. His desire
is to escape. But a prison-break is not an easy matter; you must
know all about your prison, otherwise you might spend years

THE QUESTION OF IDENTITY

in tunnelling, like the Abbé in *The Count of Monte Cristo*, and only find yourself in the next cell.

And, of course, the final revelation comes when you look at these City-men on the train; for you realize that for them, the business of escaping is complicated by the fact that *they think they are the prison*. An astounding situation! Imagine a large castle on an island, with almost inescapable dungeons. The jailor has installed every device to prevent the prisoners escaping, and he has taken one final precaution: that of hypnotizing the prisoners, and then suggesting to them that *they and the prison are one*. When one of the prisoners awakes to the fact that he would like to be free, and suggests this to his fellow prisoners, they look at him with surprise and say: 'Free from what? We *are* the castle.' What a situation!

And this is just what happens to the Outsider. There is only one solution. He personally must examine the castle, draw his inferences as to its weaker points, and plan to escape alone. And this 'knowing the castle' is what we referred to at the beginning of Chapter IV: 'The Outsider's first business is to know himself.'

Naturally, the first question of the prisoner who begins to recover from the hypnosis is: Who am I?

In Chapters II and III we spoke of Outsiders who awake to the fact that *they were not what they had always supposed themselves to be* when they *felt something* that opened up new possibilities: Krebs's moments in the war when he did 'the one thing, the only thing', Strowde's 'glimpse of a power within him', Steppenwolf's vision while listening to Mozart. And the recovery of that insight depends on finding a way back to the place where it was seen. And thought alone is no use, because it is thought that has been bound hand-and-foot by the hypnosis of the jailer: by habit, laziness, ways of 'seeing oneself', etc. *Action* is necessary. A man can change his mental habits by changing his way of life; sometimes one act alone can completely change the whole mental outlook. A libertine can become a faithful married man by the mere repetition of the words 'I will', provided he is deeply enough impressed by their meaning. The main thing is that a man should feel an act of Will to be *unreversible*. These definitions, that have evolved logically from the last chapter, place us in a strange, half-lighted landscape, where the Outsider is half-hidden in an

intangible prison of angles and shadows. His purpose is clear—
to himself: to find his way back into a daylight where he can
know a single undivided Will, Nietzsche's 'pure will without
the troubles of intellect'. His first step is to repudiate the false
daylight of the once-born bourgeois. His next problem is to
find an *act*, a definite act that will give him power over his
doubts and self-questionings.

At this point, we can pass the threads of the argument into
the hands of another Russian writer, and leave him to unravel
them further for us.

*   *   *

There were a number of events in Fyodor Dostoevsky's life
that were 'turning-points', sudden, violent experiences that
raked across his mental habits and placed him in the Outsider's
position of seeing himself as a stranger. This gives him a peculiar
value in our study, as combining the characteristics of the Van
Gogh Outsider and the Herman Hesse type: men who write
about their problems, and the men who live them.

Dostoevsky's father was murdered by his peasants; they
attacked him one day when he was drunk, and killed him by
the strange method of crushing his testicles. They succeeded
so well in hiding the fact that he had died by violence that they
were never brought to justice. Dostoevsky learned of the death
of his father while he was an engineering student in Petersburg.

Fame broke on him suddenly when he was only twenty-four;
his short novel *Poor Folk* was hailed by the foremost Russian
critics as the most outstanding novel since *Dead Souls*. The
unknown engineering student was acclaimed as a great writer.
Three years later, the reversal came when he was arrested for
being involved in a nihilistic plot. The story of the fake 'execution' in the Semyonovsky Square is well known (Dostoevsky
makes Prince Myshkin retell it in *The Idiot*). By the time the
'pardon' arrived at the last moment, one of the condemned
men had gone insane, and never recovered. Dostoevsky spent
the next ten years in exile in Siberia.

His later life is equally a story of sudden brilliant successes,
and catastrophes that fell on him without warning. In his
dealings with people, especially women, he often showed
revolting weakness and stupidity; in his recovery from dis-
asters and in the writing of his books he revealed extraordinary

spiritual strength. It is the same with his books. *The Brothers Karamazov*, *The Devils*, *The Idiot* are surely the sloppiest great novels ever written; this must be qualified by adding that they are also among the greatest novels ever written.

The Outsider theme is present in everything that Dostoevsky ever wrote; his five major novels represent an increasingly complex attack on it. Since the English edition of his works runs into fifteen volumes, it is obvious that our attention must be very strictly limited to his most important work. (The alternative would be to extend this section on Dostoevsky out of all proportion to the sections on other writers.) This means that certain works that would well repay our study must be ignored completely: *The Double*, *The House of the Dead*, *The Gamblers* and *A Raw Youth*.

The novels that are most important for our purpose are *Notes from Underground*, *Crime and Punishment* and *The Brothers Karamazov*.

Notes from Underground is the first major treatment of the Outsider theme in modern literature. With Hesse's *Steppanwolf*, it can be considered as one of the most important expositions of the Outsider's problems that we shall deal with in this study. Written sixty-four years before Hesse's and forty-six before Barbusse's book, when no other 'Outsider' literature existed, it stands as a uniquely great monument of Existentialist thought.

Its title in Russian, *Notes from Under the Floorboards*, carries the suggestion that its hero is not a man, but a beetle. This is just what he makes himself out to be; his first words are: 'I am sick. I am full of spleen and repellent. . . .'

And the character-analysis that follows shows us why he considers himself a beetle. He has been like this, he says, for twenty years, living alone in his room, seldom going out, nursing his dyspepsia and ill-temper, and thinking, thinking. . . . For fifty pages he rambles on, expounding his ideas. He is neurotically over-sensitive: 'No hunchback, no dwarf, could be more prone to resentment and offence than I. . . .'

Yet all this rings false; we begin to grow impatient of the beetle-man's word-spinning, when suddenly we become aware that, in spite of the longwindedness, he is really trying to define something important. He is full of fantastic illustrations of his 'complicated state of mind'. Here is an example (greatly abridged): 'People who are able to wreak vengeance on an assailant, and in general to stand up for themselves—how do they do it? It can only be supposed that *momentarily their whole being is possessed* by a desire for revenge, and no other element is . . . in them. A man of that sort goes straight to his goal as a mad bull charges. . . . I do not consider a man of that type to be the "normal", as his mother Nature—would have him be. Yet I envy him with all the power of my spleen. . . .' [Italics mine.][11]

We are reminded of T. E. Lawrence's envy of the soldier with a girl or a man caressing a dog. Yes, we know all about this aspect of the beetle-man. He thinks too much. Thinking has thinned his blood and made him incapable of spontaneous enjoyment. He envies simpler, stupider people because they are undivided. That is nothing new. What more has the beetle-man to tell us?

Well, there is the odd fact that he *likes* suffering.

. . . it is just in this same cold, loathesome semi-mania, this same half-belief in oneself . . . this same poison of unsatisfied wishes . . . that there lies the essence of the strange delight I have spoken of.[12]

And this 'strange delight' is the centre of the beetle-man's dialectic. For upon it pivots the whole question of *freedom*. Is man really incapable of absolute evil, as Boethius (following Plato) asserts? Does he always strive for what he instinctively apprehends as the Good? The arguments for it are strong. For the criminal, crime is a response to the complexities of his social life. In that case, is the soul, then, governed by natural laws like Einstein's gravitational formulae? '*Tout est pour le mieux dans ce meilleur de mondes possible*'; and Hegel, with a grand sweep, completes the System begun by Leibniz. (It was Leibniz, after all, who originated the conception of philosophy as glorified logic that has had such depressing results in modern philosophy.) So after Hegel, Reason governs all; men are cogs in a great machine that makes for ultimate Good.

And suddenly, Dostoevsky's beetle-man starts up, with his bad teeth and beady eyes, and shouts: 'To hell with your System. I demand the right to behave as I like. I demand the right to regard myself as *utterly unique*.'

And now we can see what the beetle-man is really getting at, with his nasty leers and shrill giggles. His belligerence is a reaction against something, and that 'something' is rational humanism. And before long we recognize the Nietzschean note:

> To maintain theories of renovating the human race through Systems ... is about the same thing as to maintain that man grows milder with civilization. Logically, perhaps, this is so; yet he is so prone to Systems and abstract deductions that he is for ever ready to mutilate the truth, to be blind to what he sees or deaf to what he hears, so long as he can succeed in vindicating his logic. ... Civilization develops in man nothing but an added capacity to receive impressions —that is all. And the growth of that capacity increases his tendency to seek pleasure in spilling blood. You may have noticed that the most enthusiastic blood-letters have always been the most civilised of men. ... [13]

This is the essence of Nietzsche's vision on the hilltop ... unreason, the smell of blood, violence, and utter contempt for mere intellect. We can imagine how disgusted the beetle-man would have been with Freud's psychology, which expounds the most picturesquely complicated accounts of the 'mechanisms' that produce 'irrational' human actions.

> ... On the contrary, you say, science will in time show that man does not possess any will or initiative of his own— but that he is as the keyboard of the piano. Above all, science will show him that there exist certain laws of nature which cause everything to be done. ... Consequently, you say, those laws will only have to be explained to man and at once he will become divested of all responsibility, and find life much easier to deal with. All human acts will then be mathematically computed according to nature's laws and entered in tables of logarithms. ...
> But who would care to exercise his will-power according to a table of logarithms?

And here we can pause to observe that this dialectic of the beetle-man, this anti-rationalist tirade, was published many years before the name Kierkegaard was heard outside Denmark, or Nietzsche outside Germany. Kierkegaard's *Unscientific Postscript*, which is the bettle-man's case extended to several

hundred pages, had been published under the curious pseudo-
nym 'Johannes Climacus' in the same year as *Poor Folk*, but it had
made no impression comparable to Dostoevsky's story. Neither
was Kierkegaard the first exponent of *Existenzphilosophie*:
half a century earlier, another unknown man of genius had
written:[14]

> All bibles and sacred codes have been the cause of the
> following errors:
> That man has two really existing principles, viz., a body
> and a soul
> That Energy, called Evil, is alone from the body, and
> Reason, called Good, is alone from the soul.
> But the following contraries to these are true:
>
> Man has no body distinct from his Soul—for what is called
> body is that portion of the soul discerned by the five senses. . . .
> Energy is the only life, and is from body, and Reason is the
> bound or outward circumference of energy.
> Energy is eternal delight!

William Blake also had no love of philosophers and their
'logarithms', and he detested systems as much as did Kierkegaard. Yet he had to labour at his own attempt at an existence-
philosophy, for:

> I must create my own System or be enslaved by another
> man's
> My business is not to reason and compare; my business
> is to create.[16]

So we can see at a glance that we have here a strange group of
men—Blake, Kierkegaard, Nietzsche, Dostoevsky: two violently
unorthodox Christians, one pagan 'philosopher with a hammer',
and one tormented half-atheist-half-Christian, all beginning
from the same impulse and driven by the same urges. Since we
can see plainly, after our painstaking analysis, that this impulse
is fundamental in the Outsider, it is not a bold step to assert
that *these men held basically the same beliefs*. The differences that
seem to separate them are only differences of temperament
(imagine Blake's reaction to Kierkegaard's *Diary of the Seducer*,

or Nietzsche's to Dostoevsky's *Life of Father Zossima!*); the basic idea is the same in all four.

To recognize this conclusion is, in fact, to have made a great step towards conceding the contention of this book, that the Outsider's values are religious ones, but elaboration of this point can wait until we have finished with Dostoevsky.

The beetle-man's argument reaches a climax with this important statement:

If you say that everything—chaos, darkness, anathema—can be reduced to mathematical formulae—*then man will go insane on purpose* to have no judgement, and to behave as he likes. I believe this because it appears that man's whole business is to prove that he is a man and not a cog-wheel. . . . And perhaps, who knows, the striving of man on earth may consist in this uninterrupted striving for something ahead, that is, *in life itself*, rather than some real end which obviously must be a static formula of the same kind as two and two make four—I am sure that man will never renounce the genuine suffering that comes of ruin and chaos. Why, suffering is the one and only source of knowledge.[16] [Italics mine.]

What I must stand for is my personal free-will, and what it can do for me when I am in the right mood to use it.[17]

After these gigantic analyses, this beetle-man cannot resist Evan Strowde's conclusion: 'So we have reached the belief that the best thing we can do is to do nothing at all—is to sink into a contemplative inertia.'

But he knows, as well as Strowde, that this is not really what he wants; it is a second-best for something else, 'Something for which I am hungry, but which I shall never find'. So ends the beetle-man's preamble to the reader.

The second part of his 'confession' is a tale of his own past, and of a glimpse of that 'something he can never find'. It is not a particularly good story. He tells how he forced his company on a party of old schoolfellows, who openly disliked him, and how, after some humiliations, he followed them to a brothel. In bed with a prostitute named Lisa he begins a conversation—about death. And as he talks his own imagination fires. He begins by speaking of love and religion and God. When she mockingly accuses him of talking like a book, he grows more eloquent; and suddenly it is Dostoevsky, the great artist-psychologist of *Poor Folk*, who is creating a picture of human misery and redeeming love, who is speaking into the darkness to the young prostitute who lies by his side. This is the Outsider's moment, his feeling of harmony, his glimpse of a 'power within him'. The girl suddenly begins to cry, and quietly, the Outsider slips out of bed and takes leave of her, after giving her his address.

But when the girl calls on him a few days later, a complete change of attitude has occurred in him; the 'glimpse' has been completely lost; he is his old irritable, violent self again. He curses her, insults her. When, with the insight of a woman in love, she divines that he is desperately unhappy, and suddenly offers herself to him, his self-contempt turns to hatred for her. He takes her body, and then offers her payment for her 'services'. She leaves, and he is alone again, suddenly feeling lost and miserable, hating himself, and his inability to resolve the everlasting conflicts within him.

Notes from Underground is an unpleasant story, so unnecessarily unpleasant as to be barely readable. What it does convey, more than any other work we have quoted, is the tortured, self-divided nature of the Outsider. The nasty taste it leaves in the mouth is due to its failure as a work of art, its obsessive caterwauling about the weakness of human nature, etc. A lot of Dostoevsky's work leaves the same taste, his 'Eternal Husband' and many of the short-stories arouse a mixed feeling of boredom and disgust, the sort of irritation one feels in watching Mr. Aldous Huxley's systematic butchery of all his characters. If we were to judge Dostoevsky by such work, the final verdict on him would be the same as Shaw's on Shakespeare—that he understands human weakness without understanding human strength.

In point of fact, this is not true; Dostoevsky's evolution as a novelist is a slow development of understanding of human strength. The heroes of the early books are in every sense 'Godless'; then little by little, they cease to be vain and trivial. Raskolnikov is followed by Prince Myshkin, then by Kirilov and Shatov, finally by the Karamazov Brothers, who are giants compared to the beetle-man.

Crime and Punishment has suffered greatly at the hands of

critics who insist on treating it as a moral tract upon the wickedness of taking human life, in spite of Dostoevsky's plain statements about its real purpose, which is far less obvious. Even Nicholas Berdyaev, whose book on Dostoevsky is the most stimulating ever written, adopts the Christian standpoint and condemns Raskolnikov as a 'cold monster'.

Having already seen what happens when the Outsider makes the 'attempt to gain control', we can dismiss this interpretation without fear of finding ourselves in the position of condoning murder. In *Crime and Punishment*, Raskolnikov is in the same position as the beetle-man, living alone in his room, morose, too self-conscious, hating human wretchedness, and disliking the human weakness which he holds to be its cause. With his whole being, he wants to establish contact with the 'power within him', and he knows that, to do this, he must arouse his will to some important purpose, to find *a definitive act*. In a later chapter of the book (after the murder) Dostoevsky describes Raskolnikov's awakening: 'His movements were precise and definite; a firm purpose was evident in him. "Today," he muttered to himself. He understood that he was still weak, *but his intense spiritual concentration gave him strength and self-confidence*'.[18] [Italics mine.]

And a little later:

> ... a sort of savage energy gleamed suddenly in his feverish eyes and his wasted, yellow face. He did not know or think where he was going, but had one thought only: 'that all this must be ended today ... that he would not return home without it, because he would not go on living like that.'

Now we can see that *Crime and Punishment* is actually simply a study in what we have spoken of in Chapter IV—the definitive act. Raskolnikov's position has much in common with Nietzsche's: he hates his own weakness, he hates human weakness and misery. His deepest instinct is towards strength and health, 'pure will' without the troubles and perplexities of intellect'. He does not believe that he is rotten to the core; he does not believe 'there is no health in us'. There *is* strength— he is certain of that—but a long way down, and it would take a great deal of will to blast one's way down to it. Very well, show him a way, any way. Show him an enemy worth his strength.

And here is the difficulty. For Raskolnikov, like Barbusse's hero, has 'no genius, no special talent'.

A writer, a thinker, a preacher, a soldier, all might find worth-while work to do in that environment of social misery and decay. But Raskolnikov has no faith in his mission. He sees Petrograd as Blake saw London, the Industrial Revolution:

> I wander through each dirty street
> Near where the dirty Thames does flow
> And on each human face I meet
> Marks of weakness, marks of woe.

The misery that provoked young Russian students to become followers of Herzen and Bakunin aroused in Dostoevsky a deeper feeling than a desire for social revolution. And in *Crime and Punishment*, the suffering, fevered Raskolnikov is Dostoevsky's spokesman. His reaction to it all is a fictionalized version of Dostoevsky's feeing about it.

Now here the problem of interpretation becomes difficult. For Raskolnikov's reaction to his perception of universal misery is to commit a crime, to kill an old pawnbroker, whose death will serve the double purpose of providing him with money to escape his binding poverty, and of being a gesture of defiance, a definitive act. The murder achieves neither of these purposes; he finds no money and solves no problems. The Reader asks, Why does he solve no problem? and it is only too easy to 'identify' his horror of the bloodshed with a moral intention on the part of the author. Berdyaev writes:

> The spiritual nature of man forbids the killing of the least and most harmful of men: it means the loss of one's essential humanity . . . it is a crime no higher end can justify. Our neighbour is more precious than any abstract notion. . . . That is the Christian conception and it is Dostoevsky's.[19]

Now, this is a convenient simplification that completely obscures the real meaning of the novel. Raskolnikov rejects this point of view and there is no evidence that Dostoevsky accepts it. Dostoevsky does *not* state: 'Murder is wrong because the Christian conception of the sacredness of human life is right.' His theme is far more subtle; and although it is true that his final conclusions are Christian, it would be downright dishonesty to accept Berdyaev's short-cut to them. It would involve the assumption that Dostoevsky created Raskolnikov as Shakespeare created Iago, to be a pure villain: we should then agree with Berdyaev: 'There is no humanitarianism in Raskolnikov, who is cruel and without pity'; whereas, in point of fact, a glance at almost any page of *Crime and Punishment* will show us that this is nonsense. The central theme of *Crime and Punishment* is pity; pity is Raskolnikov's undoing. The idea that obsesses him is Van Gogh's 'Misery will never end'. From the beginning of the book, all the situations are devised to drive this home: the drunken Marmeladov (who enjoys suffering, like the beetle-man) and his starving family; the dream of the horse being beaten to death; the long recital of woes in the letter from Raskolnikov's mother; there are even little episodes that have no relation to the plot, but were interposed simply to intensify the picture of human suffering: the young girl who has been drugged and seduced, the woman who tries to drown herself as Raskolnikov leans on the bridge. To add to all this, there are Raskolnikov's humiliations: his poverty, his landlady dunning for rent, etc. And underneath all this, even more fundamental, there is the beetle-man's problem: What is worth doing?

For the beetle-man, the problem was complicated by his emotional anaemia: he thinks much more than he enjoys or suffers. Raskolnikov is a little better off: the world's misery unites his whole being with a mixed feeling of revolt and pity. Particularly, his feeling about 'lower forms of life' (Lawrence's detestation) are unambiguous—about vile old pawnbrokresses, for instance. He is a dissatisfied man and therefore a dangerous man. There is human misery, and he asks himself the question: What can be done about it? His healthy-minded answer is: '*You* can do nothing as you are.' And why? Because as he is he suffers from all the Outsider's disabilities; he is aware of his strength, but has no idea of how to use it; he thinks instead of acting.

He is not quite such a fool and neurotic as the beetle-man. Nevertheless, he *is* over-sensitive, and he over-estimates his own callousness. Besides which, he has intended to kill only the old woman; when he is interrupted, he has to kill her sister too. Later two painters are accused of the crime and there is a possibility they may be executed; in which case he will have committed four murders. All this contributes to his breakdown. Finally, the last indignity, the murders do not alter his life; he derives no benefit from them. With two murders to his credit, possibly four, he is back where he started. No wonder he breaks down and confesses!

But before the end of the book, he has caught a glimpse of 'a way out'. There is the scene with the prostitute Sonia, in which she reads aloud the story of raising Lazarus. And Raskolnikov recognizes his own problem. For he too needs to be raised from the dead. Like another Outsider we have considered, the idea both fascinates and revolts him. For the spiritually dead, the idea of rebirth is terrible. Sonia who is simple and docile and, like Susan Kitteredge in *The Secret Life*, has no spiritual problems, can somehow divine Raskolnikov's misery; she too could tell him: 'You'll *have* to be, somehow.' His attempt at solution of the Outsider's problems is a failure; he has tried to gain self-control and has not succeeded. But it would be a mistake to suppose that this is because his method was *wrong*. He has already advanced to Nietzsche's position of 'beyond good and evil'. Although he tells Sonia, in confessing the murder, 'I murdered myself, not her,' this is not an indication that he accepts the murder to have been evil, for later he asked frenziedly: 'Crime? What crime? That I killed a vile, noxious insect. . . .'

And it is apparent, at the end, that he has no feeling of 'Christian repentance' for the murder. He is not giving himself up because he wants to 'expiate' it:

> Only now I see clearly the imbecility of my cowardice. . . . It's simply because I am contemptible and have nothing in me that I have decided to [give myself up]. . . . I wanted to do good to men, thousands of good deeds to make up for that one piece of stupidity; not stupidity even, simply clumsiness, for the idea was by no means so stupid as it seems now it has failed. . . .[20]

This is unambiguous, and unless we assume that Dostoevsky completely dissociates himself from Raskolnikov's ideas, we can hardly persist in the belief that Raskolnikov fails because his solution is *morally wrong*. He fails for the very different reason that he is not strong enough *to cease to be an Outsider*. This, of course, does not mean that we must accept Raskolnikov's belief that murder is *not* morally wrong. It is simply that the question is *irrelevant* to the Outsider's problems; and *Crime and Punishment* is first and foremost a book about the Outsider's problems.

The transition from *Notes from Underground* to *Crime and Punishment* is obviously very much like the transition from Barbusse's hero to Van Gogh and T. E. Lawrence. The beetle-man is a passive (Barbusse) Outsider; Raskolnikov is an active (Van Gogh) Outsider. Dostoevsky's treatment of the theme has taken an immense leap forward from one book to the next. When we note the fact that *Poor Folk* and *The Double* (both written before the years in Siberia) are also about the Outsider, and about Outsiders even weaker and stupider than the beetle-man; we might hazard a generalization, and say that the Outsider theme was one of Dostoevsky's central preoccupations, and that, as he grew more mature as an artist, his Outsiders tended to grow in stature.

This is borne out by a glance at the later novels: even Myshkin in *The Idiot* is an Outsider, although in a different sense than anyone we have dealt with so far. He is an imaginative picture of the Chinese 'man of Tao':

> He is modest, like one who is a guest,
> He is yielding, like ice that is going to melt,
> He is simple, like wood that is unplaned,
> He is vacant, like valleys that are hollow,
> He is dim, like water that is turbid. . . .*

This is Myshkin, described by Lao Tze 500 years before Christianity. His secret is simple: he is still a child. Men do evil because they attach importance to the wrong things, because they are 'grown-up'. Myshkin has perfect *instinctive* simplicity. But the criticism we can aim at him has already been developed in this study: you cannot solve the problem of evil by remaining a child. Chaos must be faced; there must be a descent into the dark world. In *The Idiot*, there are, as for Emil Sinclair, two worlds—the light world of the General's family (especially Aglaya), and the world of nervous tension, guilt,

* *Tao Te Ching*, XV.

chaos (Nastasia and Rogojin). Myshkin cracks up under the strain between the two; like Vaslav Nijinsky, he goes insane. Clearly, the lesson here is the same as in *Demian*: childlike innocence is no solution of the Outsider's problems.

There are two more major novels of Dostoevsky which we must analyse in detail (if we except *A Raw Youth*, which is technically so botched as to be almost unreadable). Both of these make a completely new attack on the Outsider's problems. From the nature of Dostoevsky's achievement so far, from the fertility of his intellect and his tremendous creative impulse, we can expect some important new treatment of the theme; and in fact we shall find that in *Devils* and *The Brothers Karamazov* Dostoevsky succeeds in analysing the problems as no one else has.

Of these two novels *Devils* develops the idea of *Crime and Punishment*, and must be examined in the remainder of this chapter. The greatest attack on the Outsider problems—the last great novel—will carry us forward into an entirely new field, and must be reserved for the next chapter. For in *Devils*, as in *Crime and Punishment* and *Notes from Underground*, the ethical ideas are still in solution as it were. In *The Brothers Karamazov* they have crystallized in concrete concepts of good and evil.

Devils is a logical development from the earlier novels: this is to be expected. Dostoevsky simplifies his treatment of the Outsider by dividing it in two, and distributing the parts between the two chief characters, Stavrogin and Kirilov. Before we speak of these, it may be advisable to say something about the genesis of the book.

Its original idea sprang from the 'Netchaev affair'. Netchaev was an anarchist-nihilist who undoubtedly deserves to be the subject of a detailed biography. Where anarchism was concerned he was a fanatical idealist; apart from this, his personal character was as base and immoral as anything in criminal history. His intrigues show him to have been as degraded as Lacenaire, and he was as ruthless and brutal as any Nazi thug. Yet his life shows an extraordinary, perverted heroism. There is even a story that he helped to plan the assassination of Alexander II while he was imprisoned in the Peter and Paul Fortress (Russia's 'Devil's Island'), and that when his associates asked whether they should concentrate on rescuing him or on killing the Tsar, he answered without hesitation, 'Remove the oppressor'. The 'oppressor' was removed, and Netchaev died of scurvy in prison.

Netchaev, 'the tiger cub', was one of the world's most remarkable deceivers; he tried to build up a vast revolutionary movement solely on lies, bluff and play-acting. He deceived everybody (including the arch-revolutionaries Bakunin and Herzen) and might easily, with a little more luck, have intrigued his way to absolute dictatorship of Russia (which was obviously his ideal).

The affair that provided the plot of *Devils* led to Netchaev's downfall. In Moscow, posing as the representative of a certain 'European Revolutionary Alliance', Netchaev organized small groups of students and disillusioned ex-Army officers into 'revolutionary committees'. A student named Ivanov was suspected of planning to betray them, and was murdered by Netchaev, with the complicity of the 'group'. The murder was soon discovered; arrests followed. Netchaev escaped to Switzerland, then to England, while the affair occupied the front pages of Russia's newspapers. Later, Netchaev, with misplaced confidence in the authorities' short memory, walked back into the lion's mouth, and ended in the Peter and Paul Fortress.

Another interesting point was utilized in the novel. It transpired in the trials that a certain student who intended to kill himself had agreed to await the convenience of the 'European Revolutionary Alliance', and was to leave a death note in which he would take responsibility for any crimes the 'Alliance' cared to saddle him with. Out of this episode came the conception of Kirilov, the 'suicide maniac', and, incidentally, one of the most important treatments of the Outsider theme in Dostoevsky.

The structure of the novel is loose and unsatisfying. It opens with a long section about an old Russian liberal of the 40's, and the General's widow who supports him. These two are typical inhabitants of the small town where the action takes place. Having carefully set the scene and provided the background, Dostoevsky is then prepared to allow his terrible, maniacal characters to erupt into it. Enter Netchaev,* who is the old liberal's son, and Stavrogin, who is the widow's son.

Netchaev's part of the novel provides the 'plot' and continuity of the story; in spite of which, it has an odd air of

* Called Pyotr Verkovensky in the novel.

irrelevancy. Stavrogin is the 'hero' of the novel, but there is no counterpart between him and Netchaev as hero and villain; from the point of view of the Netchaev affair, Stavrogin is irrelevant. Actually, the novel is really absorbing only when Stavrogin (or Kirilov) is on the scene, and it is Netchaev who seems to have intruded where he has no business.

The horrors and mystifications reach a climax when Netchaev's terrorists set the town on fire and murder an ex-Captain and his imbecile sister (who is also Stavrogin's wife). The old Russian liberal leaves home and dies; the student Shatov (Ivanov) is murdered, Kirilov commits suicide to Netchaev's specification and Netchaev catches a train to Switzerland.

The Stavrogin story is the centre of gravity of the novel. Stavrogin is the outcome of a much earlier project of Dostoevsky's to write *The Life of A Great Sinner*. Dostoevsky always found crime absorbing; it is one of those limits of human character that can spring from the Outsider's sense of exile. The great criminal is as distant from the average bourgeois as the great saint. In practice, of course, most 'great criminals' turn out to be mindless gorillas or Freudian neurotics; still, in theory, in the imagination of the artist, they could easily be men of unusually independent mind who simply give a different expression to the greatness of the saint or artist. In *The House of the Dead*, Dostoevsky gives accounts of the criminals he met in Siberia; and there is about all these men, mostly murderers, that slight element of the more-than-human that instantly grips the reader's interest (in contrast with the all-too-human characters of most modern novelists, who produce acute intellectual constipation after fifty pages). At the same time, the criminal, in choosing crime (if he chooses it, and doesn't just drift into it from laziness), has made the voluntary descent into the dark world which places him a step nearer the resolution of good and evil that the saint achieves. Salvation through sin recurs constantly in Dostoevsky's work.

In *Devils*, Stavrogin's story is told with many mystifications that are intended to define him as an Outsider. Actually, no reader who has grasped the concept of the Barbusse Outsider will find anything mystifying about Stavrogin's actions. Conceive him as a Russian combination of Evan Strowde and Oliver Gauntlett, add a touch of Pushkin's Eugene Onyegin, and you have a reasonably accurate picture. His story unfolds as a series of romantically paradoxical acts: he kisses someone's wife in the middle of a respectable social gathering; he pulls the nose of a retired General and bites the ear of an inoffensive old man. In short, he plays the Rimbaud-roaring-boy in the drawing-room atmosphere of the town. 'Old men and invalids are so respectable they ask to be boiled.'* For the inhabitants of the town, Stavrogin's conduct is explained when he has a mental breakdown and has to be sent to a sanatorium to recuperate. For the discerning reader, of course, his strange actions and the brainstorm are *both* results of his Outsider tendencies.

As the novel goes on, Stavrogin does even stranger things: he accepts a slap in the face from Shatov; he engages in a duel in which he allows his opponent to shoot, and then fires his own pistol into the air; he acknowledges a poverty-stricken imbecile to be his wife (although most of the women in the town are willing to fling themselves at his head). Finally, he produces a 'confession' that is nightmarish in its horror** and hangs himself. 'The verdict of our doctors', the narrator states, 'was that it was most definitely *not* a case of insanity.'

An important assertion, this; Dostoevsky will allow his readers no easy way out. Stavrogin was his most important attempt, to date, to summarize his ideas of good and evil. To interpret Stavrogin as a psychopath is as shallow as to interpret Raskolnikov as a 'cold monster'.

On the other hand, there is no point in the novel at which Stavrogin gets on a soapbox to explain himself. Dostoevsky wrote no systematic treatise on the Outsider, in spite of his exhaustive treatment of the theme. His business was 'not to reason and compare, but to create', and although it is only slovenly thinking not to recognize that the critical faculty is eighty per cent. of the creative, it would still be unreasonable

---

* It always seemed to me that Henry Miller caught the very essence of this type of revolt in one of the 'Tropic' books, where he tells a story of how he managed to have sexual intercourse with a girl on a crowded dance-floor without anyone noticing. He emphasizes the pleasure that the *situation* gave him. The episode has psychological significance, and might almost be the foundation of a treatise on the revolutionary mentality.

** This 'confession' chapter was rejected by Dostoevsky's printer, and only appeared in print many years later, when the Soviet Government opened the Dostoevsky archives. Merezhkovsky has described it as 'the concentrated essence of horror'. It has been published as a booklet by the Hogarth Press in England, but for some reason, has not yet been incorporated into any complete edition of *Devils*.

to expect Dostoevsky's people to be as lucid in self-analysis as Pirandello or Shaw characters. Fortunately, from our point of view, there is no problem touched on in *Devils* that we have not already examined in this study; and Stavrogin presents no problems. The suicide letter, for instance, might be an epilogue to *The Seven Pillars of Wisdom*:

> I've tried my strength everywhere. You advised me to do that so as to learn to 'know myself'. When I've tried it for my own sake and for the sake of self-display, it seemed infinite, as it has been before in my life. Before your eyes I put up with a blow in the face from your brother; I acknowledged my marriage in public. *But what to apply my strength to— that's what I've never seen and don't see now.* My desires are never strong enough. They cannot guide me. You can cross the river on a tree-trunk, but not on a chip. . . .[21] [Italics mine.]

Stavrogin, the Evan-Strowde Outsider who has lost motive, can acknowledge the power of motive in others, in Kirilov, the 'suicide maniac':

> . . . Kirilov, in his magnanimity, could not compromise with an idea and shot himself.

But Stavrogin knows he cannot imitate him:

> I can never be interested in an idea to the same extent. I could never shoot myself.

In spite of which, he commits suicide, although he has no hopes from suicide:

> I know it will be another delusion, a delusion in an infinite series of delusions.

Nothing is real—consequently he has nothing to live for and no reason for dying:

> My love will be as petty as I am myself. . . . I know I ought to kill myself, to brush myself off the earth like some loathsome insect. . . .

Always in Dostoevsky there is this comparison of men to insects: half a dozen passages spring to mind. It is the Hemingway position, 'Most men . . . die like animals', or the comparison of Catherine Barkely's death with that of ants on a burning log. There is no belief. Men's lives are futile, and they die 'not with a bang but a whimper'. And when they *are* inspired by a belief, it depends on their blinding themselves with their emotions. This is Stavrogin's position, and he hates it. He would like to breathe clean air and feel a sensation of power. But how? To do good? That is out of the question; he sees it as a game of emotional profit, self-flattery, nothing more. Then evil? His 'confession' is an account of his attempt to do evil. It is a deliberate sensation-seeking, rather like Dorian Gray's, except that Dorian goes in for sensual pleasures, and Stavrogin experiments with moral depravities too, robbing a pathetic bank clerk of his last rouble notes, seducing a ten-year-old girl and then deliberately allowing her to kill herself. Reading the 'confession', we begin to feel a stifled irritation with Stavrogin. Why doesn't he get away from his effete surroundings, and discover how powerfully the urge to live inheres in the body itself? We feel that ten years in Siberia would teach him the value of life; and, in fact, we shall find that this is the solution that Dostoevsky produces for another of his characters who had allowed himself to be blinded by his own pettiness in *The Brothers Karamazov*. Stavrogin thinks that he has explored life from end to end and found it all hollow, when actually he is only constipated with his own worthlessness. He fails to apply his intellect to the question, Why do all living things prefer life to death?

Stavrogin missed the point, but his creator was not fooled. The man who had stood in front of a firing squad in the Semyonovsky Square knew all about the value of life. In *Crime and Punishment*, Raskolnikov meditates:[22]

> . . . someone condemned to death says, or thinks an hour before his death, that if he had to live on a high rock, on such a narrow ledge that he'd only have room to stand, and the ocean, everlasting darkness, everlasting solitude, everlasting tempest around him, if he had to remain standing on a square yard of space all his life, a thousand years, eternity, it were better to live so than die at once.

Only to live, to live and live. Life, whatever it may be . . .

In opposition to this, there is the vision of Svidrigailov, the criminal sensualist who speculates whether eternity may not be like a dusty corner of a small room, full of spiders and cobwebs. Svidrigailov shoots himself; Raskolnikov prepares to endure a ten-year ordeal in Siberia that will 'raise him from the dead'.

In *Devils*, Stavrogin is the criminal sensualist who cannot conceive eternity, except in terms of his own dreary, imprisoned existence. Kirilov, the suicide maniac, also kills himself, but it is Kirilov who had seen the way out of the nightmare of unreality. It is in Kirilov that Dostoevsky embodies the highest vision of the novel. Kirilov is to kill himself when Netchaev gives the order, but he has already decided to die. His reason is Outsider-logic. If God exists, then everything is his Will. If he doesn't exist, then Kirilov himself is God and must show his Will by the Ultimate Unreversible definitive act—to kill himself.

> Because all will has become mine. Is there no man on this planet who, having finished with God, and believing in his own will, will have enough courage to express his self-will in its most important point? It's like a beggar who has inherited a fortune and is afraid of it. . . .[23]

Kirilov has finished with God because he cannot believe in an external principle that is more important than his own subjectively known reality. Kirilov reasons: 'If God exists, he must be an external reality, like the Old Testament Jehovah.' His Existentialist logic disposes of such a God. It is the opposite of Lawrence's Bedouin, who 'could not look for God within him; he was too certain he was in God'; but, unfortunately, Kirilov does not believe in 'God within him' either.

But the decision that life was valueless compared with his own Will gives Kirilov the insight he needed. Without realizing it, he has attained the ideal non-attachment that is the religious ideal. Being willing to give up his life at any moment, he has voided it of the pettiness that ties most men to their delusions. He has destroyed the 'thought-riddled nature'. He asks Stavrogin:

'Ever seen a leaf—a leaf from a tree?'
'Yes.'

'I saw one recently—a yellow one, a little green, wilted at the edges. Blown by the wind. When I was a little boy, I used to shut my eyes in winter and imagine a green leaf, with veins on it, and the sun shining. . . .'

'What's this—an allegory?'

'No; why? Not an allegory—a leaf, just a leaf. A leaf is good. Everything's good.'

'Everything?'

'Everything. Man's unhappy because he doesn't know he's happy . . . he who finds out will become happy at once, instantly. . . .'

'And what about the man who dies of hunger, and the man who insults and rapes a little girl. Is that good too?'

'Yes, it is. And the man who blows his brains out for the child, that's good too. Everything's good. . . .'

'When did you find out you were so happy?'

'I was walking about the room. I stopped the clock. . . . It was twenty-three minutes to three.'[24]

Dostoevsky was haunted by that passage from 'Revelation':

And the angel which I saw stand upon the sea . . . lifted up his hand and sware . . . that there should be time no longer, but the mystery of God should be finished. . . .[25]

Possibly Dostoevsky's knowledge of 'Moments of timelessness' came only in the strange insights before his epileptic seizures: this is how he describes one in *The Idiot*:

The next moment, something seemed to explode in front of him; a wonderful inner light illumined his soul. This lasted perhaps half a second, yet he distinctly remembered hearing the beginning of a cry, the strange dreadful wail that escaped him without his volition. . . . Then he was unconscious. . . .[26]

The moment of 'inner light' is Nietzsche's moment of 'pure Will, free of the perplexities of intellect. . . .' His willingness to die to express the absolute supremacy of the Will is the supreme act of renunciation. St. John of the Cross writes of it:

And therefore, the soul that sets its affections upon created beings . . . will in no way be able to attain union with the infinite being of God: for that which is not can have no communion with that which is.*

Without religion, without even belief in God, Kirilov has achieved the saint's vision. His perfect non-attachment has made him into a visionary. He lives all the time in the insight that Meursault achieved only on the eve of his execution: 'I had been happy and I was happy still.'

Dostoevsky did not stop to argue or explain his point; he dramatized it and now the novel is drawing towards its close; everything is moving faster. In the last hundred pages, he rises to a pitch of prophetic intensity that cannot be paralleled elsewhere in literature. Netchaev has arranged for the same night the murder of Shatov, the firing of the town and the murder of Stavrogin's imbecile wife and her drunken brother. Shatov is to meet five 'comrades' on Stavrogin's estate to hand over the printing-press. Before he sets out, his wife arrives, in the last stages of pregnancy (she had deserted him three years before, only a fortnight after their marriage, to go and live with Stavrogin). In a wild state of excitement, Shatov rushes off to borrow money and find a midwife. Then he looks on as the baby is born, and the revelation stirs him profoundly. He mutters: 'There were two, and now there's a third human being, a new spirit, whole and complete . . . a new thought and a new love . . . it makes me feel afraid. There's nothing bigger in the world. . . .'[27] Then a comrade arrives to fetch him away. Shatov asks him, as they walk through the dark, 'Erckel, have you ever been happy?'

The murder that follows is perhaps the most terrible single episode in Dostoevsky; after the birth-scene, it is almost unbearable to read. But it is not the end of Netchaev's work. After he has seen the body consigned to a pond, he goes to call on Kirilov. The moment has arrived for Kirilov to kill himself for the 'European Revolutionary Alliance'. But first, there is a slight formality. Kirilov is to write a suicide note, confessing to having murdered Shatov. Again the scene reaches a dramatic tension that cannot be paralleled in modern literature, apart from the murder scene in *Crime and Punishment*. At first, Netchaev is convinced that Kirilov won't do it; he encourages him to talk about his reasons for committing suicide; his cunning is

* *Ascent of Mount Carmel*, IV, 4.

rewarded, and finally Kirilov shoots himself through the head. Netchaev hurries off, a handkerchief bound around his hand where Kirilov had tried to bite off the top of his finger, and catches an early train out of the town. He leaves behind him a blazing town, three murdered bodies and a suicide; and the death-toll is not yet complete. That is the last we see of 'the tiger cub'. He is not important; he is only the Iago of the story, He is no Outsider. The most important figure in the book lies dead in a shuttered room, the revolver still in his hand, to be found by Shatov's wife the next morning when she goes to his room seeking her husband.

The nightmare is almost over. Dostoevsky's last great study in the Outsider will bring it to a close.

CHAPTER SEVEN

THE GREAT SYNTHESIS. . . .

THE BROTHERS KARAMAZOV is Dostoevsky's biggest attack on the Outsider theme.

We have seen Dostoevsky beginning with a portrait of the Barbusse-type Outsider—the spineless beetle-man, the underground man who cannot escape his loathing for human stupidity—and applying the formula 'The Outsider's Salvation lies in extremes', until he has created Raskolnikov, Myshkin, Stavrogin, all Outsiders who know who they are and where they are going. Extremes of crime or extremes of asceticism, murder or renunciation, both have the same effect. Both free the Outsider from his fundamental indecision, so that the problem is carried to a higher stage.

In *The Brothers Karamazov*, all that Dostoevsky had learned from his earlier experiments with Outsiders is summarized. We have, at once, the beetle-man, Raskolnikov, Myshkin combined in this, the great synthesis. They are the three brothers Karamazov—Mitya, Ivan, Alyosha—the body, the intellect, the emotions. And since Dostoevsky himself was the intellectual Outsider, it is Ivan who claims the centre of the stage in his biggest novel. In Ivan the question of the 'evil principle' is attacked from *within*.

The plot of the novel is simple; Mitya and his vile, sensualist father are rivals for the love of the same girl. When the father is murdered by Mitya's bastard half-brother Smerdyakov, the evidence against Mitya is overwhelming, and he is convicted and sent to Siberia (Smerdyakov in the meantime having committed suicide).

Together with this story there are two parallel themes, connected with Ivan and Alyosha. Alyosha has Van Gogh's temperament, but fortunately he has fairly early found orientation in religion; when the novel opens he is a novice in the local monastery (like Narziss in Hesse's book). Alyosha's story concerns his mental upheaval caused by the death of Father Zossima, the Abbot (or Elder) whom he idolizes; it ends with

Alyosha going into the world (like Goldmund and Joseph Knecht) to look for his salvation.

Ivan's story is almost static; it lies in his position as an intellectual Outsider, a man who thinks too much to enjoy living. There is something of Raskolnikov's ruthlessness about Ivan. And his bastard half-brother worships him and apes him; a constant reminder that he is not all intellect, but fifty per cent. flesh and crass stupidity. Nothing *happens* to Ivan. Dostoevsky uses him to pose the question: What happens when a man believes that life is unlivable? The answer appears when Ivan is visited by an embodiment of his unbelief, by the Devil.

The Brothers Karamazov was never finished. We are not told whether Ivan found an answer or whether he went mad. Neither are we shown what happens to Alyosha when he goes 'into the world'. (This was to be the subject of a sequel that Dostoevsky never lived to write.) For all that, we have in *The Brothers Karamazov* a more conclusive attempt at solution of the Outsider's problems then any we have yet considered.

Of the three 'stories', Mitya's tells us least. Dostoevsky was always a bad craftsman. (*Crime and Punishment* is his only complete *artistic* success; the other novels are as unshapely as pillow-cases stuffed with lumps of concrete.) The central 'plot' of the novel is no more than a background for the more important stories of the other two brothers, and in fact it has hardly any direct bearing on their stories at all. The idea that Ivan is *morally* responsible for his father's death, having wished it, is completely irrelevant to his problems as an Outsider. (This particular view is made much of by the 'Christian' school of commentators, who always try to treat the novels as Just-so-stories with a moral on the last page.) If a moral can be drawn from Ivan, it is an Outsider's moral: that the man who thinks too much is likely to go to exhausted extremes where the world becomes a shadowy paradigm of ideas. To keep sane he must continually come back to reality.

Alyosha is not such a fool. There is no danger of his leaving reality behind by overworking his brain. But he falls into the same pit as Van Gogh instead; he allows emotional problems, problems about human beings, to obscure fundamentally sane vision. That is his 'moral'.

And Mitya? Well, Mitya seems to be one of those characters who meant more to his creator than he does to us (like Shatov

in *Devils*). He embodies Dostoevsky's obsession about shame;
he strikes himself on the chest and calls himself an insect; he
plunges from towering rages into ecstasies of self-abasement, and
behaves generally with a complete lack of emotional discipline
that is repugnant to a Western European. Certainly he is
'Russian', and perhaps for that reason he fails to awaken the
interest of the Western reader as Ivan and Alyosha do. His
'moral' seems doubtful, unless we can interpret his acceptance
to prison-sentence as his recognition that he needs to discipline
himself, and will *have* to discipline himself, or sink into utter
degradation, in Siberia.

This of course is not to dismiss Mitya; for Mitya, in a sense,
knows better than Ivan. Primarily, he is 'a man of motion',
like Nijinsky; and if he finds 'salvation', that is, unity of
his impulses and certainty of purpose, it must be through
action. At the end of the novel, Mitya's story too is only half-
finished.

So none of the three stories *The Brothers Karamazov* is finished:
which is to say that none of the Outsider's problems is finally
solved. Yet the analysis of these problems is on a scale we have
not considered before. Here is Ivan, for instance, the thinker,
so like Raskolnikov in many ways. Where his detestable father
and his uncontrolled brother are concerned, he is ruthless. 'One
reptile will devour the other—and serve them both right too.'
He has no sentimentality. Yet he is obsessed by pity, pity for
human misery, and with the intellectual question that, since
human beings *are* such a wretched lot, what is there to do
except call them beetles and acknowledge yourself one of
them? Ivan's instinct is like Nietzsche's, towards great health.
And, like Nietzsche, he is always aware of the Pro and Contra,
Ultimate Yes and Ultimate No. The chapter called 'Pro and
Contra', in which Ivan analyses the problems at length, is an
Outsider Scripture, a monumental piece of summarizing.
Critics are agreed in regarding it as the apex of Dostoevsky's
creative edifice. We must now examine this at length.

Alyosha and Ivan are alone together for the first time.
Immediately, without preamble, Ivan states his credo:

'. . . if I lost faith in the order of things, if I were convinced
that everything is a disorderly, damnable, devil-ridden chaos,
if I were struck by every horror of man's disillusion—still I
should want to live. . . .'[1]

And here is Ivan's denunciation of the 'thought-riddled nature':

'I want to travel in Europe, Alyosha. I know it is only a graveyard, but it's a most precious graveyard. Precious are the dead that lie there; every stone over them speaks of such burning life in the past, such passionate faith in their work. . . . I shall steep my soul in my feeling. I love the leaves in spring, the blue sky—that's all. It's not a matter of intellect or logic—it's loving with one's inside, with one's stomach.'

'I think everyone should love life above everything else in the world,' Alyosha tells him.

'Love life regardless of the meaning of it?'

'Certainly—it must be regardless of logic—'it's only then one can understand its meaning.'

We can see how far Dostoevsky has advanced beyond Lawrence's horror of 'lack of pattern and purpose in Nature'. Behind man lies the abyss, nothingness; the Outsider knows this; it is his business to sink claws of iron into life, to grasp it tighter than the indifferent bourgeois, to build, to Will, in spite of the abyss. Ivan has half-solved the Outsider's major problem. Alyosha recognizes this; he tells him:

'Half your work is done. It only remains to do the other half now.'

'What other half?'

'To raise up your dead, who have perhaps not died after all.'[2]

Alyosha is right, but he does not understand the magnitude of the problem of 'raising up the dead'. Ivan goes on to explain this. He also has the makings of a monk, for he tells Alyosha:

'I accept God and I accept his wisdom, his purpose, which are unknowable to us; I believe in the underlying order and meaning of life; I believe in the eternal harmony. . . . I believe in the Word to which the Universe is striving. . . . I seem to be on the right path, don't I? Yet—in the final result, I don't accept God's world.'

Then begins the great discussion, or rather, the great monologue, for it is mostly spoken by Ivan. What Ivan now

explains in full is the difficulty of the 'second half' of the solution.
Cruelty and misery: that is Ivan's theme. He confines himself
to cases of cruelty to children, and mercilessly describes these
for a dozen pages. He concludes with his well-known statement:
'It's not God I don't accept, Alyosha—only that I most respect-
fully return him the entrance ticket.'

It is an Existentialist argument. To build on the abyss, you
must have a foundation. For Ivan, the sufferings of one
tortured child are enough to blast any foundation apart.
Lawrence asserted that bodily sufferings have ultimately no
power over the Will. That would be a good enough foundation
to build on, to Will on. But what about the children's sufferings?
A child cannot be expected to exert tremendous Will-power.
The child's sufferings just *are*; they cannot be reduced or
resolved into a universal harmony, a System.

Not a rational solution, perhaps, Alyosha admits; but what of
the irrational solution, the religious solution that Christ died as
a pledge that the world's suffering would be ultimately
resolved? Ivan has an answer for that too; his Legend of the
Grand Inquisitor.[3]

Christ returned to earth once, Ivan tells Alyosha, in Seville,
at the time of the Inquisition. The Grand Inquisitor had him
seized and cast into prison. The same evening he visited him,
and explained why he could not allow him to resume his
ministry in Seville. This, in summary, is what he tells Christ:
'What message did you preach in Palestine? That all men must
strive for more abundant life, that they must Will unceasingly
to realize that "The Kingdom of God is within them", that
they should not be content to be men, but should strive to be
"Sons of God"? You raised the standard of conduct of the Old
Testament; you added to the Ten Commandments. Then you
left us to build a Church on your precepts. What you didn't
seem to realise is that all men are not prophets and moral
geniuses. It is not the Church's business to save only those few
who are strong-willed enough to save themselves. We are
concerned about raising the general standard of all the race,
and we can't do this by telling every man that he had better
be his own Church—as you did. That is tantamount to telling
every man that he must be an Outsider—which God forbid!
The Outsider's problems are insoluble, and we, the elect,
know this. You raised the standard too high, and we have had

to haul it down again. We the elect, are unhappy—because we know just how terribly difficult it is to "achieve salvation". But we have always kept this a secret from the people—who are not much better than dogs and cats, after all. Now you come back, proposing to give the show away! Do you suppose I can allow that? I am afraid I shall have to have you quietly done away with and it is entirely your own fault. Prophets are all very well when they are dead, but while they are alive there is nothing for it but to burn or crucify them. . . .'

As the Grand Inquisitor ends his indictment, Christ leans forward and kisses him on his pale lips. This is his reply: Your reasoning is powerful but my love is stronger.

But Ivan has stated the case against religion as it has never been stated, before or since. Christ's love is no answer to that.

Dostoevsky's avowed intention in writing *The Brothers Karamazov* was to analyse and refute atheism. There are many critics who believe that in this his artistry overcame his intention, and that he made Ivan's case unanswerable. Let us agree at once that 'The Grand Inquisitor' is an artistic *tour de force*, and the statement of the opposite case (in the 'Russian Monk' section) cannot compare with it in power and conviction. But let us not confuse the dramatic effectiveness of an argument with its final truth. What Ivan has done is to express the ultimate No that drove Lawrence to mind-suicide, and Van Gogh, Nijinsky and Nietzsche insane. He has done this so brilliantly, so finally, that we must pay a great deal of attention to his argument, and get its full significance quite clear, before we go on to consider the 'refutation' of it. It is the most tremendous Outsider indictment ever written. The picture we have built up of the Outsider shows him as a half-way house to a higher type of man than the 'once-born' man; he loses more sleep, eats less, and suffers from all kinds of nervous diseases. Nevertheless, when we have analysed the Outsider's uneasiness, his state of nervous tension, we have found it to have an *objective cause* in his sense of the precariousness of human life, as exemplified in the passage from Beddoes quoted on p. 108.

Now the once-born bourgeois might object that the precariousness *is there*; everybody knows it; it would be folly to live in a state of nervous tension on account of it. (He might instance the ancient Greeks, that nation of healthy, once-born optimists whose art is full of the consciousness of death and its inevitability.) But this is to ignore the biological truth that the preservation of life depends on awareness of death. If you inoculate a man with a small quantity of a disease he becomes immune to a large quantity; if you subject a man to extremes of heat and cold, he develops a resistance to both and can survive under conditions that would kill another man. The Outsider can regard his exacerbated sense of life's precariousness as a biological measure to increase his toughness; in fact, to make him capable of 'living more abundantly'. This is the conclusion that Steppanwolf reached.

Dostoevsky has considered the question from the angle of *freedom*. His beetle-man stated his credo, 'that man's whole business is to prove that he is man, not a cog-wheel'. Freedom means life; it has no meaning in relation to a chest of drawers or a dead body. It has less meaning for a tree than for a man. In the same way, it has less meaning for an incurable dipsomaniac or drug-addict than for a normally healthy person. The more life, the more possibility of freedom.

Now we can begin to see the full meaning of Ivan's arguments. His argument builds up carefully to the conclusion of James's vastation: *'There is no freedom.'* He agrees, there *is* life; he loves life, 'the sticky buds in spring', but he cannot accept any meaning of life.* It just 'is'—a senseless, devil-ridden chaos. In the section on cruelty to children, Ivan paints his Nietzschean picture of human nature: human, all too human, futile, deluded; the intelligence that makes him man only making him (as Mephistopheles says) more brutal than any beast. Now Ivan passes on to Christ; and here we are reminded of a speech by Kirilov, when he tells Netchaev:[4]

'Listen to a great idea: there was a day on earth and in the middle of earth were three crosses. A man on one cross had such faith that he said to another: "Today you will be with me in paradise". The day ended, both died, and neither found paradise nor resurrection. . . . Listen, that man was the greatest of all on earth. . . . The whole planet . . . is sheer madness without that man. And so if the laws of Nature didn't spare even him . . . if they made even him live among lies and die for a

* Or compare 'Chehov: *Three Sisters*, Act II:
Mary: There must be some meaning?
Tuzenbach: A meaning, did you say? Look there—the snow is falling; what is the meaning of that?'

lie, then the whole planet is a lie, and is based on a lie and a stupid mockery.'

Ivan also believes that 'that man was the greatest of all on earth', and his 'Grand Inquisitor' legend is an expansion of Kirilov's speech. The Inquisitor is a man of spiritual insight; he has starved in the desert to achieve freedom; but, as Ivan says, 'he saw it was no great moral blessedness to achieve perfection if at the same time one gains the conviction that millions of God's creatures have been created as a mockery: that these poor rebels can never turn into giants!' The Inquisitor's feeling about mankind is one of deep pity. Perhaps the Outsider can be aware of depths of human misery, but these poor insects, leading their blinded lives, who would open their eyes to their own bondage and wretchedness? What good would it do, anyway? Give them bread and amusements; give them shallow little creeds to fight for and silly little superstitions to sing hymns about, but don't ask wisdom of them. Christ asked: Which of you can drink of the cup that I drink of? Yet he behaved as if everyone could. He said: 'My Yoke is easy and my burden light,' but this is a lie, for freedom is the greatest burden of all: to tell every man to think for himself, to solve the problem of good and evil and then act according to his solution: to live for truth and not for his country, or society, or his family. It is kinder to men to think of them as insects; eternal life for such creatures must be a monstrous superstition. There will always be those few who strive to realize the ideal of freedom by being their own judge; these will know the agony of standing alone. 'For only we, who guard the mystery, shall be unhappy,' the Inquisitor tells Christ. This is the conclusion of the 'Treatise on the Steppenwolf'. The Outsider is always unhappy, but he is the agent that ensures happiness for millions of 'Insiders'. Haller's reaction to this truth, we remember, was the decision to cut his throat. Alyosha asks Ivan: 'How can you live, with such a hell in your heart and head?' And Ivan answers: 'There is a strength to endure everything.' This is Ivan's case, case for Ultimate No. What of the other side?

'The Recollections of Father Zossima' are Dostoevsky's reply to the 'Legend of the Grand Inquisitor'. Zossima is the Abbot of the Monastery where Alyosha makes a record of his last conversations; these form an autobiography, with appended 'moral exhortations'. Zossima begins by speaking of his elder brother, who died of consumption when Zossima was a child. This brother was an intelligent youth, a free-thinker, who declared that Lenten facts were twaddle, and there was no God. But when the disease confined him to bed, a change came over him; suddenly he became tolerant of his mother's devotions; a curious mystical frame of mind possessed him (which the doctors attributed to the disease). 'Life is a paradise; we are all in paradise but we won't see it.' When the doctor told him he might have many days yet to live, or months and years, he answered, 'Why reckon days? One day is enough for a man to know all happiness.'⁵

This made a deep impression on his young brother's mind. Connected with this was an occasion when he heard the Book of Job read in Church: 'Naked I came out of my mother's womb and naked shall I return to the earth . . .' and 'for the first time I understood something read in the Church of God'. It is the mystical sentiment of Blake's 'Go, love without the help of anything on earth'; the experience laid the foundation for Zossima's later religious fervour.

Zossima's story of his youth seems to follow the pattern of other Outsiders' (Emil Sinclair and Tolstoy in particular): he forgets the childish impressions when he becomes a cadet in the army; he 'sins', and riots, does his best to behave like a 'young blood'. The turning-point comes when he has challenged someone to a duel; suddenly the realization of his folly bursts on him; he allows his opponent to fire at him, and then throws away his pistol, and preaches a sermon: 'Nature is sinless . . . only we are sinful; we don't understand that life is paradise, for we have only to understand it and all will be fulfilled in all its beauty. . . .'

It is not the idea of the duel that has produced this conversion; it is his bad conscience about a servant he has beaten the day before; suddenly he remembers his brother, who died expressing the doctrine of Christian equality. 'No man is good enough to be another man's master.' After the duel, he resigns his commission and becomes a monk.

This is the essence of Father Zossima's life, and it constitutes Dostoevsky's answer to Ivan's rebellion. Zossima is an orthodox Christian; but more important, he is a mystic. His message is not 'Christ died for man: therefore you must love your neighbour'; that would fail to meet Ivan's argument on any level.

He does not *begin* by denying Ivan's point that men are contemptible; in fact, he fully admits it. The centre of Zossima's message is Blake's mystical doctrine: 'If the doors of perception were cleansed, everything would appear infinite', including human beings. So Zossima's 'Life' is not a reply to Ivan's argument, any more than adulthood is a reply to childhood. Ivan could not be expected to grasp Zossima's insights; he is still in the early stage of trusting to Reason; and the belief that everything is infinite is an *existential* truth not accessible to reason. As far as it goes, Ivan's analysis of the world is completely right. Misery will never end: that is true; but that does not negate the saint's vision, because he sees that life can never end either. They are not even two eternal *warring* principles; they are on a completely different level.

Man can live on Ivan's level or Zossima's. Or he can do infinitely worse and live on the level of the common bourgeois. What is important is that he leave the world of common daylight; when he enters the no-man's-land between hell and heaven, he is an Outsider. Now the difficulties begin. Unless he is very lucky he will find his face turned towards hell; human delusion, corruption, pain, stupidity, ultimate defeat, these are the realities that suddenly occupy his whole field of vision. And behind them, the canvas on which these are merely shadows, the terror of complete emptiness, unbeing, the abyss.

It is not easy to escape; it is not easy because there seems to be no reason for escaping; this negates even the concept of freedom. The release, if it comes, involves a complete retracing of the steps through the human ground; back to the essential Will to live that underlies all existence. And this recognition of the world's unreality, this insight that comes between death and morning, brings a certainty in its wake. It is naked insight into the purpose of the force that demands life at all costs. This insight is called mysticism.

Ivan is half a mystic; as Alyosha says: he has only half solved the problem. Zossima is less aware of the world's misery and man's weakness than Ivan. He does not even hope that all men will become 'guardians of the mystery'. He does not preach life after death, heaven for the good, hell for the wicked. 'What is Hell? I maintain it is the suffering of not being able to love—and for that, you do not need Eternity; a day will do, or even a moment.'

In *The Brothers Karamazov*, there are two more chapters that enforce the meaning of Zossima's words, and these chapters *are* artistically comparable with Ivan's 'Legend'. The first is Alyosha's vision of the first miracle. After the death of Zossima, the body begins to decompose immediately. The people interpret this unfavourably; Zossima was a saint, why should he rot? Perhaps it is a 'sign', sent to warn them not to honour Zossima as a saint. Alyosha is disturbed too, not because he doubts Zossima's sanctity, but because this unpleasant anti-climax to his Abbot's death seems an omen of the ultimate triumph of evil.

In a state of wretched discouragement, he falls asleep at the side of the coffin. He has a dream that completely restores his faith: he is present at Cana in Galilee, when Christ changes the water into wine; an old man whispers to him: 'He is changing the water into wine that the gladness of the guests may not be cut short. He is expecting new guests. He is calling new ones unceasingly for ever and ever. . . .' Alyosha wakes from his dream, with a feeling of renewed life. He goes out, and, under the night sky, he is overwhelmed with 'universal conscious-ness'. The stars inspire him: 'there seemed to be threads from all those innumerable worlds of God, linking his souls to them. . . . It was as if some *idea* had seized sovereignty in his mind.' He flings himself on the earth, weeping: 'He could not have told why he longed to kiss it—and to love it for ever and ever.' In such a moment, Alyosha can see and touch the answer to Ivan's rebellion. Ivan's indictment is valid for men as they are; but if all men could see as he sees, Ivan's words would cease to be true.

There is no need to point out that Alyosha's vision can be paralleled by others described in this book: by Meursault's, by Nietzsche's. What is the content of this vision of Alyosha's? Recalling Nietzsche's 'pure Will, without the troubles of intellect', we can say that it seems to be a vision of power, of Yea-saying—ἡ δύναμις καὶ ἡ δόξα. Normally man's mind is composed only of a consciousness of his immediate needs, which is to say that this consciousness at any moment can be defined as *his awareness of his own power to satisfy those needs*. He thinks in terms of what he intends to do in half an hour's time, a day's time, a month's time, and no more. He never asks himself: What are the *limits* of my powers? In a sense, he is like

a man who has a fortune in the bank, who never asks himself,
How much money have I got?, but only, Have I enough for a
pound of cheese, for a new tie?, etc. In such moments as
Alyosha's vision he pushes aside all these minor affairs, and
takes stock of his powers in not terms of *doing* but simply of
being. Since it is normally the things we do that make up our
idea of what we are, this 'stocktaking of energy' tends to jump
the personality and all 'perplexities of intellect'; it is in other
words a vision of pure Will, pure power, pure possibility. The
personality temporarily disappears: this is the most important
aspect of the vision.

At the same time, of course, Alyosha has realized the truth
that Zossima and Kirilov also knew: that everything is good.
Evil is ultimate bondage; this suggests the possibility of ultimate
freedom.

Mitya has a vision too; and his vision, as we would expect, is
of a totally different kind from Alyosha's. Mitya lacks self-
control, and he is completely self-centred. To escape the prison
of his own self-regard, he needs to become an Outsider; he
needs to discover that he is in a world that is so full of misery
that his only business is to love. Mitya is not basically bad or
selfish; it is only that he has never had to think of anyone but
himself. He has almost driven himself mad, lusting after a
sloe-eyed Russian wench who (the author cynically admits)
will run to fat in another ten years. Now he is accused of
murdering his father and stealing his money. There has been a
long cross-examination scene (more than fifty pages of it)
in which Mitya has been subjected to something like a third-
degree. The irony, the stupidity of it, bewilder him; he seems
to have lost touch with reality. I quote the scene that follows in
full; it is a supreme instance of Dostoevsky's artistic power of
evocation:

He felt more and more oppressed by a strange physical
weakness. His eyes were closing with fatigue. The examination of the witnesses was, at last, over. They proceeded to a
final revision of the protocol. Mitya got up, moved from his
chair by the corner to the curtain, lay down on a large chest
covered with a rug, and instantly fell asleep.

He had a strange dream, utterly out of keeping with the
place and time.

He was driving somewhere in the steppes, where he had been stationed long ago, and a peasant was driving him in a cart with a pair of horses, through snow and sleet. He was cold, it was early in November, and the snow was falling in big, wet flakes that melted as soon as they touched the earth. And the peasant drove him smartly; he had a long, fair beard. . . . Not far off was a village; he could see the black huts, and half the huts were burnt down, with only the charred beams sticking up. As they drove in, there were peasant women drawn up along the road, a lot of women, a whole row, all thin and wan, with their faces a sort of brownish colour—especially one woman at the edge, tall and bony, who looked forty but might have been twenty, with a long, thin face. And in her arms was a little baby, crying. And her breasts seemed so dried up that there was not a drop of milk in them. And the child cried and cried, and held out its little bare arms, with its little fists blue from cold.

'Why are they crying, why are they crying?' Mitya asked, as they dashed gaily by.

'It's the babe,' answered the driver, 'the babe's weeping.'

And Mitya was struck by his saying, in his peasant way, 'the babe', and he liked the peasant calling it a 'babe'. There seemed more pity in it.

'But why is it weeping?' Mitya persisted stupidly, 'Why are its little arms bare? Why don't they wrap it up?'

'The babe's cold. Its clothes are frozen and don't warm it.'

'But why is it? Why?' Mitya foolishly persisted.

'Why, they're poor people, burnt out. They've no bread. They're begging because they've no bread.'

'No, no.' Mitya, as it were, still did not understand. 'Tell me why it is these poor mothers stand there. Why are these people poor? Why is the babe poor? Why is the steppe barren? Why don't they hug each other and kiss? Why don't they sing songs of joy? Why are they so dark from black misery? Why don't they feed the babe?'

And he felt, though the questions were unreasonable and senseless, that he wanted to ask just that, and he had to ask it in just that way. And he felt that a passion of pity, such as he had never known before, was rising in his heart, that he wanted to cry, that he wanted to do something for them all, so that the babe should weep no more, so that the dark-faced, dried-up mother should not weep, that no one should shed tears again from that moment, and he wanted to do it all at once, regardless of all obstacles, with all the recklessness of the Karamazovs.

'And I am coming with you. I won't leave you now for the rest of my life' he heard close beside him Grushenka's voice, warm with emotion. And his heart glowed, and he struggled towards the light, and he longed to love and live, and to go on and on, towards the new beckoning light, and to hasten, hasten, now, at once.

'What? Where?' he exclaimed, opening his eyes and sitting up on the chest, smiling brightly. Nicolay Parfenovitch was standing over him, suggesting that he should hear the protocol read aloud, and sign it. . . . He was suddenly struck by the fact that there was a pillow under his head that had not been there when he fell asleep, exhausted, on the chest.

'Who put that pillow under my head? Who was so kind?' he cried, with a sort of ecstatic gratitude. . . .

He never found out who the kind man was—perhaps one of the peasant witnesses . . . but his soul felt tense with the emotion. He went to the table and said he would sign whatever they liked.

'I've had a good dream, gentlemen,' he said, in a strange voice, with a new light, as of joy, in his face.[6]

Again we see, in the phrase 'he longed to live and live, and to go on and on', the same Yea-saying vision as had happened to Alyosha, as well as to Kirilov and Shatov. We can even parallel it with Raskolnikov's in the scene of *Crime and Punishment* in which Sonia reads him the Gospel:

How it happened he did not know. But all at once something seemed to seize him and fling him at her feet. He went and threw his arms round her knees. He had risen again and knew it, and felt it with all his being'.[7]

Even Stavrogin has experienced something of the kind;[*] he tells about it at the end of his 'confession': his dream of a

---

[*] It is interesting to compare this with Thomas Mann's scene in *The Magic Mountain* of Hans Castorp's dream, in the 'Snow' chapter.

golden age as in the Claude picture: warm sea and perfect harmony of human beings. Then the face of the dead child he raped rises in his memory and destroys the vision. Here again, Mitya evokes the Golden age: 'Why don't they sing songs of joy?' just as Ivan had evoked it at the end of the 'Rebellion' Chapter. This is Dostoevsky's Pro and Contra: in one balance-pan, human misery; in the other, the unconquerable force of Life from which human beings cut themselves off with their trivial, tied-to-the-present personalities. Mitya learns that man can become aware of that pure Will to live only by ceasing to care about his own little affairs.

We now come to Ivan's 'vision', one of the most important sections in the book.

For some reason, critics who have acclaimed the Grand Inquisitor section as 'the concentrated essence of Dostoevsky'* have paid no attention to Ivan's scene with the Devil, although it is obviously intended to supplement the earlier chapter. Actually, as I hope to show, Ivan's 'vision' is the climax of the book. In it there is not only a summary of the Outsider's dialectic, there are seeds of the development of a whole field of modern literature.**

Ivan is sick. The narrator tells us he is on the eve of a brain-storm. This is the point to which unending thinking has brought him. After a last interview with Smerdyakov (his 'ape'—a reminder of his baser part), in which he wrings a confession of the murder from his half-brother, he goes back to his empty room. And now occurs the scene towards which the Outsider's destiny has always tended. The room is no longer empty. There is Another.

The Devil is a seedy would-be gentleman, wearing a reefer jacket and check trousers. Dostoevsky's portrait of him is as circumstantial as a description by Balzac of some small trades-man. This is a very human devil. Ivan had told Alyosha in the Pro and Contra section:

'I think if the Devil doesn't exist, and man has created him, he has created him in his own image and likeness.'

Here he is: human, all too human; something of a buffoon, like Ivan's dead father; something of the ape, like Smerdyakov.

---

* See *The Grand Inquisitor*, Introduction by D. H. Lawrence (Hogarth Press).
** Tchehov's 'Black Monk', whose metaphysical themes are repeated in Piran-dello, Andreyev, Sartre and in England in Mr. Eliot's *Family Reunion*. Mann's *Doktor Faustus* is also indebted to it.

Is he real? And here is Dostoevsky's point: He is as real as anything in a world of unrealities. Ivan believes he is unreal and tells him so: the Devil laughs and admits it. All is unreal. Being? What is it? Perception. What you see exists for you. If I am delusion of your mind, you are also a delusion of mine, the Devil tells him. Each man exists in a solipsist universe in which he treats his delusions as realities. Exploding logic; reason, tired of proceeding forward, tries to erupt out of the page. You, the reader holding this book—one level of reality; Ivan, another—less real; the Devil another—less real still; but all is relative. Are you reading for amusement? No? You have some serious interest in reading? You don't mind reading of Ivan's confusion between real and unreal, but when you put down this book, what then? You must take up your own life. Real or unreal? The intellect pretends to be sincere, pretends to question everything, but the arm-chair you are sitting in, the chest of drawers, the fire, you don't question their existence, nor the work you must do tomorrow and the day after. The intellect can go off on quixotic voyages, but you, the being, the personality, have to go forward along your destiny, what Minkowski would call your 'geodesic'.

This uncoils from Ivan's interview with the Devil; it is always latent in it. It will always be there until human beings have attained ultimate reality and can read *The Brothers Karamazov* from an ultimately real arm-chair which *is* just what it appears to be, facing their lives with an ultimate knowledge of who they are, what life is, what death is, where they come from and where they are going. Then they can *know* that Ivan's Devil was unreal, but then, *The Brothers Karamazov* is only a book, and Dostoevsky was only a man, and for unreality there is not much to choose between them. Behind Ivan there is a universe of chaos, cinders. Ivan accuses the Devil of re-hashing the ideas from his student days; but what does that matter? It may be one more evidence of the Devil's unreality, but does it prove the ideas unreal? Are the ideas realler than Ivan? Plato would say yes; Kierkegaard and the modern Existentialists, no. This too lies latent in the situation between Ivan and the Devil.

And these 'ideas' of Ivan's: as soon as we touch them it sets the whole merry-go-round off again. As a student, Ivan had argued that good and evil have no relation to the soul. They are only two poles in life, two lumberjacks at either end of a double-handed saw. Or compare evil to the clapper of a bell; remove it and the bell is silent, unmanifest. Good and evil, what are they? the Devil asks. When man is uncivilized, his good and evil are completely arbitrary; his gods are immoral and his devils are only graveyard bogies. As he learns to use his reason, he sorts out good from evil. But where does it end? Only at the Outsider's 'Truth, what do they mean by it?' He does not reason himself towards God, or towards becoming a god himself, but only into the position of Burridan's ass, starving between two equal loads of hay. The notions of good and evil evaporate. He finds himself—in his room, staring at the wall; and if Another exists, then he is like this one, a shabby vulgarian in check trousers. This is the end of the great God Reason, when it goes far enough; eternity, a dusty room with cobwebs; the Devil, a human being, and Heaven, perhaps, as in Rupert Brooke's sonnet, where:

> An idle wind blew round an empty throne
> And stirred the heavy curtains on the walls . . .

And belief? It is not that Ivan does not want to believe. Spiritual starvation has made him sick and afraid of his own existence.

> Will the veiled sister pray
> For the children at the gate
> Who will not go away and cannot pray?

If he can recover from this 'terrifying insight' and find belief, he may become more passionately religious than Alyosha; he will believe with the unwavering certainty of one who has been lost for a long time and is determined never to be lost again.

But we are not to know what happened, because Dostoevsky never finished the story. There *are* hints in the Devil chapter. There is the story of the free-thinker, who believed there was no life after death, and when he died, was indignant to find he was wrong. As a punishment for his unbelief he was sentenced to walk a quadrillion miles. He lay down and refused to move, and a thousand years went by before he grew tired of lying down, and set out to walk the quadrillion miles. And when he had finished—(and here Ivan interrupts to ask where he got the billion years to do it in? The Devil explains that our earth has lived and died a thousand times—Zarathustra's Eternal Recurrence)—when he had finished, and was admitted into heaven at last, he cried immediately that two seconds in heaven were worth walking for a million times as long. . . .[8]

Here Ivan interrupts with a shout, 'You are repeating a story I made up when I was a student.' The Devil has proved again that he is a figment of Ivan's imagination. So!

But consider the story itself. Its content is the same as Nietzsche's vision on the hilltop: reconciliation, a Vision of pure Being that makes up for all the apparent terrors and miseries of living. The unbeliever walks for a quadrillion miles, yet one moment of reality makes up for it. It is like Steppanwolf's idea that he might one day look back on himself from his ultimate goal 'to which the difficult path seems to be taking him', and smile with 'a mixture of joy and pity', or even to realize, like Meursault that 'he had been happy and was happy still'. It is an idea, this, that turns up repeatedly in world religions; that life is such a tissue of delusions that man can never have the remotest idea of who he is or what he is doing, but that the dream can break suddenly, and the resulting glimpse is sudden complete understanding. The Bhagavad Gita expresses it:

'Even if you are the most sinful of sinners, this insight will carry you like a raft above all your sin' (IV, 36).

Chuang Tzu says:

'While they dream, they do not know that they are dreaming. Some will even interpret the dream they are dreaming (i.e. Hegel and the systematizing philosophers) and only when they wake do they know it was a dream. By and by comes the great awakening, and then we find out that this life is really a great dream. . . .'

And here is the very essence of *Existenzphilosophie*. The poet-philosopher has an intuition that man is so completely sunk in delusion that he can never hope to know himself consistently and act upon his knowledge. A moment comes, and it seems a moment of deeper insight than man normally has, of recognition that man does not know the world or himself. He is so sunk in delusion and a high opinion of himself that there is no hope at all of his ever knowing himself. This is a way of seeing that comes easily to Outsiders, because the Outsider sees with such penetration through the usual self-deluding, the way in which all men and women blind themselves with their emotions. The consequence is usually a Swiftian contempt for men and women, the kind of feeling that finds full expression in the last pages of Gulliver's *Voyage to the Houyhnhnms*:

My reconcilement to the Yahoo kind in general might not be so difficult if they were content with those vices and follies only which Nature has entitled them to. I am not in the least provoked at the sight of a lawyer, a pickpocket, a colonel, a fool, a lord, a gamester, a politician, a physician, an evidence, a suborner, an attorney, a traitor, or the like; this is all according to the due course of things; but when I behold a lump of deformity and diseases, both in body and mind, smitten with pride, it immediately breaks all the measures of my patience. . . .

This is not pathological loathing; there is not the slightest touch of insanity about it (in spite of the prevailing modern opinion to the contrary). It is the ordinary Outsider attitude to men, and it is also the religious attitude. The same savage indictment of human folly can be found in the Book of Ecclesiastes, as well as in the New Testament and the *Pensées* of Pascal. The common mob, the philistines and moneychangers, are 'flies in the market-place'. Then, as the Outsider's insight becomes deeper, so that he no longer sees men as a million million individuals, but instead sees the world-will that drives them all like ants in a formicary, he knows that they will never escape their stupidity and delusions, that no amount of logic and knowledge can make man any more than an insect; the most irritating of the human lice is the humanist with his puffed-up pride in Reason and his ignorance of his own silliness.

The answer of a man like Kierkegaard to this vision that forced itself upon his over-sensitive perceptions, is the religious solution. For nothing is more natural than that the mind that has tired of its reasoning faculty should turn to the areas of the being that lie below consciousness, to the instincts and intuitions. It may be a simple revolt, like D. H. Lawrence's, but if it is too simple, it may fall into the error that Steppanwolf

avoided, the 'back to the animal' attitude of L
Mawr' or 'The Virgin and the Gipsy'. That
But Kierkegaard had the solution when he realize
necessary intensity to fuse all his instincts and rational i.
lay in the religious attitude.

And at this point, a genuinely puzzled reader who can
sympathize with the Outsider, but cannot quite understand
how he can jump to the religious attitude, may ask: 'But is it
true? Is it true in the same way that one and one make two?'
And here an analogy might make things clearer. When
Einstein introduced his special theory of relativity, he was
careful to explain that his disagreement with the Newtonian
formulae did not matter unless you were dealing with particles
travelling at a very high speed, at a speed approaching 186,000
miles per second, in fact. Unless you were dealing with such
high speeds, you need not worry about Time being different
for different co-ordinate systems in relative motion, nor about
simultaneousness having no meaning without many more
definitions. But if you *are* dealing with high speeds, then there
is nothing for it; you *must* discard Galilei's equations and use
Lorentz's.

The same goes for the Outsider. If you are living a very
ordinary dull life at low pressure, you can safely regard the
Outsider as a crank who does not deserve serious consideration.
But if you are interested in man in extreme states, or in man
abnormally preoccupied by questions about the nature of life,
then whatever answer the Outsider may propound should be
worth your respectful attention. The Outsider is interested in
high speeds and great pressures; he prefers to consider the man
who sets out to be very good or very wicked rather than the
good citizen who advocates moderation in all things.

And this brings us back to Ivan Karamazov. Ivan is such a
man who is not contented with ordinary speeds. He feels great
spiritual power in himself. Like Raskolnikov, he does not feel
that he has been born to be a nonentity. Dostoevsky tells us
that 'he began very early—almost in his infancy—to show a
brilliant and unusual aptitude for learning'. Naturally, he
feels that his way must be the way of intellect. And what is the
business of intellect? It is to synthesize unendingly. The
Outsider naturally sees most men as failures; in fact, he may
feel that every man who has ever lived had been a failure

So the Ivan-type applies his intellectual powers to the question:
How must I live my life so as not to have to consider myself a
failure? And with a standard so high, the problem must gnaw
at him day and night, make leisure impossible, shatter his
nerves with an unending sense of tension, urgency, like the
laceration of a spur being driven into the mind. He gropes
for standards. He realizes intuitively 'If I can say: That man
was a failure, then I must have an idea of what success
means.'

And the trouble has begun. If he had time to sit in a quiet
spot, under pleasant circumstances, he might get to grips with
it. But our life as human beings in a modern society seldom
allows us those circumstances. It is a repetition of Van Gogh's
problem, the day by day struggle for intensity that disappears
overnight, all interrupted by human trivialities and endless
pettinesses. When Dostoevsky made Ivan on the eve of a
brainstorm see the Devil, he was only symbolizing what can
happen to such an Outsider. Ivan is aiming at complete synthesis, to see the world as a whole. Blake calls it 'fourfold
vision' in one of his poems:

> Now I a fourfold vision see
> And a fourfold vision is given to me
> It is fourfold in my supreme delight
> And threefold in soft Beulah's night
> And twofold always. May God us keep
> From single vision and Newton's sleep.*

Ivan's Devil is an embodiment of the last line, 'single vision
and Newton's sleep'. He is a sort of version of Roquentin's
Nausea, William James's 'stubborn unreduceable fact', brute
reality that negates spirit or, worse than that, embodies delusion.
It is this Devil who drove Van Gogh insane, who stayed at
T. E. Lawrence's elbow whispering self-distrust; no nightmare
monster of evil with three faces, *imperador del doloroso regno*, but a
breaker of wings, poisoner of the Will to live.

*   *   *

In his *Doktor Faustus*, Thomas Mann is openly indebted to
Ivan's Devil scene, and has added some interesting observations
on the psychology of the Outsider that clarify Dostoevsky's

views. Mann's Faustus (who is based on Frederick Nietzsche), argues:[10]

> . . . the contritio without hope, as complete disbelief in the possibility of mercy and forgiveness . . . only that is true contritio. . . . You will admit that the everyday sinner can be but moderately interesting to mercy. Mediocrity, in fact, has no theological status. A capacity for sin so healless, that it makes a man despair from his heart of redemption— that is the true theological way to salvation.
>
> He (the Devil): You are a sly dog! And where would the likes of you get the single-mindedness, the naive recklessness of despair, which would be the premise for the sinful way of salvation? Is it not plain to you that the conscious speculation on the charm that great guilt exercises on Goodness makes the act of mercy impossible to it?
>
> Faustus: And yet only through this ne plus ultra can the high prick of dramatic theological existence be arrived at— I mean the most abandoned guilt, and the last and most irresistible challenge to everlasting goodness.
>
> He: Not bad. . . . And now I will tell you that precisely heads of your sort comprise the population of Hell . . . your theologian in grain, your arrant wiley pie who speculates on speculation because he has speculation in his blood. . . .

Mann makes the position even clearer. It is just that position in Eliot's 'Ash Wednesday' that I analysed in Chapter V. St. Augustine's solution was *Credo ut intelligam*, believe to understand. And what if a man has not a grain of faith in him, if he is a reasoner through and through? By reasoner I do not mean simply a rationalist—like certain modern logicians who question the possibility of the synthetic *a priori*, but never doubt the utility of lecturing to students three times a week and publishing books on logical positivism; to these, the Outsider would apply Mann's harsh judgement: Mediocrity has no theological status. But the man who, like Evan Strowde, sets out to 'get past all tricks to the heart of things' . . . is he inevitably damned? This is one of the Outsider's worst dilemmas: to feel the whole being groaning for some emotional satisfaction, some solid reality to touch, and to feel the reasoning faculty standing apart, jeering at the possibility of satisfaction and discouraging its approach. What should such an Outsider do? Should he deliberately repress his reasoning faculty, accept a faith and hope that his reason will be reconciled to it one day? Accept *Credo ut intelligam*?

No. The Outsider cannot countenance such an idea. And, in fact, we have seen him solving the problem in this study. Man is not merely intellect and emotions; he is body too. This is easiest of all to forget. The life of the Outsider pivots around his intellect and emotions, and as often as not, he retreats into a cork-lined room as did Proust and forgets he has a body. It was Hemingway's main achievement to restore the sense of the body into literature; he has done this even more successfully than D. H. Lawrence, who was always getting bogged down in his emotions. In Hemingway, especially in the early volumes, there is a sense of physical freshness, a direct, intense experience of natural things that makes the 'troubles and perplexities of intellect' seem nonsense. And this was also Zarathustra's vision; in a passage that might be set as an epigraph to Lawrence's *Man Who Died*, he declares:

> While Jesus the Hebrew only knew the tears and the melancholy of the Hebrew, together with the hatred of Goodness and Righteousness, the longing for death overtook him.
>
> Would that he had remained in the desert, far from the good and righteous! Perhaps he would have learned how to live and love the earth—and to laugh as well.[11]

And this judgement, apart from its implied criticism of the founder of the Christian religion, would be endorsed by many mystics, Christian and otherwise. In speaking of Blake and Traherne in the last chapters it will be seen just how important is the part that the mystic ascribes to 'love of the earth'. This is where Mann's *Doktor Faustus* fails (and it is a very bad portrait of Nietzsche in that it ignores the Whitmanesque aspect of Nietzsche's message and concentrates on intellectual problems).* And, it would seem, it is the point where Ivan fails too, in spite of his assurance that he loves 'the blue sky and the sticky buds in spring'. And Dostoevsky makes his meaning

---

* Readers of Goethe's *Faust* will recollect the scene in which Faust is on the point of suicide because of his sense of defeat in his intellectual problems, and is called 'back to earth' by the Easter bells and memories of pure physical well-being in childhood.

unequivocal by the 'vision' scenes of the other two brothers. Alyosha is overwhelmed with sheer physical love of the earth, like Van Gogh's, and kisses it and weeps on it. And Mitya is made to realize that the earth is full of suffering human beings, and that no one can be whole and complete without a sense of kinship with the suffering of all other living beings.

In his 'Snows of Kilimanjaro', Hemingway writes of Scott Fitzgerald:

> Poor Julian and his romantic awe of [the rich] . . . he thought they were a special glamorous race, and when he found out they weren't, it wrecked him just as much as anything had wrecked him.
> He [the hero] had been contemptuous of those who wrecked. . . . He could beat anything . . . because nothing could hurt him if he did not care. . . .[12]

This book has been a study chiefly in men who 'wrecked' for different reasons, men who cared too much about something or other, and cracked under the strain.

Now Dostoevsky has brought us to the threshold of new developments, and he has helped to summarize most of the themes of previous chapters. What we cannot have failed to notice, as the analysis has taken us from Barbusse, Sartre, Hesse, towards Raskolnikov, Ivan Karamazov, is that the greatest men have been those who were most intensely concerned about the Outsider's problems, and the question of how *not* to wreck. The Outsider must keep asking the question: Why? Why are most men failures? Why do Outsiders tend to wreck?

We lack the *concept of an enemy*: that is the trouble. We talk vaguely of 'the Outsider's problems', and we even get around to defining them in terms of 'freedom', 'personality', but that only leads us into metaphysical discussions about meanings. What we haven't yet got around to is a bare statement: '*This* is where the Outsider is going, and *this* is what he often falls over, breaking his neck.' That is what we need, to sort out some of the threads we have unravelled in previous chapters: a statement of destination and a concept of an enemy (or of an 'obstacle', if the word fits the metaphor better).

Let us summarize our conclusions briefly:

The Outsider wants to cease to be an Outsider.

He wants to be 'balanced'.

He would like to achieve a vividness of sense-perception (Lawrence, Van Gogh, Hemingway).

He would also like to understand the human soul and its workings (Barbusse and Mitya Karamazov).

He would like to escape triviality forever, and be 'possessed' by a Will to power, to more life.

Above all, he would like to know how to express himself, because that is the means by which he can get to know himself and his unknown possibilities.

Every Outsider tragedy we have studied so far has been a tragedy of self-expression.

We have, to guide us, two discoveries about the Outsider's 'way':

(1) That his salvation 'lies in extremes'.

(2) That the idea of a way out often comes in 'visions', moments of intensity, etc. It is this latter possibility that we must investigate further in the next two chapters.

CHAPTER EIGHT

THE OUTSIDER AS VISIONARY

THE VISIONARY IS inevitably an Outsider. And this is not because visionaries are a relatively small minority in proportion to the rest of the community; in that case, rat-catchers and steeple-jacks would be Outsiders too. It is for the very different reason that he starts from a point that everybody can understand, and very soon soars beyond the general understanding. He starts from the 'appetite for fruitful activity and a high quality of life', the most profound and ineradicable human instinct. And before long you have him making statements like this:

> I assert for myself that I do not behold the outward creation, and that to me it is hindrance and not action; it is as the dirt upon my feet, no part of me. 'What,' it will be questioned, 'when the sun rises do you not see a round disc of fire, something like a guinea?' Oh no, no, I see an innumerable company of the heavenly host crying: 'Holy holy holy is the Lord God Almighty.'[1]

Poetic allegory, perhaps? Then consider that Blake told Crabb Robinson that he had seen the ghost of Julius Caesar on the previous evening, and that he spent more time conversing with spirits than with human beings. This is either madness or a very strange order of sanity. Another mystic who was also a brilliant scientist and a first-rate engineer stated that he had made a complete tour of heaven and hell, not in poetic fancy, like Dante, but actually, like a Sunday afternoon bus excursion, and that he habitually held conversations with angels. Nevertheless, there are thousands of followers of Emanuel Swedenborg today who believe his books to be as sane as Newton's *Principia* and as objective as the Kinsey report on sexual behaviour. It does not simplify the question to say that 'sanity' is a relative term, especially where religious sects are concerned. Swedenborg and Blake proclaimed their insights to be real, corresponding to some real object, much as

Wells made that claim for *Mind at the End of Its Tether*; our experience with Wells's pamphlet should have made us cautious about pooh-poohing these claims.

In this chapter I intend to deal with two Outsiders who formulated a religious solution to their problems, and who also asserted that they had developed a certain faculty for seeing 'visions' as a consequence of their attempts at solution. Their temperaments were completely unlike: George Fox was primarily a man of action who needed a physical outlet for the impulses that stirred in him; Blake was at once a clear thinker and a dreamer, an obstreperous iconoclast and an other-worldly poet. Fox's name became known from end to end of England; Blake remained in unrelieved obscurity all his life. These two men achieved, by sheer strength of Will, an intensity of insight that few men have known.

In speaking of them, it is necessary to remember that what they left recorded on paper was the least important part of their lives. It is the lesson that is expressed in the Chuang Tzu book in the story of the Duke of Ch'i and his wheelwright. It tells how the wheelwright saw the Duke reading, and called to ask him what the book was about. 'The words of sages,' the Duke explained. 'The lees and scum of bygone men,' the wheel-wright said; and when the irritated Duke asked him what the devil he meant by this, the wheelwright told him: 'There is an art in wheel-making that I cannot explain even to my son. It cannot be put into words. That is why I cannot let him take over my work, and I am still making wheels myself at seventy. It must have been the same with the sages: all that was worth handing on died with them. The rest they put into their books. That is why I said you are reading the lees and scum of dead men.'

This lesson should be especially taken to heart in reading the works of the visionaries dealt with in the following chapters. The essentials of what they *saw* died with them. Their value for us does not lie in the 'visions' their words can conjure up for us, but in the instructions they left for anyone who should want to see the same things that they saw. It lies, in other words, in the discipline they recommend.

Certain questions should be asked before we pass on to examine these men. There will be many readers for whom the arguments of Outsiders in Chapters I and II against religion seem unanswerable. The Outsider recognizes with penetrating clearness that all men are dishonest with themselves, that all men blind themselves with their emotions. The 'answers' of religion seem to him to be lies designed to make men comfortable. It is not a desire to be an 'Antichrist' that makes this type of Outsider reject religion; on the contrary, he may be intensely miserable that he cannot accept them. He can find authority in the Church itself for his attitude: in Meister Eckhart, for instance, with his: 'If God could backslide from truth I would stick to truth and let God go.'

The question that arises naturally, therefore, is: Is it not superfluous to quote religious men who are bound to be biased? And the answer, I think, is that it can do no harm to see what they can teach us about the Outsider. We can admit now that, for the Existentialist Outsiders of the earlier chapters, a specifically Christian solution would be untenable. For the Existentialist would like to say of his solution, not 'I believe', but '*I know*'. And this is not unreasonable. Sartre gives an example that illustrates it: that if the phone rang, and a voice at the other end said: 'This is God speaking. Believe and you are saved; doubt and you are damned,' the man holding the receiver would be justified in answering: 'Very well, in that case I'm damned.' He would be justified because all men have a right to withhold belief in something they cannot *know*.[2]

What we are trying to do in this book is to establish precisely what the Outsider does know, or can know, and our criterion is empirical. Whatever can be experienced can, within this definition, be 'known'. Very well, then we must ask the Outsider questions until we have an idea of where his experience is lacking; then we can tell him: 'Go out and look for these experiences, and your doubts will be answered.' In his rudimentary Outsider parable *The History of Mr. Polly*, H. G. Wells showed his hero setting his house on fire and leaving his wife, to tramp the roads: 'If you don't like your life you can change it.' Now, Mr. Polly's solution would have no value for most of the Outsiders we have dealt with, because they are far more complex then Mr. Polly (Hesse, perhaps, is an exception). But at least it is an example of the type of answer we are looking for, a 'go out and *do* something'.

That is why I am starting my analysis with George Fox.

Fox is one of the greatest religious teachers England has produced; compared with him, Bunyan was weak, Wesley neurotic and Wycliffe bigoted. He was strong-minded, imaginative, level-headed and sympathetic. When Fox, the religious agitator, appeared before Cromwell, the keeper of the peace, the preacher and the soldier paid their respects to each other and parted friends. They both had the same qualities—courage, will-power—and each knew his own mind and wasn't afraid to speak it.

Yet with his soldier qualities, Fox united another and totally different set, those of the poet and mystic. The combination often produced strange results:[3]

> As I was walking with several friends, I lifted up my head and saw three steeple house spires, and they struck at my life. I asked them what that place was; they said 'Lichfield'. Immediately the word of the Lord came to me, that I must go thither. . . . As soon as they were gone, I stept away, and went by my eye over hedge and ditch until I came within a mile of Lichfield; where, in a great field, shepherds were keeping their sheep. Then I was commanded by the Lord to pull off my shoes. I stood there, for it was winter, but the word of the Lord was like a fire in me. So I put off my shoes and left them with the shepherds; and the poor shepherds trembled, and were astonished. Then I walked about a mile, and as soon as I was got within the city, the word of the Lord came to me, saying: 'Cry: Wo to the bloody city of Lichfield.' So I went up and down the streets, crying with a loud voice: Wo to the bloody city of Lichfield. It being a market day, I went into the market-place, and went up and down in several places of it, and made stands crying: Wo to the bloody city of Lichfield, and no one touched nor laid hands upon me. As I went down the town, there ran like a channel of blood down the streets, and the market-place was like a pool of blood . . . so when I had declared what was upon me and cleared myself of it, I came out of the town in peace about a mile to the shepherds, and there I went to them, and took my shoes, and gave them some money, but the fire of the Lord was so in my feet and all over

me that I did not matter to put my shoes on any more. . . .

After this, a deep consideration came upon me, for what reason I should be sent to cry against that city: Wo to the bloody city of Lichfield. . . . But afterwards I came to understand that in the Emperor Diocletian's time, a thousand Christians were martyred in Lichfield. So I was to go, without my shoes, through the channel of blood, and into the pool of their blood in the market place, that I might raise up the memorial of the blood of those martyrs, which had been shed above a thousand years before, and lay cold in their streets.

The first thing that strikes us of this experience is how lucky Fox was to be able to do an apparently irrational thing without misgivings, and 'declare what was upon him until he had cleared himself of it'. Most of the Outsiders we have considered never got to the point of declaring what was upon them, to express it and clear themselves of it by a definitive act. Steppenwolf, for instance, at the end of a boring day, feeling a suppressed rage that made him want to go and do something violent . . . with the stuff of a George Fox in him, he would not have remained a bored hypochondriac for long! Dostoevsky made his Raskolnikov more resolute than Hesse's hero; but then, he made him lose courage after the definitive act, and the parable is a great idea left undeveloped.*

Now, the beetle-man Outsider, the Sartre or Barbusse hero, might well envy Fox his confidence and conviction, and yet feel that there are insuperable barriers to prevent him from doing the same sort of thing. Fox is a man who sticks at nothing. He is the perfect example of the Outsider in revolt. When his convictions are stirred, he lowers his head and charges like a bull, just like the 'man of action' that we found Dostoevsky's beetle-man admiring in Chapter VI. A brick wall does not worry him. He is the sort of man that the beetle-man can admire, and feel contempt for. Fox accepts things that the beetle-man

---

* This, of course, is not intended as a criticism of *Crime and Punishment*. Given the situation as Dostoevsky defined it in the first part, the remainder of the book may be artistically inevitable. Since writing the above (and Chapter VI) I have come across a passage in one of Rilke's letters that makes the same point; speaking of Malte, Rilke comments: '. . . like a Raskolnikov, he remained behind, consumed by his deed, *ceasing to act at the very moment when action had to begin*, so that his newly acquired freedom turned against him and destroyed him, the weaponless' (October 19th, 1907. Italics mine).

cannot accept: his own identity, for instance. 'If George Fox says: Verily, there is no altering him.' The beetle-man could never make such a boast.

Yet anyone who has read the *Journal* will know that there is a great deal more than a bull at a gate about George Fox. The self-confidence has arisen as the result of a long course in self-doubt. And this is what the beetle-man cannot understand, for his self-doubt never drives him to seek for a solution with the determination of a desperate man. Consequently, he never discovers what he might be capable of.

The one thing that no reader of the *Journal* can doubt is that George Fox was once as complete an Outsider as the hero of *Notes from Under the Floorboards*. This was in his early days, when he was barely nineteen. He tells us how, at that age, he began to feel the stirrings of the discontent that separated him from his family and friends. One holiday he joined his cousin in the local pub, and there, quite suddenly, felt a savage disgust against all the merrymaking. He stood up and left them, and: 'I returned home, but did not go to bed that night, nor could not sleep, but sometimes walked up and down, and sometimes prayed and cried to the Lord: Thou seest how young people go together into vanity, and old people into the earth, and thou must forsake all, both young and old, and keep out of all, and be a stranger to all.'[4]

> What are the roots that clutch, what branches grow
> Out of this stony rubbish? Son of man,
> You cannot say, or guess, for you know only
> A heap of broken images where the sun beats,
> And the dead tree gives no shelter, the cricket no relief. . . .

Fox's feelings at nineteen are not difficult to parallel in modern literature. The way Outsiders feel about the general mass of men doesn't change much in three hundred years.

> And many that professed religion sought to be aquainted, but I was afraid of them, for I was sensible they did not possess what they professed.[5]

Like all Outsiders, Fox was sensitive to the fact that what people call religion is mostly an ersatz substitute. He admits that:

... at Barnet a strong temptation to despair came upon me ... and some years I continued in that condition, and fain would have put it from me. And I went to many a priest to look for comfort, but found no comfort from them. ... [6]

We can imagine Fox, a serious-minded, inwardly tormented young man, moving from place to place like Van Gogh or a Hesse wanderer, feeling deeper needs than other people seem to feel, and wondering if he is not merely a misfit in the world. But Fox was a little better off than the modern Existentialist Outsider, for to the modern, all religions and creeds seem to be outworn lies; in Fox's day, the words of the Old Testament could still stir the blood with a sense of authenticity; only the year before, Cromwell's brigade of specially picked 'men of religion' had scattered the King's forces at Marston Moor, so that Cromwell could write: 'God made them as stubble to our swords.' Reform was in the air, and Fox too wanted to find other men who could share his sense of urgency; he wanted to find men and women like himself, who felt a 'hunger and thirst after righteousness', for whom the question of their salvation was of burning importance. Instead, what did he find?

From Barnet I went to London, where I took a lodging, and was under great misery and trouble there, for I looked upon those who professed religion in the city of London, and I saw all was dark and under the chain of darkness. ...

And I had an uncle, one Pickering, a baptist ... yet I could not import my mind to him, nor join with him, for I saw all, young and old, where they were.[7]

That is to say (to alter his language slightly) that he saw too deep and too much. Other people cannot help. He tells of the discussions he engaged in with the priest at his home village, where Fox talked of Christ's despair and temptations, with the terrible insight of the Outsider, and of how disgusted he felt to hear his own words repeated on Sunday in the priest's sermon. Later experiences with priests were, if anything, even more disillusioning:

After this I went to another ancient priest at Mancetter in Warwickshire, and reasoned with him about the ground of despair and temptations, but he was ignorant of my condition, and bade me take tobacco and sing psalms. . . .[8]

(We can compare this with Broadbent in *John Bull's Other Island* telling the Outsider-priest Keegan: 'Try phosphorus pills. I always take them when my brain's overworked.')

. . . then I heard of a priest living about Tamworth was accounted an experienced man, and I went seven miles to him, but I found him like an empty hollow cask. . . . Then I heard of one doctor Cradock of Coventry, and I went to him, and asked him the ground of temptation and despair, and how troubles came to be wrought in man. . . . Now as we were talking together in his garden, the alley being narrow, I chanced in turning to set my foot on the side of a flower bed, at which the man was in such a rage as if his house had been on fire. . . . I went away in sorrow, worse than when I came. . . . I thought them miserable comforters, and saw they were all as nothing to me, for they could not reach my condition.[9]

Like all Outsiders, Fox wanted to be understood, wanted someone to look into his soul and soothingly set things to right. And, like all Outsiders, he had to learn to work out his own salvation. It is the hardest message of all, that there is a final enemy whom every man and woman carries about with them, who cannot be fought vicariously. It is a truth that the doctrine of the Atonement was invented to make less terrible: this final, internal enemy, against whom there can be no appeal for outside help. All saints and religious teachers have made recognition of this last enemy the basis of their creeds.* Many great spiritual teachers have left accounts of their 'struggles for light'.** The characteristics of the struggle are often like Steppenwolf's description of his 'average day': failure, dullness, deadness of the senses, lack of a sense of urgency, often

* For the simplest form of this solipsist problem, *q.v.* St. Augustine 'I came to know where I was [as a child], and tried to express my wants to those who could gratify them, yet could not, *for my wants were inside me, and they were outside*' (*Confessions*, Bk. I, VI. Italics mine.)

** *Q.v.* the Buddha's 'early struggles' (*Sayings of the Buddha*, tr. F. L. Woodward, World Classic Series), p. 14. See also Suso's *Autobiography* (mentioned in Chapter IX).

resulting, after long effort, in a sudden relaxing, an intensity and warmth:

> And though my exercises and troubles were very great yet they were not so continual but that I had some intermissions, and was sometimes brought into such a heavenly joy that I thought I had been in Abraham's bosom. . . .[10]

And Fox's 'spiritual combat' resulted in a sudden realization:

> Then the Lord did let me see why there was none upon the earth that could speak to my condition, namely, that I might give him all the glory; for all are concluded in sin, and shut-up in unbelief as I had been, that Jesus Christ might have the pre-eminence. . . .[11]

Translating this out of its religious terminology into the language of the Existentialist Outsider, we can see that when Fox reached some kind of internal resolution of his Outsider problems, he felt glad that he had not been tempted to resolve them easily by accepting other people, or some easy creed or faith. 'That he might give God all the glory', 'that Jesus Christ might have pre-eminence', . . . even if these terms mean nothing to us, it is obvious that they have some psychological counterpart, some meaning that *is* relevant to the Outsider. It is not so far from Steppenwolf's recognition that he must 'traverse, not once more but often, the hell of his inner being', and even in this term 'the *hell* of his inner being', we have an acknowledgement of the reality of this internal enemy. Fox, like Steppenwolf, like Van Gogh and Nijinsky and Sartre's hero, has moments when all is supremely well, when he can say *yes* to everything, even to the terror of his inner conflict. And these moments are common to most poets and artists, as well as to religious men like Fox. Rilke, in the direct Nietzschean tradition, spoke of 'to praise in spite of' (*dennoch preisen*), and began the greatest of his ten Elegies:

> May I, emerging at last from this terrible insight
> Burst into jubilant praise to assenting angels. . . .[12]

All this can help us to understand what was going on in Fox's heart of hearts, what processes are described, under this terminology that in so many ways means less to us than to Fox's contemporaries, and yet which can, in all important respects, mean even more if we can grasp its inner meaning. What we can say, without fear of misrepresenting Fox, is that these struggles were of the same nature as those of Lawrence, Van Gogh, Nietzsche: that when he spoke of 'inner torments', he meant that same striving for self-expression, like a drowning man gasping for air, and that same view of the world's terror and misery that Rilke called his *grimmige Einsicht*, terrible insight. And for Fox, just as for Ivan Karamazov, the temptation was to give God back his entrance ticket.

At this point we enter into that difficulty that I spoke of at the end of the section on Nijinsky: the difficulty of telling how far an Outsider has really solved the problem, and how far he has compromised. As we read Fox's *Journal*, trying to understand what was happening to him in the terms of the Barbusse Outsider, the difficulties increase. All this torment we can understand; but passages like the following are more difficult:

> My desires after the Lord grew stronger, and zeal in the pure knowledge of God and of Christ alone, without the help of any man, book or writing. For though I read the scriptures that spoke of Christ and of God, yet I knew him not by revelation. . . .
>
> And I found there were two thirsts in me: the one after the creatures, to have gotten help and strength there, and the other after the Lord the creator and his son Jesus Christ. . . .[13]

What exactly does he mean by 'the Lord the creator and his son'? Let us dismiss at once the notion that he believed in them as a child believes in fairies, or that they may have represented vague religious emotions as Finn Macool represents vague patriotic emotions to an Irishman. Fox was an Outsider, and we know enough about Outsiders to know that his symbols usually correspond to a psychological reality. Besides, Fox's 'thirst after the creatures' is common to all Outsiders; we can recall that desire of Henry James the elder to call his wife when he felt the presence of something 'evil' in the room.* Now James turned back to 'the creatures' as his salvation: his whole solution is contained in the title of his book: *Society, the Redeemed Form of Man.* Fox's phrase would seem to intimate—and we must be very cautious about this—that he can believe in some solution quite apart from other men, quite apart from *outside sources.* He seems to mean that he does not intend to change his relation to society, or to change society's relation to him; he intends, it would seem, to change only his relation to his 'inner-self'. Fox would no doubt grow impatient if he could overhear this hair-splitting, and say roundly that he intended to do nothing of the sort, that he intended to have done with relations with men and establish a direct relation with God. ('And does not the soul, sighing after such fictions, commit fornication against thee?' St. Augustine writes, considering the years in which he cared more about human beings than about God.) But in that case, what is a 'relation with God' if not a synonym for complete self-expression? ('No man has ever achieved complete self-realization', Hesse wrote.) Self-expression is impossible in relation with other men; their self-expression interferes with it. The greatest heights of self-expression—in poetry, music, painting—are achieved by men who are supremely alone. And it is for this reason that the idea of 'the beatific vision' is easier for the artist to grasp than for anyone else. He has only to imagine his moment of 'greatest aloneness' intensified to a point where it would fill up his life and make all other relations impossible or unnecessary. They never are, of course, for the artist; his moments of highest inspiration leave him glad enough to get back to people, but at least he knows something of that complete independence of other human beings the theoretical existence of which most people prefer to doubt.

What Fox knew was that he could achieve moments when things that were going on inside him became so absorbingly interesting that he forgot everything else. And he also discovered that when he emerged from these states of watching his own interior mechanism, he was no longer the same person.

* It is interesting to contrast this with a passage in the younger Henry James's novel of 'psychological evil', *The Turn of the Screw,* where James speaks of the child who wakes up to see a ghost in the room, who, terrified, wakes up her governess for protection; but the governess is as terror-stricken as the child and can give no comfort. Both, in this symbolic situation, are in the same position as James's father and brother in their 'vastations'—utterly alone.

This, of course, is nothing so strange; anyone can notice the same phenomenon when he comes out of a theatre or concert or cinema, having been completely taken 'out of himself'. No one would expect to pass through an intense emotional experience and not feel 'a different person' afterwards. But in a cinema, you only pass out of your own life into other people's; you learn nothing new about yourself; hence the change, the mental relaxation, wrought by it can hardly be expected to last for more than a few hours. There is nothing to hold it in place. It would be a different matter if the film had shown you things about yourself that you had never realized before; told you that you were capable of things that you wouldn't have dreamed of attempting; pointed out that all your conceptions of yourself and everybody else were based on misunderstandings, and that you had only to shake off these conceptions to begin to live for the first time.

And this is what happened to Fox after three years of wandering up and down the country, in constant spiritual conflict. He began to see visions and hear voices; or perhaps it would be truer to say that he went through emotional experiences that could only be expressed by speaking of visions and voices:

> And I saw the mountains burning up and the rubbish, and the rough and crooked ways and places made smooth and plain that the Lord might come into his tabernacle. *These things are to be found in man's heart* . . .[14]

His Outsider's insight, as far as other people were concerned, was unabatedly keen:

> And I saw Professors and priests and people were whole and at ease in that condition that was my misery, and they loved that which I would have been rid of . . . their minds are in bondage. And they are brittle and changeable, and tossed up and down with windy doctrines and thoughts. . . .[15]

But now he felt he knew the way to cease to be an Outsider. Or rather, he knew how to cease to be miserable as an Outsider; for he felt by this time that to be an Outsider means to be able to perceive the corruption and delusions of 'the world', and that there can be no way *back* out of that condition: only a forward way. It meant telling the world, as loudly and as frequently as possible, that it was corrupt and deluded, that, to make no bones about it, it was damned.

For Fox, one of the chief enemies was the Church. This is often so with spiritual reformers. They may be intellectual men who find that the saints and mystics are kindred spirits, and who are therefore happy to belong to the same organization. There are others who can only see that the 'visible Church' is represented by men who are neither devout nor strong-willed, and who can therefore see no good in it. It is usually the intellectual spiritual reformers who can reconcile themselves with the Church: Newman, Hulme, Mr. Eliot. George Fox detested it and made it one of his chief targets. Tramping from town to town, wearing leather breeches for hard wear, he stood up in the market-place and preached his fiery message. He got into the habit of interrupting clergymen in Church, a proceeding that was not without physical hazards:

> But the people fell upon me in a great rage, struck me down and almost stifled and smothered me, and I was cruelly beaten and bruised by them, and their hands, Bibles and sticks. Then they haled me out, though I was hardly able to stand, and put me into the stocks, where I sat for some hours; and they brought dog whips and horse whips. . . .¹⁶

This sort of entry is a commonplace in the *Journal*; we get the impression that Fox enjoyed the beatings; they proved his toughness to himself, and gained him sympathizers and admirers.

His astounding success as a preacher must remain a mystery to our generation. There must have been 'something about him' that struck home to his listener's hearts, or perhaps it was simply that the 'dry souls' were there as tinder to his convictions. Anyone who has ever wandered around Hyde Park on a Sunday afternoon will understand what a hopeless business preaching can be; how men who are absolutely chock-full of conviction and fire can fail to arouse the slightest enthusiasm from a crowd. But Fox collected followers who were willing to go to prison for him, willing to undergo persecution from the government and the clergy and their fellow-townspeople, simply to declare themselves 'friends', to declare that they looked to their 'inner light' rather than to the church for guidance.

The rest of the story is no longer an Outsider's story; it is the story of a religious movement that belongs to history. Fox had ceased to be a Barbusse-type Outsider, a man-on-his-own in a world that did not understand him, and had become a leader of a movement that soon became thousands strong. He had accepted his 'Outsider-ishness', not as a symptom of some strange disease, but as a sign that his healthy soul was being suffocated in a world of trivial, shallow, corrupted fools. From then on, there was no more trouble. He was like a ship that had been sailing hopelessly lop-sided, shipping water, and now he had shifted his ballast and rearranged his cargo, and the whole bulk righted itself in the water. It was plain sailing henceforward. And he states:

> The pure and perfect law of God is over the flesh to keep it and its works, which are not perfect, under, by the perfect law; and the law of God that is perfect answers the perfect principle in everyone.[17]

If we look at these words in the light of what has gone before, and don't allow the words 'law of God' to put us off, we can see in this credo the Outsider's attempt to explain what has happened in him. We may, if we find his terminology old-fashioned, want to substitute our own expressions but there can be no doubt about the accuracy of his gist. There was a dynamo inside him, and while that dynamo was converted to driving the unimportant needs of the flesh—a full belly and social security—his greater needs starved. He calls these greater needs 'the perfect principle of God', and whether we like the words or not, our examination of the Outsider can have left us in no doubt whatever about their existence. He who finds a 'definitive act' to express the 'principle of God' is acting in accordance with the Law of God. As to this law, Fox adds grimly: 'He that can receive it, let him.' And the others; well, the Outsider has never known quite what to do about the others. No doubt if Fox had ever been in the position of the Grand Inquisitor, he might have been driven to the Grand Inquisitor's answer: bread and amusements and Divine

Authority. As it happened, Fox never had to face this problem, and he spent his life in the assured faith that everyone could receive the full burden of freedom and self-determination. His practice of this type of spiritual anarchism was not unsuccessful. Like Christ, he preached the doctrine that every man is responsible for his own salvation, and that he'd better look to it and do something about it. He was not a great psychologist, like Pascal and Newman, to ask himself difficult questions such as: *What degree* of self-knowledge must a man attain before he can be considered saved? (That is a question that usually leads to Hesse's answer: No man has ever achieved salvation.) His doctrine was robust and common-sensible, like Yeats's salvationist who told his street-corner audience 'The Kingdom of God is within you, and it would take a big pill to get it out.' He felt that urging people to a higher level of personal conduct was a valid method of 'saving them'. His aim, the aim he set before his followers, was not to achieve heaven after death, but to feel certainty of the presence of God in this life, just as he had.

He reasoned like this: What is wrong with the 'unredeemed' man? Well, he is lazy, he lacks high ideals, he cannot see beyond tomorrow. What, therefore, is his salvation? Not to be afraid of aiming high, not to be afraid of feeling that the mantle of all the poets and prophets who ever lived has descended on his shoulders, his alone; that upon him depends the future state of all the race. When Fox accepted this for himself, he ceased to be a miserable Outsider and became a great leader. He advised everyone to try the same remedy. But surely, one could object, all men are not Outsiders? Nonsense, Fox would say, let any man open his eyes to the world he lives in, and he'll become an Outsider immediately. He will begin by thinking he sees 'too deep and too much'; he will end by realizing that you cannot see too deep and too much.

This is obviously another way of saying (with Novalis) 'All men could be men of genius if they weren't so lazy': a doubtful and difficult proposition, fraught with difficulties. Because the answer is that it may have been true for Novalis, and for Nietzsche; it may happen to be true for me and for you because we both happen to be men of genius; but to say it is always true for everybody is a different thing. And the same goes for salvation and holiness. If salvation means self-knowledge, then it looks as if most men are predestinately damned.

Let us, at the risk of forgetting Fox, digress for a moment to take a closer look at this question of self-knowledge. The world's history is full of men who, by sheer spiritual force, escaped one set of circumstances and moved into another and higher set. This happens most frequently in the field of the arts, especially literature. A modern example would be D. H. Lawrence, who was born in the Nottingham coal country, son of a miner. If Lawrence had accepted the circumstances of his birth as the inevitable boundaries of himself (as most of us do) he would have become a coal-miner, or perhaps (being delicate) a clerk in an office or a schoolteacher. His struggles for self-expression that eventually produced *Sons and Lovers* were nothing less than a course in self-knowledge.

And this is true of many writers. The exploration of oneself is usually also an exploration of the world at large, of other writers, a process of comparison of oneself with others, discoveries of kinships, gradual illumination of one's own potentialities. In the same way, Dickens would have remained in a blacking factory, Shaw in a Dublin office, Wells in a draper's shop, Rilke in the Prussian Army, except for that persistent desire towards self-discovery that made them all into major writers and intellectual driving-forces in their age. Yet can we say that any of these men ultimately 'realized themselves'? No: Rilke was a hypochondriac; Wells was a political witch-doctor, full of quack remedies for the age; Dickens a sentimentalist who helped to poison our language, and Shaw—perhaps the greatest of the four—even Shaw became a complacent, self-satisfied old man.

So how can we speak of ultimate self-knowledge, Ultimate Salvation? D. H. Lawrence saved himself from becoming an overworked schoolteacher only to become, in the course of ten years or so, the irritating self-worshipper who wrote *Kangaroo* and *Lady Chatterley's Lover*. And this comment is not just wanton sniping at a very great writer. There is an immense problem there. Let any readers who fancy their psychological insight try reading the lives of the five men I have just mentioned, and then try, as a sort of spiritual crossword puzzle, to work out how they would have lived the same lives, given the same circumstances. Let them recognize that all these men came to suffer from a lack of self-criticism that caused a deterioration of their 'inspiration', and then ask: 'How could it have been avoided?' They will realize that there is no danger to self-knowledge so great as being universally accepted as a spiritual leader.

And this point carries us back naturally to George Fox. How far does the history of Fox's life present us with a final, convincing solution of the Outsider's problems? We must admit, it doesn't. His *Journal* can move us, even inspire us in places, but beyond a certain point, there is a sense of anticlimax. Fox wasted himself fighting the stupidities of his age. The Quaker movement, admittedly, was a fine and valuable thing. But is that all? Let us recall Evan Strowde, in Chapter II, for a moment:

> Strowde: Save me from the illusion of power! I once had a glimpse—and I thank you for it, my dear—of a power that is in me. But that won't answer any call.
> Joan: Not even that of a good cause?
> Strowde: Excellent causes abound. They are served—as they are—by eminent prigs making a fine parade, by little minds waiting for what's to happen next. Track such men down . . . search for their strength, which is not to be borrowed or bargained for . . . it must spring from the secret life.

Well, we can see that Fox made a better show than Strowde, tracking his 'inner powers' to the roots, and harnessing them to action. Fox refused second-bests, that 'devil's own second-best', and made himself into a great man. But what then?

It looks an unanswerable question, and we had better pass over it for the moment. When the Outsider's problems seem to lead to an impasse, the best thing is to go back and try another approach. If Fox had ended his life being taken up in a fiery chariot, like Elijah, we would probably still feel that he was ultimately a failure, like all other Outsiders. Or are they? Meursault realized that 'I had been happy, and I was happy still'. But what is the use of being happy if you don't realize it until you are about to die?

Fox was better off than the Barbusse Outsider or the beetle-man. He had made an 'attempt to gain control'. He was better off, in a way, than Van Gogh or Lawrence, for his attempt led to more success than theirs.

But in what sense was he not successful?

Strowde has pointed us in the direction of the answer. Illusion. Fox accepted the world as it appears. He did not accept the common moral interpretation, but he adopted the common metaphysical interpretation. Reality is what it seems to be.

Let us cast our minds back to Nietzsche for a moment, Nietzsche at twenty, discovering a tattered volume in a Leipzig bookshop, and reading it through almost immediately: Schopenhauer's *Welt als Wille und Vorstellung*, 'The World as Will and Appearance'.

> ... here there gazed at me the full, unbiased eye of art ... here I saw a mirror in which I observed the world, life and my own soul in frightful grandeur. ... [18]

Schopenhauer made Nietzsche aware of something that, as a poet *and an Outsider*, he had been subconsciously aware of for a long time: that the world is not the human bourgeois surface it presents. It is Will, and it is delusion. Schopenhauer was fond of borrowing a phrase from the Upanishads and calling it *Maya*, illusion. This is the view of the Vedantic philosophy: that the world is an appearance of the absolute Brahman, which is supreme and characterless. The Christian religion has its counterpart of this belief when it says: God is everything. But it is one thing to say it because it is in your catechism, another to see it or feel it because you happen to be an Outsider.

The Outsiders I dealt with in the first chapter had that in common, an instinct that made them doubt the 'reality' of the bourgeois world (I call it this for want of a better word; in practice, I mean the world as it appears to the human social animal). All of the meaning of this attitude is compressed in De Lisle Adam's 'As for living, our servants will do that for us'. It means that the human personality is conceived almost as an enemy; when it comes into contact with 'the world', it tells the soul lies, lies about itself and its relation to other people. Left to himself, in solitude, meditation, study, Axel believes that his soul establishes its true relation with the world. As soon as he begins to *live*, the falsehood begins. 'He wanted to meet in the real world the unsubstantial image that his soul so constantly beheld', Joyce wrote of Dedalus. So do all Outsiders. So did Fox, in those early days of wandering. But did he ever meet it? Did he create it with the power of his mind over other men?

Judging him by the Outsider's stern criterion, there is nothing for it but to answer: No. He showed a way, an approach. He showed that there is no point in getting neurotic and defeatist about it, and deciding, like Schopenhauer, that the world and the spirit are at eternal, perpetual, unresolvable loggerheads. The *Journal* is a more inspiring document than the *Welt als Wille und Vorstellung*. 'But not psychologically *truer*,' the Outsider might urge. But even that will not hold. The sense of the world as Will and delusion is as strong in the early pages of the *Journal* as in Schopenhauer. Only later, there is a sense that Fox had missed the final solution, a sense that brute reality ('stubborn, unreduceable fact', James calls it) has got the upper hand. We suspect that Fox became a little uncritically self-assertive. There was the unpleasant James Nayler affair, for instance.

Nayler was Fox's right-hand man, young, good-looking, a spell-binding orator, second only to Fox in authority in the movement. But he was a far more imaginative man than Fox, and he allowed two women disciples to persuade him that he was the Messiah, and that he had been sent to announce the more-or-less immediate arrival of the Day of Judgement. He allowed himself to be led (in a state of fever) into Bristol, riding on a donkey, and preceded by the two women disciples crying, 'Holy, holy, holy.' When the police gathered their wits together, they arrested Nayler and charged him with blasphemy. A trial followed, in which Nayler was asked: 'Do you claim to be the Son of God,' and replied: 'I am, and so is everybody.' But the judges were not to be put off by such subtle theological points, and Nayler was duly sentenced. He was to be publicly whipped in London and Bristol, to be branded on the forehead with B for blasphemer, and to have his tongue bored through with a hot iron. Everyone was appalled by the savagery of the sentence, even non-Quaker-sympathizers. But Fox was not. He was mainly irritated by Nayler's silly behaviour, and the harm it did to the movement. He refused to listen to the pleas of Friends who asked him to stand by Nayler; he ignored

Nayler's message asking him to visit him in prison (where, even after the whipping and branding, Nayler was still treated with cruelty). Finally, he wrote Nayler a letter, reproving him for accusing him (Fox) of jealousy and telling him: 'There is no pardon for you in this. . . .' Nayler was kept in jail for three years, being released in September, 1659. He died a year later, after being attacked by robbers on a journey to the North.

Fox's part in this affair is not so inhuman as it appears at first sight. He showed the same stern devotion to his principles that he had often shown before hostile judges, and he refused to falsify the religious position that he had spent his life making so clear, by giving his support to a man who *had* falsified it. As a leader, his conduct was as justifiable as that of any statesman who allows expediency to rule his personal feelings. But for the Outsider, the horror of the situation is that Fox should ever have been forced into that kind of position. He feels that, somehow, the real Outsider should be concerned with nothing except human psychology, with discriminating between the world as Will and the world as Delusion. All this business is horribly irrelevant. How could any Outsider get himself mixed up with such tomfoolery?

Perhaps it would be fairer to Fox to ask: How could he have avoided it? Philosophers will tell you that if you have a standard in your head, there must be somewhere a reality or idea that corresponds to that standard. What is this standard by which we are judging Fox?

It is difficult to formulate, because we are not certain about our ultimates. Ask the Outsider what he ultimately wants, and he will admit he doesn't know. Why? Because he wants it instinctively, and it is not always possible to tell what your instincts are driving towards. Young W. B. Yeats wanted a fairy land where 'the lonely of heart is withered away'. Dowson and Thompson and Beddoes were 'half in love with easeful death':

> They are not long, the days of wine and roses
> Out of a misty dream
> Our path emerges for a while, then closes
> Within a dream.[19]

Axel wanted to live in imagination alone, in a castle on the Rhine, with volumes on Hermetic philosophy, and Yeats even made preliminary steps to put the idea into practice, with his plans for a brotherhood of poets who would live in a 'Castle on the Rock' at Lough Kay in Rosscommon:

> I planned a mystical order that should buy or hire the castle, and keep it as a place where its members could retire for a while for contemplation, and where we might establish mysteries like those of Eleusis or Samothrace. . . . I had an unshakeable conviction that invisible gates would open, as they opened for Blake, as they opened for Swedenborg, as they opened for Boehme, and that this philosophy would find its manuals of devotion in all imaginative literature. . . . *

This idea of Yeats's is persistently an Outsider-ideal, persistent even in unromantic Outsiders: solitude, retreat, the attempt to order a small corner of the 'devil-ridden chaos' to one's own satisfaction. A Marxist critic would snap: Escapism; and no doubt he would not be entirely wrong, but let us look closer. The real difference between the Marxian and the romantic Outsider is that one would like to bring heaven down to earth, the other dreams of raising earth up to heaven. To the Outsider, the Marxian seems hopelessly short-sighted in his requirements for a heaven on earth; his notions seem to be based on a total failure to understand human psychology. (Aldous Huxley's *Brave New World* and Zamyatin's *We* are typical expressions of Outsider criticism of social idealism.)** Now George Fox combined the practical-mindedness of the Marxian with the Outsider's high standard for a 'heaven on earth', and in so far as he was practical-minded, he failed to penetrate to the bottom of the Outsider's ideal. What did he achieve? He founded the Society of Friends, a very fine thing in itself, but lacking the wearing-quality of older established sects; he conquered his Outsider's sense of exile. And there we have it! As a religious teacher, *he accepted himself and the world*, and no Outsider can afford to do this. He accepted an essentially optimistic philosophy.

* *The Trembling of the Veil*, Book III.
** It is interesting to note that Zamyatin's novel, published in Russia in 1927, has been largely drawn upon by George Orwell in his *Nineteen Eighty-Four*; so largely, it seems to me, that it is hardly conceivable that Orwell would have published his novel if an English translation of Zamyatin's novel had existed at the time. An American edition has existed for some years, but this is still unobtainable in England.

When all the Friends had got it into their heads that they had an 'inner light', they felt that evil had been finally overcome; all that was necessary was to act according to the 'inner light'. The Enemy was minimized. The evil in this was the same as in all sects that set out to give their followers the feeling that they have a monopoly of divine benevolence. For the Outsider, the best place to watch the eternal comedy of human beings deluding themselves (apart from the Jehovah's Witness and the Christian Scientist meetings), is a Quaker congregation on a Sunday evening. The distinction between reality and unreality is lost; neither is it recognized that good is traditionally associated with the real, evil with the unreal; human beings accept themselves and their personalities with no sense of bondage, for all have an 'inner light', and the inner light can do no wrong. This criticism may seem unduly harsh, but it must be remembered that we are looking at these things from the Outsider's point of view, and it is Roquentin who condemns men who think their existence is necessary as *salauds*. The Outsider's business is to discriminate between real and unreal, necessary and unnecessary. Where Fox fell short of this standard, we must not hesitate to condemn him; the problem is difficult enough without blurring the lines with compromise.

Fox, then, was too much the man of action; his method of trying to persuade all men to become Outsiders was too unsophisticated. It failed to do justice to the complexity of the problem. Consequently, he failed to solve it.

Before we leave Fox, we should acknowledge the greatness of his effort to solve the Outsider's problems; he is perhaps England's major religious teacher, and his faith is an Outsider's faith. Under different circumstances, in another age, he might have been the founder of a new religion instead of a new sect, and the founders of the great religions did not compromise less than Fox, in trying to make the Outsider's solution valid for everybody.

Fox began to solve his own Outsider problem when he accepted his destiny as a prophet. The Outsider is primarily a critic, and if a critic feels deeply enough about what he is criticizing, he becomes a prophet.

William Blake prefaced his epic poem 'Milton' with a quotation from the Book of Numbers: 'Would to God that all

the Lord's people were prophets.' This is a sentiment that Fox
heartily endorsed. Yet Fox made it his business to try to make
all the Lord's people into prophets, and his approach was so
popular that he had a great deal of success. Blake, on the other
hand, spent his life in complete obscurity; the prophetic note
never left his voice, but he never spoke from the popular
pulpit. During his lifetime, he was considered a madman and a
crank; even his friends would have refused to vouch for his
genius. Blake didn't worry; he worked on steadily, producing his
unpopular paintings and his even less popular epic poems,
living as best he could. He took the healthy view of the Greek
Stoic, that he lacked nothing that he really needed:

> I have mental joy and mental health
> And mental friends and mental wealth
> I've a wife I love and that loves me
> I've all but riches bodily.[20]

Blake's struggle was very like Nietzsche's; and the re-
semblances between the two men's way of seeing the world are
astonishing, considering the eighty years between their births
that made Blake a contemporary of Dr. Johnson, and Nietzsche
of Dostoevsky. Blake, at all events, was lucky in having a wife
to share his struggle, a completely docile girl who always
regarded her husband as a great man. Such a wife might have
saved Nietzsche's sanity.

Fame, Blake believed, is unnecessary to the man of genius.
Man is born alone and he dies alone. If he allows his social
relations to delude him into forgetting his fundamental loneliness, he is living in a fool's paradise. From the beginning he
was preoccupied with the problem of Solipsism, that you cannot
be certain of the existence of anything or anybody except
yourself:

> Nought loves another as itself
> Nor venerates another so
> Nor is it possible to thought
> A greater than itself to know.[21]

This is Ivan Karamazov's starting-point; in the face of it,
what meaning has the Christian idea of loving your neighbour

as yourself, or a love of God that could lead Abraham to sacrifice Isaac? Blake was determined to get his foundations right before he began, and if getting his foundations right meant attacking the 'fundamentals' of religion, well, so much the worse for the fundamentals. He states his principle in the opening paragraph of one of his earliest works:

As the true method of knowledge is experiment, the true faculty of knowing must be the faculty that experiences.[22]

This is scientific common sense; it would not be out of place in a Secular Society pamphlet. But in the next paragraph, Blake plunges into his own mysticism:

... the poetic genius is the true man, and that the body, or outward form of man, is derived from the poetic genius. Likewise, the forms of all things are derived from their genius, which by the ancients was called Angel and Spirit and Demon.

The poetic genius is everywhere called the spirit of prophecy.

Again, the emphasis on prophecy. We can see that Ivan's Grand Inquisitor would have felt inclined to add Blake to his bonfire as well as George Fox and Christ.

I have already quoted passages that show Blake thinking along Nietzschean lines—'Energy is eternal delight'; that is, not towards a Christian ethic that proclaims: Blessed are the poor in spirit, but towards a vitalist ethic that exalts the man of genius. Before the end of this book, we shall have to analyse these terms 'Christian' and 'vitalist', but at this point, I should only like to observe that vitalism is not necessarily a philosophy that regards life as the be-all and end-all, to which all other moral values are subservient. It may be only a way of deriving those values or of renewing them. When Aristotle wrote: 'Not to be born is the best thing, and death is better than life'; he expressed the view that can be said to lie at one extreme of religion. At the other extreme is vitalism; Kirilov's 'everything is good' (note that Kirilov professed himself an atheist). In this sense, vitalism can be regarded as an antinomian reaction:

The worship of God is: Honouring his gifts in other men, each according to his genius, and loving the greatest men best . . .[23]

and Blake ends a demonstration that Jesus broke all the ten commandments with the statement:

I tell you, no virtue can exist without breaking these ten commandments. Jesus was all virtue, and acted from impulse and not from rules.[24]

We can see in such a statement the beginnings of a defence of Raskolnikov and Stavrogin. All impulse is good. 'Energy is eternal delight.' In 'Jerusalem', Blake wrote—

When thought is closed in caves
Then love shall show its root in deepest Hell. . . .[25]

In other words, when self-expression is denied, then energy will find its outlet in crime or violence. Repeatedly in his work, Blake shows indifference to moral issues when self-expression is at stake: 'Rather murder an infant in its cradle than nurse unsatisfied desire',

That he who will not defend truth may be compelled to defend a lie . . .
That enthusiasm and life shall not cease.[26]

In many other ways Blake was an iconoclast; on the subject of sex, for instance. A century and a half before D. H. Lawrence wrote *Lady Chatterley's Lover*, Blake had preached that sex can raise man to visionary insight. He also preaches that the way to overcome vices is to give them full self-expression; the result will be virtue:

> But Covet was poured full
> Envy fed with fat of lambs
> Wrath with Lion's gore
> Wantonness lulled to sleep
> With the virgin's lute
> Or sated with her love

Til Covet broke his locks and bars
And slept with open doors
Envy sung at the rich man's feast
Wrath was followed up and down
By a little ewe lamb
And wantonness on his own true love
Begot a giant race.[27]
('Book of Los', IV and V.)

There is even a tradition that Blake was so confirmed in his opinion of the senses' fundamental innocence that he proposed to go to bed with his wife's maid, an arrangement that Mrs. Blake refused to permit. But the proposal had been in accord with his teaching in the Prophetic Books. In 'Visions of the Daughters of Albion', he makes his heroine promise her husband (Theotormon):

. . . to catch for thee girls of mild silver or of furious gold
I'll lie beside thee on a bank and view their wanton play
In lovely copulation, bliss on bliss, with Theotormon.[28]

This was not mere libertinism; it was a part of Blake's religious doctrine. He makes Oothoon ask:

How can one joy absorb another? Are not different joys
Holy, eternal, infinite? and each joy is a love.

The question that must be asked is obviously: What was the end of Blake's system? From these extracts, it seems to have a suspicious smell of Rousseau's 'back to Nature' doctrine.

The end, in a word, was Vision, Yea-saying. This was Blake's ultimate, just as it was Nietzsche's and Rilke's. 'To praise in spite of', *dennoch preisen*.

For, like Van Gogh and Nietzsche after him, Blake had had moments when he had seen the world as entirely positive, entirely good. Blake also was a painter. Van Gogh had painted cornfields so that they seemed to blaze upward; he painted self-portraits against the same distorted, brilliant background, as if he could not even look at his own face in a mirror without all his vital energies breaking loose and trying to flow out of his paint-brush. Blake's outlook was the same, but his training was different; he knew how to express vital energy only in two ways: through the human form, and through colour. He preferred water-colours because they are less heavy than oils, and he painted Michelangelesque men and women against vivid backgrounds of light. Unfortunately, Blake was not a great draughtsman like Michelangelo, nor did he know as much about the effects of light as Turner or Monet. His painting is often vivid and electrifying, but it is too light-weight to be really great, in the way that Van Gogh's painting is great. There is not the intensity.*

Nevertheless, the paintings are valuable as a part of Blake's exposition of his 'world view' in a way that Van Gogh's are not.

Van Gogh's mysticism was all unconscious, and there is no exposition of it in his prose. Blake made all of his work, as well as his life, a systematic exposition of his mysticism.

At this point, it would not be unreasonable to ask: What exactly do we mean by mysticism? And, in fact, there could be no better point at which to ask it, for Blake can provide us with the answer.

Mysticism is derived from the Greek μύειν, to shut the eyes: exactly what Blake meant by it. 'Seeing' is not simply using the eyes. The retina of the eye records impressions which are carried to the brain, which interprets them. If the brain becomes lazy and ceases to interpret the impressions that the eye carries to it, one literally ceases to see. The experience is familiar to everyone. You are reading a book, and you are tired; your mind begins to drift, and suddenly you realize you have read half a page without its meaning anything to you. Your eyes have read it, but your brain failed to interpret it; therefore, to all intents and purposes, you have not read it. It is the same with seeing. You are on a long train journey; at the beginning of the journey you watch the fields passing with interest; the new sights stimulate all kinds of thoughts and impressions; at the end of the journey, you are almost asleep; nothing arouses the interest, nothing makes an impression. You are no longer seeing.

Rimbaud grasped the essence of this experience when he wrote to a friend: 'The poet should be a visionary; one should

---

* This, of course, is arguable, and I do not pretend that it is any more than a personal opinion.

make oneself a visionary. . . .' 'One makes oneself a visionary by a long, immense, ordered derangement of the senses.' He claimed that he had trained himself to visual hallucinations, to see 'a mosque instead of a factory . . . calashes on the roads of the sky, a drawing-room at the bottom of a lake'. Rimbaud had realized that seeing is an affair of the brain, and the brain can be affected by the will. Man's own inner being orders what he sees.

Rimbaud's 'ordered derangement of the senses' may strike us as being rather silly, or at least rather youthful, but it is not entirely so. Rimbaud was not advocating drug-taking or alcohol; he was advocating the use of the Will. He set out to use his Will-power on the senses. The result was a sharpening, an intensifying, a cleansing of the senses, that altered everything he saw. He was seeing differently; he was seeing visions.

I have already spoken of that cleansing of the senses in connexion with Lawrence. This is Blake's most important utterance on it:

> The ancient tradition that the world will be consumed by fire at the end of six thousand years, is true, as I have heard from Hell.
>
> For the cherub with his flaming sword is hereby commanded to leave his guard at the tree of life; and when he does, the whole creation will be consumed and appear infinite and holy, whereas it now appears finite and corrupt. This will come to pass by an improvement of sensual enjoyment.
>
> But first, the notion that man has a body distinct from his soul is to be expunged, this I shall do by printing in the infernal method, by corrosives, which in Hell are salutary and medicinal, melting apparent surfaces away and displaying the infinite that was hid.
>
> If the doors of perception were cleansed, everything would appear to man as it is, infinite.
>
> For man has closed himself up, til he sees all things thro' chinks of his cavern.[29]

This can be supplemented by another quotation from the introduction to 'Europe':

Five windows light the caverned man; through one he breathes
   the air,
Thro' one hears music of the spheres; through one the eternal
   vine
Flourishes that he may receive the grapes; thro' one can look
And see small portions of the eternal world which ever groweth,
Thro' one himself pass out what time he please; but he will not
For stolen joys are sweet, and bread eaten in secret pleasant![30]

   This is clear enough; Blake claims that the outside world is
infinite and eternal, and would appear so to everyone if everyone could see things without the grime on their windows of
perception. No doubt if Blake could have lived long enough to
see Van Gogh's 'Starry Night' or the 'Road at Dusk with
Cypresses', he would have said without hesitation: This man
sees things as they are.
   There is another great passage in 'Visions of the Daughters
of Albion' where Blake makes clear what happens when the
brain refuses to do its work of interpretation, or what happens
when something affects it to warp its interpretations:

They told me that the night and day were all that I could see
They told me that I had five senses to inclose me up
And they inclosed my brain into a narrow circle
And sunk my heart into the abyss, a red round globe, hot
   burning,
Til all from life I was obliterated and erased.
Instead of morn arises a bright shadow, like an eye
In the eastern cloud; instead of night, a sickly charnel
   house. . . .[31]

   What Blake is intimating here is that the vision of things
as 'infinite and holy' is not an abnormal vision, but the perfectly
normal emotional state. And yet man is not born with such a
vision, and he can live so far from it that he can decide at the
end of his life that 'not to be born is the best thing, and death
is better than life'. Why? Blake cannot say why; he can only
account for it by utilizing the legend of a Fall; by saying, as it
were, 'Men are born like smashed radio sets, and before they can
function properly, they must repair themselves'. (Blake lived
before the machine-age, or no doubt he would have used the

same kind of simile.) In short, he used the legend of Original Sin.

For readers who approach this argument for the first time, the most doubtful part about it is the proposition that men *ought* to see the world like Van Gogh's *Nuit Etoilé* as a matter of course. They may object: 'We agree that man *could* see a starry night that way, but to claim that he *ought* to, perhaps that he *did*, once upon a time, and lost the faculty because he ate an apple from a forbidden tree. . . .' This is reasonable, and it can be answered by saying that the concept of Original Sin does not insist on the Garden of Eden, or even that man did possess the visionary faculty once upon a time and has lost it since; it only insists that the visionary faculty is man's norm. Just as you would not count a man 'normal' if he had a mouth but no voice, or eyes but no sight, so you cannot count him normal if he has a brain but no visionary faculty. Most men live from moment to moment, with no fore-sight or hind-sight. Immediate physical needs occupy all their attention, just as with animals. The average man is distinguished from dogs and cats mainly because he looks farther ahead: he is capable of worrying about his physical needs of six months hence, ten years hence. The dogma of Original Sin insists that man lost his visionary faculty because he spends all his energy thinking about practical things. At least, that is the interpretation that the great religious teachers seem to put on it: Jesus telling the Jews not to waste so much time getting and spending, but to observe the lilies of the field.

Another example might make clearer what I mean by 'visionary faculty'. T. E. Lawrence tells that when he showed the Arabs the portraits of themselves that Kennington painted for *The Seven Pillars*, most of them completely failed to recognize that they were pictures of men; they stared at them, turned them upside-down and sideways, and finally hazarded a guess that one of them represented a camel, because the line of the jaw was shaped like a hump! This seems incomprehensible to us because we have been looking at pictures all our lives. But we must remember that a picture is actually an abstraction of lines and colours, and that it must require a certain mental effort to interpret those lines and colours as a man or a sunset. We make the effort unconsciously, and so are not aware of it. There are some mathematicians who can see the answer to a complex geometrical problem by merely glancing at a diagram;

again, this is because their brains do all the work subconsciously, and can perceive relations where most of us would only see a confusion of lines and angles. *None of our senses would operate if the brain did not do all the work.* If a European can see a sunset on a canvas where a practical-minded Arab can only see a blur of colours, it is not illogical to suppose that a development of the same faculty might lead the practical-minded European to see things where he saw nothing before. And this is the faculty that Blake possessed instinctively, and claimed that all men could possess, if they spent less time being practical, and more time trying to discipline the visionary faculty. Such an injunction is a commonplace in religion:

> My Lord taught my brother and myself to concentrate our attention on the tip of the nose, and as I did this, I began to notice, after three weeks, that my in and out breathing seemed like smoke coming out of a chimney. At the same time, my body and mind became bright internally, and I could see the whole world becoming clear and transparent like a crystal ball. . . . Then my mind became enlightened, and I attained to a state of non-intoxication. . . .[32]

This is a quotation from the Surangama Sutra, a Buddhist scripture, written down about A.D. 100 from a tradition that was probably a great deal older. A hundred similar examples could be chosen from the world's scriptures. All of them point to the same truth: that a discipline of the mind leads to a completely different way of *seeing* the world. Blake, like Nietzsche, only rediscovered something fundamental about human nature. And we can learn from Blake that the 'visionary faculty' is not something you might just happen to have, or something you could catch like the measles, but is the result of a long, rigorous discipline of the senses, a discipline that tries to force the mind in a direction that is completely foreign to its everyday activities, and as different from it as vertical is from horizontal.

Perhaps the simplest approach to Blake, in a section as necessarily short as this, would be to examine his works briefly in chronological order. But first, a reference to some earlier points might be advisable.

In Hesse's *Steppenwolf* and *Demian*, we have a summary of

those problems that Blake must certainly have known from a very early age. There are two worlds; or rather, two distinct ways of looking at the same world, and they can be called (for convenience) the Inspired and the Uninspired. It is the task of the artist to connect them; Steppanwolf bored, irritable, sick, and Steppanwolf touched by music or poetry and made to feel suddenly harmonious, whole; the world of practical things, hard work, dreariness, and the world of art, music, intellectual pleasure. But where do the two worlds meet? Certain men are acutely susceptible to this second world, to harmony in art or nature, and we say of these men that they are 'sensitive', 'artistic', etc. But they will tell you that art is one thing, living another. There is a poignant section in Thomas Mann's *Buddenbrooks* that describes the young Hanno Buddenbrooks going to a performance of *Lohengrin*, and how, the next morning, he gets up to go to school, now hating the world he lives in, the cold dawn, the thin drizzle, the smell of wet garments in the schoolroom. There is the romantic Outsider's problem in essence; and there are the two worlds, the ecstatic, vital world of *Lohengrin* and the dull world of the schoolboy.

Thomas Mann is, like Hesse, a descendant of Novalis and the German Romantics, and the way he states the problem makes the two worlds seem tragically, impossibly distant. But there are other artists and poets who are more optimistic about the relation of the two, who can stand with a foot in both worlds without undue discomfort: Synge, Joyce, Herrick, Shakespeare, Rabelais. And Blake belongs with these men.

His first step, as a poet, was to make a very elementary picture of the two worlds: *The Songs of Innocence*, and *The Songs of Experience*. After this, he set out to treat the problem more complexly in his first long poem, 'The Book of Thel'. Thel, the innocent virgin, is troubled by the problem of death; she questions a lily, a cloud and a worm, and all assure her of the fundamental harmony of the world, the Fatherhood of God. Then she enters the grave (there are signs that Blake added this episode as an afterthought), and is terrified by a voice from her own grave-plot that speaks of the Contra in the universe, the element of discord:

Why cannot the ear be closed to its own destruction
Or the glistening eye to the poison of a smile?[33]

'Thel' is Blake's own version of *Demian*, and its message is the same: Chaos must be faced.

In the poems that Blake engraved after 'Thel', the atmosphere of innocence is gradually dissipated. In 'Visions of the Daughters of Albion', Oothoon is raped, and her husband is possessed by morbid hatred and jealousy at the thought that another man has known her body. (It is interesting to compare this with modern versions of the same situation in D. H. Lawrence's *Shadow in the Rose Garden* and William Faulkner's *Sound and the Fury*.) The greater part of the poem consists of Oothoon's pleas, assuring her husband that innocence is undefilable. It is useless; Theotormon has allowed the emotion to cloud the 'doors of perception'. In him, a version of the Fall has taken place.

In 'America', Blake uses the American Revolution and the freeing of the slaves as symbols of release from the imprisonment of the five senses. The poem contains the tremendous lines:

The times are ended, shadows pass, the morning 'gins to break,
The fiery joy that Urizen perverted to ten commands
What night he led the starry host through the wide wilderness.
That stony law I stamp to dust, and scatter religion abroad
To the four winds as a torn book, and none shall gather the
  leaves. . . .
To renew the fiery joy and burst the stony roof
That pale religious lechery, seeking virginity
May find it in a harlot, and in coarse clad honesty
The undefiled; tho' ravished in her cradle night and morn.
For everything that lives is holy, life delights in life
Because the soul of sweet delight can never be defiled
Fires inwrap the earthly globe, yet man is not consumed,
Amid the lustful fires he walks; his feet become like brass
His knees and thighs like silver, and his breast and head like
  gold.[34]

In 'Europe', he uses woman as a symbol of imprisonment, for the female temperament is literal, practical, down-to-earth.*

---

* Most women writers I know of bear out Blake's verdict. It has always seemed to me that one of the great omissions from world literature is a female *Portrait of the Artist*, a soul history of a sensitive woman. Even men seem unable to write convincingly of women. There is evidence of how it can be done in Jacobsen's portrait of the artist's mother in *Niels Lynne*.

Enitharmon, the female counterpart of Los, the Outsider-principle, cries:

> Go, tell the human race that woman's love is sin
> That an eternal life awaits the worm of sixty winters
> In an allegorical abode where existence hath never come...[35]

The symbolism here is plain enough: literal thinking perverts the inspired truths of religion into superstitions. And Blake's accusation, hurled at the whole world, is that it thinks literally. Blake's particular bugbears were the rationalists and the 'natural-religionists', Gibbon, Voltaire, Rousseau, and the scientists Priestley and Newton. (Modern counterparts of these would be the Secular Society, or thinkers like Dewey and Russell.) Such men, Blake swore, were 'villains and footpads', men subjugated to the woman's literal way of thinking.

In 'Europe', Newton's heresies bring about the Last Judgement (and anyone who will take the trouble to look into Newton's *On the Prophecies* will see why Blake detested him so much); and Los, symbol of imaginative vitality, 'calls all his sons the strife of blood'. Blake, like Shaw after him, toyed with the idea that one day it might be necessary for the 'men of imagination' to shed the blood of the literal-minded who make the world unfit to live in.*

'Europe' is the first of a series of poems that deal with the narrow, literal state of mind, 'single vision and Newton's sleep'. This, Blake believed, was the real enemy. To facilitate his analysis of Outsider problems, he divided man into the same three divisions that we arrived at in Chapter IV: body, heart and intellect, calling them respectively Tharmas, Luvah and Urizen. His major poems, the three epics 'Vala', 'Milton' and

---

* Q.v. Shaw: *Heartbreak House*, Act I:

Captain Shotover: What then is to be done? Are we to be kept forever in the mud by these hogs for whom the universe is nothing but a machine for greasing their bristles and filling their snouts? . . . We must win powers of life and death over them both. I refuse to die until I have invented the means.

Hector: Who are we that we should judge them?

Shotover: Who are they, that they should judge us? Yet they do, unhesitatingly. There is an enmity between our seed and their seed. They know it and act on it, strangling our souls. They believe in themselves. When we believe in ourselves, we shall kill them. . . .

Hector: They are too stupid to use their power. . . .

Shotover: Do not deceive yourself; they do use it. We kill the better half of ourselves every day to propitiate them. The knowledge that these people are there to render all our aspirations barren prevents us having the apirations. . . .

'Jerusalem', deal with the interaction of these three in a series of Apocalyptic scenes, that, on the surface, seem to lack simple coherence. Yet in spite of their confusion, it is in these epic prophecies that we can see Blake's creative thought most clearly at work. All the action takes place *inside* the hero, the Giant Albion (man), as he lies stretched out on the rock of ages. (This method will bring to mind in most readers that other epic of obscurity *Finnegans Wake*, which also takes place in the hero's mind while he lies asleep.) And perhaps the best idea of the import of these poems is contained in the line from 'Milton' (put into the mouth of an ancient bard, and repeated at intervals to drive it home):

Mark well my words—they are of your Eternal Salvation. . . .

It is a line that could be put as an epigraph on the title-page of Blake's Works.

To his three principles, Luvah, Tharmas, Urizen, Blake added a fourth, Los, symbol of the imagination, identified at times with the saviour, Christ. But by 'imagination' Blake did not mean what Milton meant when Satan 'His proud imaginations thus displayed', nor what Schiller meant in his distinction between imagination and fancy; Milton's imagination was primarily a matter of intellect, Schiller's a matter of emotion. Blake's was a complex that involved intellect, emotions and even body. For Blake knew the importance of the body as well as Nietzsche; no poet sings the body so frankly (except perhaps Whitman); for, after all, 'body is only that portion of soul discerned by the five senses'; body has its place in imagination.

And the function of imagination was to look inward. In 'Jerusalem' Blake avowed his intention:

To open the eternal worlds, to open the immortal eyes
Of man Inwards, into the worlds of thought, into Eternity.[36]

Imagination is the instrument of self-knowledge.

But what must be grasped about Blake's conception is that imagination is not purely emotional or intellectual; for Blake, knowledge involved the whole being, body, emotions, intellect.

Los is only a half of Blake's picture of man's inner states. The other half is the strange being called 'the Spectre':

> Each man is in his spectre's power
> Until the arrival of that hour
> When his humanity awakes
> And casts his spectre into the lake. . . . [37]

The Spectre is the dead form. He is static consciousness. Los is kinetic, always pushing, expanding. When life recedes, the limits of its activities seem to be alive, just as the dead body looks like the living one. The Spectre is the dead, conscious part of man that he mistakes for himself, the personality, the habits, *the identity*. 'Man is not of fixed or enduring form' Steppenwolf realized, in a moment of insight. But when man is in 'the Spectre's power' (and most of us are, every day) he sees himself and the whole world as of 'fixed and enduring form'.

Blake has defined the two worlds of Hanno Buddenbrooks and Steppenwolf: one is the world of Los; the other of the Spectre. The Spectre is invisible, like a shadow, but when he has the ascendancy in man, everything is solid, unchangeable, stagnant, unreal.

And now we can begin to see how far Blake has solved the Outsider's problems. His system with its terminology is the only one we have considered so far that provides a skeleton key to every Outsider in this book. Roquentin, Meursault, Lawrence, Krebs, Strowde and Oliver Gauntlett: all are men in 'the Spectre's power', in the stranglehold of their own identity, and they mistake their own stagnation for the world's. The Spectre's mark is Unreality.

Consider the root cause of the Vastation experience in these men; Tolstoy's madman admitting that he could not escape 'the horror' because he carried its source about with him, and that source was himself; Lawrence confessing that 'I did not like the myself I could see and hear', William James's 'panic fear of his own existence'. All point to the accuracy of Blake's diagnosis.

The cause, as T. E. Lawrence realized, lies in the 'thought-riddled nature', in the intellect dominating the other two faculties. Blake symbolized the intellect as Urizen, the 'king of light'. It is Urizen who tries to play dictator over the other two. But man was never intended to be a dictator-state; it makes him lopsided, and if he goes on too long in that condition, something is bound to happen. It is bound to happen even if the dictator happens to be one of those far more genial characters, Luvah and Tharmas, the emotions and the body (and Tharmas is 'the mildest son of Heaven'), for the simple reason that the crises of living demand the active co-operation of intellect, emotions, body, on equal terms.

And now we are back again in the heart of Blake's myth. His longest and most confused epic, 'Vala, or the Four Zoas', is Blake's own way of writing *The Brothers Karamazov*. It is a psychological novel that takes place in the human brain. The hero, the Giant Alvion, dreams the whole poem. It begins at the point where Urizen has tried to seize dictatorship. Tharmas laments:

> Lost, lost, lost are my emanations . . .

i.e. self-expression is now denied to him. ('Emanation' in Blake means a form of self-expression.) In the course of the poem, we watch the confusion that results when one or the other of the faculties takes over completely; symbolically we watch the mutations of the hero Albion—T. E. Lawrence, Nijinsky and Van Gogh, Ivan, Mitya and Alyosha. Urizen is the chief villain always, because Urizen is not merely intellect; he is also personality, identity, the Spectre. As soon as man begins to think, he forms a notion of who he is. If man were entirely body or emotions, he would have no conception of his identity, consequently he could never become unbalanced like Nijinsky, Lawrence, Van Gogh. It is Urizen who starts the trouble. The Bible recounts the same legend when it ascribes the first discord in the universe to Lucifer and his pride. Lucifer is light; consciousness, Urizen.

Yet it is the Outsider's belief that life aims at more life, at higher forms of life, something for which the Superman is an inexact poetic symbol (as Dante's description of the beatific vision is expressed in terms of a poetic symbol); so that, in a sense, Urizen *is* the most important of the three functions. The fall was necessary, as Hesse realized. Urizen must go forward alone. The other two must follow him. And as soon as Urizen has gone forward, the Fall has taken place. Evolution towards God is impossible without a Fall. And it is only by this recognition that the poet can ever come to 'praise in spite of'; for if evil is ultimately discord, unresolvable, then the idea of *dennoch preisen* is a self-contradiction. And yet it must be clearly recognized and underlined that this is *not* the Hegelian 'God's in his heaven, all's right with the world'. Even if the evil is necessary, it remains evil, discord, pain. It remains an Existential fact, not something that proves to be something else when you hold it in the right light. It is as if there were two opposing armies: the Hegelian view holds that peace can be secured by proving that there is really no ground for opposition; in short, they are really friends. The Blakeian view says that the discord is necessary, but it can never be resolved until one army has completely exterminated the other. This is the Existential view, first expressed by Søren Kierkegaard, the Outsider's view and, incidentally, the religious view. The whole difference between the Existentialist and the Hegelian viewpoint is implicit in the comparison between the title of Hegel's book, *The Philosophy of History*, and James Joyce's phrase, 'History is a nightmare from which I am trying to awake' (*Ulysses*, p. 31). Blake provided the Existentialist view with a symbolism and mythology. In Blake's view, harmony is an ultimate aim, but not the primary aim, of life; the primary aim is to live more abundantly at any cost. Harmony can come later.

Blake, then, agrees with Nietzsche, Dostoevsky, Hesse; the way forward leads to more life, more consciousness. Suicide is no answer, nor mind-suicide, nor the idea of 'an allegorical abode where existence hath never come'. Heaven-after-death is irrelevant. The way lies forward, into more life. Van Gogh shot himself and Nietzsche went insane, but Raskolnikov and Mitya Karamazov went through with the terrifying crucifixion of the answer to the Outsider's problems: to accept the ordeal; not death, but 'ever further into guilt, ever deeper into human life', into the ten years' exile, the purgation. Life itself is an exile. The way home is not the way back.

It is unfortunate that lack of space prevents a longer examination of Blake's work. But from the brief survey above, it should be clear that Blake's philosophy began as an Outsider-philosophy, like Fox's, Nietzsche's, Dostoevsky's. And the most important point to emerge from our analysis is the essentially religious nature of Blake's solution. The ideas of original sin, salvation and damnation are the natural outcome of his attempt to face the world as an Outsider.

We can summarize Blake's argument briefly: All men should

possess a 'visionary faculty'. Men do not, because they live wrongly. They live too tensely, under too much strain, 'getting and spending'. But this loss of the visionary faculty is not entirely man's fault, it is partly the fault of the world he lives in, that demands that men should spend a certain amount of their time 'getting and spending' to stay alive.

The visionary faculty comes naturally to all men. When they are relaxed enough, every leaf of every tree in the world, every speck of dust, is a separate world capable of producing infinite pleasure. If these fail to do so, it is man's own fault for wasting his time and energy on trivialities. The ideal is the contemplative poet, the 'sage', who cares about having only enough money and food to keep him alive, and never 'takes thought for the morrow'. This is a way of thought that comes more easily to the Eastern than to the Western mind. Professor Whitehead has acutely observed:

The more we know of Chinese art, Chinese literature, Chinese philosophy of life, the more we admire the heights to which that civilization attained. . . . And yet Chinese science is practically negligible. There is no reason to believe that China, if left to itself, would have ever produced any progress in science. The same may be said of India. . . .*

The reason for this should be obvious enough. The Eastern way of thought is essentially Blake's way. It does not make for a mechanical civilization with atom bombs and electronic brains. Hence Blake's detestation of Newton and the Industrial Revolution. It is difficult for the Western man to think of the word 'contemplative' without instantly thinking: 'dreamy' 'unworldly', 'impractical'. He finds it hard to realize that whole civilizations have made contemplation the basis of their culture, and have, in most respects, been flourishing, prosperous and well-regulated. Blake is a good example of the contemplative temperament. There is nothing of the futile dreamer about him; all his values are clean and clear-cut:

Men are admitted into heaven, not because they have curbed and governed their passions, or have no passions, but because they have cultivated their understandings. The

* *Science and the Modern World*, Chapter I.

treasures of heaven are not negations of passion, but realities of intellect, from which all the passions emanate, uncurbed in their eternal glory. The fool shall not enter into heaven, be he ever so holy.[38]

The culmination of the Western misunderstanding of the contemplative temperament can be seen in the Marxian viewpoint that states: 'I have no use for religion because it's not practical.' It is a failure to grasp the mental attitude that sees religion as completely practical, completely commonsense.

Our civilization has grown steadily closer, in its everyday life, to the Marxian attitude. That is why we are producing Outsiders. Because the Outsider is a man who feels in the Chinese way. His revolt against Western standards takes the form of a sense of their futility, the sense that is expressed in Eliot's 'Hollow Men'. He asks questions about things that all his fellow Westerners take for granted, and his final question tends to be the cry of Bunyan's Pilgrim: What must I do to be saved? It is a cry that springs out of bewilderment. He sees the world as a 'devil-ridden chaos' and he is not sure of his own identity in it. Steppenwolf expresses the sense of sin:

> Every created thing, even the simplest, is already guilty, already multiple. The way to innocence lies ever further into guilt, ever deeper into human life.[39]

and this view is close to the orthodox Christian conception. Newman writes:

> I look out into the world of men, and see a sight that fills me with unspeakable distress. The world seems simply to give the lie to the great truth, of which my being is so full. I look into this busy, living world, and see no reflection of its creator. To consider . . . the defeat of good, the prevalence and intensity of sin, the dreary, hopeless irreligion . . . all this is a vision to dizzy and appal, and inflicts upon the mind the sense of profound mystery which is absolutely beyond human solution. . . . And so I argue . . . 'If there be a God . . . the human race is implicated in some terrible, aboriginal calamity.[40]

Note the phrase 'which is absolutely beyond human solution'. Humanism denies that there are problems that are beyond human solution. And in using the word 'human', let us also bear in mind Steppenwolf's: 'Man is a bourgeois compromise.'

The passage from Newman is a classic exposition of the doctrine of Original Sin, 'some terrible, aboriginal calamity'. Newman's way of seeing the world is pessimistic. It is Dostoevsky's way, Blake's way, Kafka's way; we can find the same vision in a modern novelist like Graham Greene (although Greene's deliberately conceived 'popular' devices exclude him from serious consideration). It is the way of the Western Outsider.

Yet Blake and Dostoevsky are pessimistic only up to a point. Then, it seems a ray of light enters from a direction we had forgotten, from the poetic genius, the faculty of Yea-saying:

Ethinthus, queen of waters, how thou shinest in the sky
My sister, how do I rejoice, for thy children flock around
Like the gay fishes on the wave when the cold moon drinks the
    dew. . . .[61]

It is the strange faculty that can see 'a world in a grain of sand' or in a leaf 'just a leaf, slightly brown at the edges'. Newman lacked it, in common with Kafka and Greene.

From this tentative definition of the idea of Original Sin, we can see the outline of the meaning of 'salvation' and 'damnation'. Damnation is to belong hopelessly to the 'devil-ridden chaos', to be of it, in it, hopelessly lashed to it. From the Outsider's viewpoint the world justifies complete pessimism. 'We have not begun to live', Yeats writes, 'until we conceive life as a tragedy.' Newman confessed that he considered most men to be irretrievably damned, although he spent his life 'trying to make that truth less terrible to human reason'. Goethe could call his life 'the perpetual rolling of a rock that must be raised up again forever'. Martin Luther told a woman who wished him a long life: 'Madam, rather than live forty more years, I would give up my chance of paradise.' No, the Outsider does not make light work of living; at the best, it is hard going; at the worst (to borrow a phrase from Eliot) 'an intolerable shirt of flame'.

It was this vision that made Axel declare: 'As for living, our servants will do that for us.' Axel was a mystic; at least, he had the makings of a mystic. For that is just what the mystic says: 'I refuse to live.' But he doesn't intend to die. There is another way of living that involves a sort of death: 'to die in order to live'. Axel would have locked himself up in his castle on the Rhine and read Hermetic philosophy. He saw men and the world as Newman saw them, as Eliot saw them in 'Burnt Norton':

> . . . strained, time-ridden faces
> Distracted from distraction by distraction
> Filled with fancies and empty of meaning
> Tumid apathy with no concentration
> Men and bits of paper, whirled by the cold wind
> That blows before and after time. . . .[42]

But he was not willing to regard himself as hopelessly damned merely because the rest of the world seems to be. He set out to find his own salvation; and although he did it with a strong romantic bias for Gothic castles and golden-haired girls, he still set out in the right direction.

And what are the clues in the search for self-expression? There are the moments of insight, the glimpses of harmony. Yeats records one such moment in his poem 'Vacillation':

> My fiftieth year had come and gone
> I sat, a solitary man
> In a crowded London shop
> An open book and empty cup
> On the marble table-top
>
> While on the shop and street I gazed
> My body of a sudden blazed
> And twenty minutes more or less
> It seemed, so great my happiness
> That I was blessed, and could bless. . . .[43]

It is an important experience, this moment of Yea-saying, of reconciliation with the 'devil-ridden chaos', for it gives the

Outsider an important glimpse into the state of mind that the visionary wants to achieve permanently.*

It will be seen at once that 'visionary', in this context, does not mean literally 'a seer of visions', like the St. John who wrote the Apocalypse, but only someone who sees the world as positive. It might be objected that a drunken man conforms to this requirement; and this, in fact, is quite true. I have already quoted William James on the subject of drunkenness, and his point that alcohol stimulates the mystical faculties of mankind. There is obviously even a point to which ordinary physical well-being, the feeling after a good dinner, can be interpreted as 'mystical affirmation'; but here we must walk carefully. The point about ordinary once-born affirmation, the attitude of the good-natured, eupeptic vulgarian who sees life through rose-tinted spectacles, is that it cannot be controlled. If it disappears, due to illness or some misfortune, then it has disappeared for good, unless it comes back of its own accord.

The Outsider cannot regard such affirmation as meaningful or valid because it is beyond his control; he wants to say 'I accept', not because fate happens to be treating him rather well, *but because it is his Will to accept*. He believes that a 'Yea-saying' faculty can actually be built in to his vision, so that it is there permanently. There is a premonition of such a faculty in Van Gogh's 'Green Cornfield' and 'Road with Cypresses'; there is a premonition in the last movement of Beethoven's 'Hammerclavier' Sonata, as well as certain canvases of Gauguin, and page after page of *Also Sprach Zarathustra*. The Outsider believes that he can establish such a way of seeing permanently in himself. But how?

By knowing himself better. By establishing a discipline to overcome his weakness and self-division. By making it his aim to become harmonious and undivided. These are the answers we have extracted from our analysis. Most men have nothing in their heads except their immediate physical needs; put them on a desert island with nothing to occupy their minds and they would go insane. They lack real motive. The curse of our

* It is interesting to compare this with Poe's description of the feelings of a convalescent at the beginning of his 'Man of the Crowd': '. . . and, with returning strength, found myself in one of those happy moods which are so precisely the converse of ennui, moments of the keenest appetancy when the film from the mental vision departs . . . and the intellect, electrified, surpasses its everyday condition. . . . Merely to breathe was enjoyment. . . .'
Poe's hero is also seated in a London café, watching the crowds.

civilization is boredom. Kierkegaard observed this acutely:

> The Gods were bored, so they created man. Adam was bored because he was alone, so Eve was created. . . . Adam was bored alone, then Adam and Eve were bored together; then Adam and Eve and Cain and Abel were bored *en famille*, then the population of the world increased, and the people were bored *en masse*. To divert themselves, they conceived the idea of constructing a tower high enough to reach the heavens. This idea itself is as boring as the tower was high, and constitutes a terrible proof of how boredom had gained the upper hand. (Tr. D. F. Swenson.)[44]

This is penetrating commentary; but then, it is only a reversal of Hesse's statement that every man has a residue of unfulfilment at the bottom of him: boredom, unfulfilment, they amount to the same thing.

They do not know themselves. They live in prison. How can an individual hope to escape the general destiny of futility?

Blake's solution was: Go and develop the visionary faculty. Good. But how?

It is a question to which, I must admit, I shall not be able to offer a selection from the full range of answers, as I have been able hitherto. The field is too big. In the next chapter, it must be deliberately limited to a few typical examples.

CHAPTER NINE

BREAKING THE CIRCUIT

In the vault of Axel's castle, Sara and the young Count Axel stand clasped in one another's arms. Sara has just shot at Axel with two pistols at a distance of five yards, but missed him both times. Sara rhapsodizes about the 'world' which they now hold in their hands: the markets of Bagdad, the snows of Tibet, the fjords of Norway, 'all dreams to realize'. But Axel, 'grave and impenetrable', asks her: 'Why realize them? . . . Live? No, our existence is full. The future? Sara, believe me when I say it—we have exhausted the future. All the realities, what will they be tomorrow in comparison with the mirages we have just lived? . . . The quality of our hope no longer allows us the earth. What can we ask from this miserable star where our melancholy lingers on, save pale reflections of this moment? . . . It is the Earth—don't you see—that has become illusion. Admit, Sara, we have destroyed in our strange hearts the love of life. . . . To consent, after this, to live would only be a sacrilege against ourselves. Live? our servants will do that for us. . . . Oh, the external world! Let us not be made dupes by the old slave . . . who promises us the keys to a palace of enchantments, when he only clutches a handful of ashes in his black fist. . . .'[1]

Sara is convinced; they drink the goblet of poison together and die in ecstasy.

There can be no doubt what Nietzsche's comment on this scene would have been; Axel, like his creator, is the most extreme type of other-worlder, and other-worlders are 'poisoners, whether they know it or not'.

Yet is this quite fair? Nietzsche himself began as an other-worlder, agreeing with Schopenhauer that 'Life is a sorry affair', and that the best way to spend it is in reflecting on it. We began this study of the Outsider with a man who spent his evenings looking through a hole in his wall and 'reflecting' on what he saw. Van Gogh retired from life when he spent his days painting in the yellow house at Arles; Gauguin went to the South Seas pursuing the same dream, *luxe, calme et volupté*.

And even Zarathustra councilled self-surmounters to 'fly to solitude' and escape the stings of the 'flies in the market-place' (i.e. other men).

No, Axel is on the right path, even if killing himself is a poor way out. 'What can we hope from this miserable star . . . ?' But Sara has just spoken of 'the pale roads of Sweden' and the fjords of Norway. A visionary like Van Gogh would find a great deal to hope from such a world. It is the world of human beings that Axel is condemning. Other people are the trouble.

To confirm this point, we can appeal to another visionary, Thomas Traherne. It is Traherne who gives the famous description of his childhood in *Centuries of Meditation*, when

> All appeared new and strange at first, inexpressibly rare and delightful and beautiful. . . . I was entertained by the works of God in their splendour and glory; I saw all in the peace of Eden. . . . The corn was orient and immortal wheat, which never should be reaped nor ever was sown. . . . The dust and stones of the streets were as precious as gold. . . . And young men [were] glittering and sparkling angels, and maids strange seraphic pieces of life and beauty. . . .[2]

Why Traherne asks, did these 'intimations of immortality' cease? He answers:

> It was eclipsed . . . by the customs and manners of men. Grit in the eye or yellow jaundice will not let a man see those objects truly that are before it. And therefore it is requisite that we should be as very strangers to the thoughts, customs and opinions of men in this world. . . . They all prized things I did not dream of. I was weak and easily guided by their example.[3]

And he concludes with a statement that sounds like a form of the Pelagian heresy.*

---

* Pelagius, the 'arch-heretic', denied the doctrine of original sin (as taught by St. Augustine), and wrote: 'Everything good and everything evil . . . is done by us, not born with us . . . we are begotten without virtue as without vice, and before the activity of our own personal Will, there is nothing in man but what God has stored in him' (*Pro Libero Arbitrio, ap Augustine*).

And that our misery proceeds ten times more from the outward bondage of opinion and custom than from any inward corruption or depravation of Nature; and that it is *not our parents' loins so much as our parents' lives, that enthralls and blinds us.* [Italics mine.]

But Pelagian or not, this is the Blakeian attitude, and the attitude of most mystics. And in it, we can see how closely Traherne's mystical Christianity approaches the romantic attitude. Compare Yeats's lines:

All things uncomely and broken, all things worn-out and old
The cry of a child by the roadside, the creak of a lumbering cart,
The heavy steps of the ploughman, splashing the wintry mould
Are wronging your image that blossoms a rose in the deeps of my heart.[4]

Yeats is implying that it is the sheer ugliness of the world, or certain aspects of it, that destroys his 'intimations of immortality':

The wrong of unshapely things is a wrong too great to be told

and this is what Axel would say. But Traherne and Blake hold a different view. Other people are the trouble. In another place Traherne tells of his moment of great decision:

When I came into the country, and being seated among silent trees and meads and hills, had all my time in my own hands, I resolved to spend it all, whatever it cost me, in search of happiness, and to satiate that burning thirst which nature had enkindled in me from my youth. In which I was so resolute that I chose rather to live upon ten pounds a year and to go in leather clothes, and feed upon bread and water, so that I might have all my time clearly to myself. . . .[5]

This is an Outsider's decision. When we met it in Hesse's *Siddhartha* it did not seem abnormal, because it happened in India. But this decision to become a 'wanderer', a 'seeker' in a European country, to wear leather clothes like George Fox (who was roughly contemporary with Traherne), this seems strange to our Western mentality, and would probably lead us to doubt the sanity of any of our acquaintances who decided to do the same. And yet it is a sensible, straightforward decision. A man only has need of the common sense to say: 'Civilization is largely a matter of superfluities; I have no desire for superfluities. On the other hand, I have a very strong desire for leisure and freedom.' I am not attempting to assert the validity of this solution for all Outsiders; in fact, the practical objection to it is that the wandering life does not make for leisure or contemplation, and it certainly fails to satisfy the Outsider's need for a direction, a definitive act.

Nevertheless, the *act of willing* is important; the result, whether it proves a success or a disillusionment, is only secondary. Again, we might turn to Yeats for an example, an example that is admittedly rather less serious than the discussion we have in hand, but it would be a pity to leave it unquoted on that account. In the Introduction to 'A Vision', a young man called Daniel O'Leary tells of how, one night in the theatre, he suddenly felt an urge to express his dislike of the insipid way in which the actors were speaking *Romeo and Juliet*:

> Suddenly this thought came into my head: What would happen if I were to take off my boots, and fling one at Mr. . . . and one at Miss . . . ? *Could I give my future life such settled purpose that the act would take its place, not among whims, but among forms of intensity?* . . . 'You have not the courage,' I said, speaking in a low voice. 'I have,' said I, and began unlacing my boots. . . .⁶ [Italics mine.]

The sentence I have italicized is the important one. It is precise definition of the definitive act: To give one's future life such settled purpose that the act would be a *form of intensity*. Admittedly, 'forms of intensity' may be a bit vague, but there can be no doubt of what Yeats is getting at. When Raskolnikov killed the old woman, he had committed such an act, that would give his future life a settled purpose; or at least, that is what he hoped. When Stavrogin raped the ten-year-old girl and stole a banknote from a poor clerk, he had not succeeded in committing a 'form of intensity'. For, unfortunately for himself, Stavrogin was not really mean-souled enough to rape or steal,

and his attempt to commit an act *which should have a meaning
independent of the emotion he put into it* was a failure. For him,
Blake's dictum that 'the true soul of sweet delight can never be
defiled' was all against him. Stavrogin had to learn that no
act is evil in itself; man puts the evil into it by the motive with
which he commits it, and the final standard of motive is
Blake's 'that enthusiasm and life shall not cease'. Evil cannot
co-exist with the striving 'to live more abundantly' which is the
ultimate aim of religion.* Stavrogin completely lacked motive.

It is unfortunate that we do not know enough about
Traherne's life to observe what happened when he made his
decision to live on bread and water and wear leather clothes.
We know in Fox's case, though; we know that Fox was not a
complete success by the Outsider's stern criterion of success.
Traherne became a priest to a country family, where he lived a
quiet, meditative life, dying at the age of thirty-eight. To judge
by the *Centuries of Meditation*, Traherne succeeded in permanently adjusting his vision until he saw the world with
the same eyes as Van Gogh, the Van Gogh of the 'Road with
Cypresses'. That adjustment, I am inclined to believe, can
only be achieved in solitude: Nietzsche understood that society
is a hall of distorting mirrors.

By way of comparison with the Western mystics we have been
dealing with, we might turn to the life of a great Hindu mystic,
Ramakrishna. Here the environment is different. India has its
tradition of contemplation and 'self-surmounting' (although at
the time of Ramakrishna's birth, 1836, Western ideas were
pushing that tradition into the background). Here we can see
what happens when the Outsider can slip into a tradition
where he ceases to be a lonely misfit.

(In the following pages I am quoting from the anonymous
Life of Ramakrishna issued by the Advaita Ashrama in Madras.
It is, on the whole, informative and well-balanced; in its latter
more than in its earlier part.)

Sri Ramakrishna was born of Brahmin parents in a little
Indian village in Bengal. From a very early age he showed
that he saw the world with the same eyes as Traherne. Acting in
plays at the local religious festival, he would plunge into a

* This is admittedly a controversial and difficult point, which I shall return to in
speaking of T. E. Hulme.

trance of joy, so that onlookers felt as if he really were the 'baby Krishna' whom he was acting. He was an imaginative child who loved to read religious stories and legends aloud to the villagers (these, of course, would be the only imaginative literature available to him); in fact, he so obviously entered into the spirit of the stories that his parents thought it was a sign of hysteria or nervous instability.

When Ramakrishna was only seven, he had an important experience, which I give in his own words:

> One day in June or July . . . I was walking along a narrow path separating the paddy fields, eating some puffed rice, which I was carrying in a basket. Looking up at the sky, I saw a beautiful, sombre thundercloud. As it spread rapidly over the whole sky, a flight of snow-white cranes flew overhead in front of it. It presented such a beautiful contrast that my mind wandered to far-off regions. Lost to outward sense, I fell down, and the puffed rice was scattered in all directions. Some people found me . . . and carried me home. . . .[7]

It is immediately obvious that this experience has something in common with Nietzsche's two 'vastations'; Nietzsche was older, he was a child of a self-critical civilization that could not give itself so easily to extreme emotions. Yet both Nietzsche and Ramakrishna experienced a sense of harmony, a possibility of a way of seeing the world that would make life a continuous 'form of intensity'. Or remember Nietzsche, walking around the lake of Silvaplana and crying 'tears of joy'. 'I have seen thoughts rising on my horizon, the like of which I have never seen before'; 'Calm and peace spread over the mountains and the forests'; 'Six thousand feet above men and Time'.

But there is an enormous difference. Ramakrishna lived in a little village. He was a Brahman's son; his life was reasonably well shielded from violent and unpleasant things. His life was idyllic (all his life he could be plunged into ecstasy, literally, by considering the country-idyll episode of Krishna's life). He was like a fine string that could resound sympathetically to the slightest vibrations of beauty or harmony in his surroundings. We might be excused for asking: Would he still have felt the world so harmonious if he had been born into Raskolnikov's

Petersburg, or the environment Graham Greene pictures in *Brighton Rock*?

It is true, I think, that Ramakrishna was lucky to spend his formative years in a peaceful environment, but that is not the whole answer. Nietzsche had his vision of 'enthusiasm and life' on the Strasbourg road, after days spent among the brutality and stench of a battlefield. But we must return to this point later. Ramakrishna's spiritual temperament, or perhaps we should say his imaginative sensitivity, continued to develop throughout his youth. His elder brother became a priest in the Kali temple at Dakshineswar, a privately-owned place of worship, built by a wealthy Sudra woman and maintained by her, and in due course his younger brother joined him there.

Now Ramakrishna tended to think of God in terms of harmony, which was natural, since his mind dwelt constantly on a legendary Golden Age of Krishna's life on earth, and since his 'mystical experiences', like the one of the paddy field, gave him an insight into a state of perfect internal serenity. Traherne said he was seeking 'happiness'; Ramakrishna said he was seeking God; but they meant the same thing. Blake would have called it Vision. Ramakrishna recognized, just as Traherne had done, that serenity comes in moments of contemplation, by directing the thoughts towards the idea of harmony. So he began to go alone into places where he was not likely to be disturbed—a grove with a reputation for being haunted was his favourite—and would sit cross-legged, and try to make his emotions and intellect co-operate to give him perfect detachment from the world. In other words, he would try to achieve the state that Nietzsche could achieve listening to *Tristan und Isolde* or reading Schopenhauer: detachment.

Now, anyone who has ever tried this knows what immediately happens. Unless the imagination can keep the high ideal in sight, the thoughts tend to get earthbound, like a bird that cannot quite take off and flutters along the ground. You sit down intending to make the mind soar up to the sky, but after a few hours, the trees and the ground seem realer than ever, and the idea of 'celestial regions' seems nonsense. *Things are too real.* It is Roquentin's Nausea again. This dead weight of uninterpretable reality is always one of the major difficulties of the solitary. Mixing with other people at least stimulates one to emulation, to strive to make comparisons favourable to oneself.

Would Joyce's Stephen Dedalus have taken such pride in regarding himself as an artist if he had not been able to tell himself that 'their silly voices made him feel that he was different from other children'? That is what Zarathustra means when he tells the aspiring solitary:

A day shall come when you shall see your high things no more, and your low things all too near, and you will fear your exaltation as if it were a phantom. In that day you will cry: All is false.

Ramakrishna has told of how he too went through this stage; he prayed to the Divine Mother, Kali: 'Are you real or are you a delusion? Am I making a fool of myself imagining that I can ever know you?' He began to feel that all his worship and meditation were getting him no nearer to a vision of 'pure Will'. He tells:

I was suffering from excruciating pain because I had not been blessed with a vision of the mother. I felt as if my heart were being squeezed like a wet towel. I was overpowered by a great restlessness, and I feared that it might not be my lot to realize her in this life. I could not bear the separation any longer: life did not seem worth living. Then my eyes fell on the sword that was kept in the Mother's temple. Determined to put an end to my life, I jumped up and seized it, when suddenly the blessed mother revealed herself to me. . . . The buildings . . . the temple and all vanished, leaving no trace; instead there was a limitless, infinite, shining ocean of consciousness or spirit. As far as the eye could see, its billows were rushing towards me from all sides . . . to swallow me up. I was panting for breath. I was caught in the billows and fell down senseless.[8]

It is obvious what happened; long meditation had tired him until he had lost sight of his aim. The decision to kill himself was a sudden danger to his vital power that aroused all his sleeping life-energies. His vision was the same as Nietzsche's on the hilltop again. The Outsider suddenly knows himself. It is Alyosha's vision of love of the earth, love of life, or, like the unbeliever in Ivan's story who had walked a quadrillion miles and declared that a few seconds of heaven were worth every minute of it. It is Chuang Tzu's 'Great Awakening', the interior gates that opened for Swedenborg and Boehme and Blake. It is a blazing of all the senses, the complete opposite of Roquentin's Nausea.

Now, Blake has told us that this vision would be possible for everyone if 'the doors of perception were cleansed', so that, under the circumstances, we cannot contend that the vision is something purely objective, like sitting in a cinema and just watching what goes before your eyes. No; what had happened to Ramakrishna is that the threat of death awoke the sleeping Will; the Will did the rest. It is important to understand this. It is this realization that is the final salvation of the Outsider. When we read of Biblical prophets or saints seeing visions, we tend to think that the vision *appeared to them*, whereas it would be truer to say that the saint appeared to the vision. Modern scepticism is quite right to doubt the possibility of such visions, if they are simply a matter of *something happening*. But they are not. They are an example of the Will *making* something happen. The Western way of thinking tends to staticize the Will.

It is necessary to get this clear before we go on with Ramakrishna's life. The fact is difficult to grasp, because our thought is always aware of such things, but is not aware that it is holding them upside down.

Go into any London library and look in the philosophy section until you find some book with a title such as 'What is Man?' or 'Is Life Worth Living?' Read half a page of it, and you will see what I mean by 'staticizing the Will'. It is as if the author were saying: 'Well, here am I, sitting in my armchair, looking out at the Panorama of Life. What is it all about?' He looks outward and accepts what he sees; he does not ask what elements in himself are making him see the world as he does. Moreover, even if he turns his eyes inwards and asks, in a Freudian or Kantian frame of mind, 'How far do my perceptions affect the way I see things?' he still sets out examining those perceptions as if they were something at the other end of a microscope, and he were a permanent and static person looking at them.

The reverse of this happens in a 'moment of vision' like Alyosha's or Nietzsche's. The bombardment of the 'self' with emotions and sensations like so many shooting stars make the visionary realize that his interior being is more like a mill-race. He is struck forcibly by the kinetic nature of the world itself. While before, he had seen the world as rather a static place, where all sorts of trivialities assumed importance as they would in a dull country village, he now sees the world as a battle-ground of immense forces. At once he becomes aware of two things, the kinetic nature of the world, and the kinetic nature of his own soul. Instead of seeing the surface of things and feeling that it is rather dull, he sees the interior working of the force of life, the Will to more life. This Will is normally hidden, leaving the conscious mind to carry on with its own affairs. The con-scious mind is left in exile in the world of matter, left to make-itself-at-home as best it can by setting up its own conception of identity and permanence. In most men, the conscious and the unconscious being hardly ever make contact; consequently, the conscious aim is to make himself as comfortable as possible with as little effort as possible.

But there are other men, whom we have been calling, for convenience, 'Outsiders', whose conscious and unconscious being keep in closer contact, and the conscious mind is forever aware of the urge to care about 'more abundant life', and care less about comfort and stability and the rest of the notions that are so dear to the bourgeois. I have tried to show in the course of this book, how the Outsider's one need is to discover how to lend a hand to the forces inside him, to help them in their struggle. And obviously, if he is only vaguely aware of these interior forces, the sensible thing is to become more aware of them and find out what they are aiming at. The Outsider usually begins by saying, 'I must have solitude to look inside myself'; hence the room on his own. Unfortunately, he also discovers that he often gets to know himself better under the stimulation of new experiences; and new experiences are out of the question when he is in a room on his own. A conflict is set up at the beginning of the 'new life', all of which is expressed so fully in *Steppenwolf*.

Ramakrishna succeeded in administering the stimulus him-self. He seized a sword to kill himself, and immediately the life-force in him revealed itself and told him: 'Nonsense; you are not going to die; look at all the work I have for you to do.' And Ramakrishna had his first vision of the 'Mother', a sudden realization that the universe is full of life, is nothing *but* life, life engaged in an unending attempt to reinforce its grip on matter. Van Gogh had become aware of the same interior vortex when he painted the 'Road with Cypresses' and the 'Starry Night', just as Beethoven had become aware of it when he wrote the 'Hammerclavier'. The sensitivity of Ramakrishna's interior harmony made it easy for him to re-establish contact with that recognition. The image of Kali in the Temple became a symbol of that recognition.

Kali is depicted as a fierce, black-visaged woman, holding a sword and a dripping human head in two of her four hands, and offering blessing to her children with the other two. She stands on the prostrate body of her husband Shiva, for Shiva only symbolizes conscious life; she is the life-force; around her neck is a necklace of human skulls. Whoever devised the first image of Kali must have been some Hindu Nietzsche who realized that the life-force is higher than the mere individual will to self-preservation, and may aim at more life through the deaths of individuals.* Hindu hymns recognize this demoniac quality in the life-force; one begins:

All creation is the sport of my mad mother Kali.

Another:

Crazy is my father, crazy is my mother [i.e. Shiva and Kali].

Another (which brings out the demoniac quality even more):

This time I shall devour thee utterly, mother Kali
For I was born under an evil star
And one so born becomes, they say, the eater of his mother....⁹

It is the same conception that Dostoevsky puts into Kirilov's mouth: '... the man who insults and rapes a little girl—that's good too, and the man who blows his brains out for the child, that's good too. Everything's good.' Nietzsche's expression of the same conception has led to his condemnation as an 'Antichrist', 'cold monster', etc. Admittedly, the abuse of the idea of Kali as

* The extent to which this conception is foreign to Western minds can be seen in the Indian room of the British Museum, where the statue of Kali—the divine mother of the universe—is labelled: 'Kali—Destroying Demon'!

destroyer led to the terrible curse of thuggism in India,* just as the ideas of Nietzsche are popularly supposed to have led to the Nazi policy of murder-camps and race-extermination.

Ramakrishna became a priest in the Kali temple after the death of his brother, and soon his reputation as a holy man spread. He was a strange priest, seldom bothering to observe the formalities of worship, on one occasion even offering the food intended for the Mother to the temple cat. When challenged about this, he replied simply that he saw everything as an embodiment of Kali. The least thing could awaken 'God-consciousness' in him and plunge him into samadhi (ecstatic trance); once, a glimpse of an English boy leaning against a tree with his body bent in three places like the traditional pictures of Krishna sent him into 'communion with God'.

When Ramakrishna was forty-six, the headmaster of a local school happened to visit him; Mahendranath Gupta became one of Ramakrishna's chief disciples, and kept the record of his daily conversations that has come down to us as the magnificent *Gospel of Sri Ramakrishna*. It is impossible to overpraise this great religious biography; it is the only complete, exhaustive record we possess of the day-to-day utterances of a God-intoxicated saint (the complete English version contains over half a million words, three times the length of the New Testament). Here is one of Ramakrishna's parables from it:

> Once a tigress attacked a flock of goats. As soon as she sprang on her prey, she gave birth to a cub and died. (A hunter had fired at her from a distance.) The cub grew up in the company of the goats. The goats ate grass and the cub followed their example. They bleated; the cub bleated too. Gradually it grew to be a big tiger. One day another tiger attacked the flock. It was amazed to see the grass-eating tiger. Running after it, the wild tiger at last seized it, whereupon the grass-eating tiger began to bleat. The wild tiger dragged it to the water, and said: 'Look at your face in the water; it is just like mine. Here is a little meat; eat it. . . .' But

---

* The thugs (pronounced tugs) were a religious sect who believed in killing human beings as a sacrifice to the Divine Mother. Their method was to accost travellers and strangle them, then bury the bodies. Sleeman (who stamped-out thuggism in India in the middle of the last century) estimated that the thugs killed some thousands of people every year, and over a million in five years!

the grass-eating tiger would not swallow it, and began to bleat again. Gradually, though, it got to know the taste of blood, and came to relish the meat. Then the wild tiger said: 'Now you see there is no difference between you and me; come along and follow me into the forest. . . .'

Eating grass is like enjoying 'woman and gold'. To bleat and run away like a goat is to behave like an ordinary man. Going away with the wild tiger is like taking shelter with the guru, who awakens one's spiritual consciousness, and recognizing him alone as one's relative. To see one's face rightly is to know one's real Self.[10]

It is tempting to compare this parable with Steppenwolf's division of himself into man and wolf, goat and tiger. The goat part is the ordinary bourgeois who bleats tamely in the world; the tiger is the Outsider part, the part that Raskolnikov chose when he murdered an old pawnbrokress, or the savage who is tired of being a goat. But the comparison is not quite accurate. It is true that Ramakrishna has accepted his destiny as an Outsider, and spends his time trying to persuade other men to become Outsiders too. But Steppenwolf's goat part enjoyed music and poetry, and so could hardly be accused of completely lacking 'spiritual consciousness'. Clearly, when the Outsider reaches Ramarkrishna's degree of spiritual consciousness, his divisions become clearer; there is now no question of murdering old women or deliberately embracing crime.

One of the most striking of Ramakrishna's teachings is the belief in the unity of all religions. The *Life* tells us how Ramakrishna first practised various religious disciplines of different sects (which is as strange in India as it would be for someone in England to declare himself at once an ardent Methodist; Quaker and Roman Catholic); later he turned to other religions, and studied in turn Christianity and Mohammedanism, worshipping the Virgin Mary instead of Kali, and then the all-pervasive Allah. Ramakrishna knew the basic reality of the universe; it made no difference what symbols he used to call it to mind; the result was always the same: ecstatic God-consciousness.

Again, before we leave Ramakrishna, we might try to cla what exactly is meant by 'God-consciousness'. There is

passage in *The Varities of Religious Experience* in which James
speaks of 'melting moods':

> The rest of us can ... imagine this by recalling our state of
> feeling in those temporary 'melting moods', into which the
> trials of real life, or the theatre, or a novel, sometimes throws
> us. Especially if we weep! For it is then as if our tears broke
> through an inveterate inner dam and let all sorts of ancient
> peccancies and moral stagnancies drain way, leaving us now
> washed and soft of heart, and open to every nobler leaning.
> With most of us, the customary hardness quickly returns, but
> not so with saintly persons. . . .[11]

We have already noted that Ramakrishna was lucky in
having spent his early life in a quiet village, where his susceptibility to these moods, his imaginative sensitivity, was in
no danger of having to put a shell on itself to protect it against
the world's brutalities. (Readers of Dickens's *Christmas Carol*
will recall the scene in which Scrooge reads *The Arabian Nights*
in his schoolroom, and the description of his delight and
absorption in the book; and of how the older Scrooge, now
hardened and bitter, recalls the scene and is plunged into a
'melting mood'.) We must understand that Ramakrishna
preserved his childlike sensitivity all his life. We, among the
complexities of our modern civilization, are forced to develop
hard shells; therefore it would not be false to say that it is our
civilization that is responsible for the prevailing humanistic and
materialistic modes of thought. Ramakrishna, at the opposite
extreme, could plunge to a depth of imaginative ecstasy which
few Westerners have ever known, except those mediaeval
saints who also were able to give up their minds as he did to
contemplation and serenity.

In the last years of his life, Ramakrishna was widely regarded
as an Avatar, an incarnation of God, like Christ, Krishna,
Gautama. (Even today his picture is worshipped by thousands
of Indians who regard him as God.) In his forty-ninth year,
Ramakrishna developed a sore throat, which developed into a
cancer, and finally killed him in August, 1886. Many of his
disciples retired into a monastery, and later set out to spread his
message over the world; the best known of them, Narendra,
Ramakrishna's favourite disciple, became Swami Vivekananda,

who made his master's name known throughout England and America.

In the course of the past two chapters, certain conclusions about the Outsider have become steadily more apparent, and we can express the most important one by saying that the Outsider would seem to be a basically religious man, or imaginative man, who refuses to develop those qualities of practical-mindedness and eye-to-business that seem to be the requisites for survival in our complex civilization. It must be again emphasized that by 'religion' I am not trying to indicate any specific religious system. Religious categories, as I have tried to show, are such simple ideas as 'Original Sin', 'salvation', 'damnation', which come naturally to the Outsider's way of thinking.

Moreover, both the Eastern and the Western ways of thinking tend to identify Original Sin with delusion. Ramakrishna never tired of telling his disciples not to think of themselves as sinners; yet he never ceased to refer to men who are 'in the world' as 'bound souls', 'deluded souls'. As to the way of escaping this delusion, there is no division of opinion: Go to extremes. That is the first necessity. The Buddha advocated a 'middle way', yet this was only after a preliminary course of extremes: the Majjhima Nikaya tells how he was 'a penance worker, outdoing others in penance; I was a rough-liver, outdoing others in roughing it; I was scrupulous, outdoing others in my scruples; I was a solitary, outdoing others in solitude'. I offer only one example of the description of the 'extremes' that followed (interested readers can find a fuller account in Woodward's *Sayings of the Buddha* in the World's Classics series):

> Then, Aggivesana, I said to myself: 'Suppose I practice still further the musing of breath suppressed?' Accordingly, I stopped my breathing in and out from mouth and nostrils, and I closed my ears.
> Then, just as if a strong man with a sharp pointed sword should crash into the brain, so did the rush of air, all outlets being stopped, crash into my brain. Then was my energy strenuous and unyielding indeed. Mindfulness was indeed established undisturbed, yet my body was perturbed; it was

not calm thereby, because I was overpowered by the stress
of the painful struggling. But even then such feelings as
arose could not lay hold of and control my mind. . . .

Finally, the scripture tells us, Gautama starved himself until
he was a living skeleton. One day when he was bathing in the
river, he found he had not strength to climb out. He finally
saved himself from drowning by clutching an overhanging
branch; but the near-experience of death had the same effect
upon him as upon Ramakrishna; a realization that he wanted
more life, not less. Then another memory came to him:

> Then . . . I thought: 'I call to mind how when the Sakhyan
> my father was ploughing I sat in the cool shade of the rose-
> apple tree, remote from sensual desires and ill-conditions, and
> entered upon and abode in the First Musing, which is
> accompanied by thought directed and sustained, which is
> born of solitude, full of zestful ease.' And then I said: 'Is this,
> I wonder, the way to Wisdom?'

This realization was followed by a decision to eat and drink
normally, and to rely upon the sensitivity of his imagination and
power of discrimination to bring about the desired result.

> Then . . . I came to Uravela, a suburb of the captain of the
> Host. There I beheld a lovely spot, a pleasant forest grove
> and a river of clear water flowing by, easy of access, and
> delightful, and hard by was the village, where I could beg
> my food. . . . So, brethren, I sat down, thinking. 'A proper
> place for striving in.'[12]

And it was here that Gautama meditated his way to 'freedom', Nirvana, perfect knowledge, self-realization. (We, of
course, are welcome to doubt whether such an ultimate is
attainable by man; but, all the same, we can recognize the
value of the Buddha's method.)
We can find even more extreme examples in the Christian
saints; there is Heinrich Seuse (or Suso) (1295-1366), who, in his
Autobiography, tells how he invented appalling bodily penances
for himself, wearing a gown of hair and an iron chain that cut
his body; then having an undergarment made of leather straps

with brass tacks pointing inwards, which he wore for several
years; he made a cross with nails pointing inwards, which he
strapped to his back and carried for eight years. He slept on an
old, studded door with no covering but a thin straw mat in
winter or summer. He continued these ascetic practices for
sixteen years until he considered that he had completely sub-
dued the body. He was inspired by a passage in Meister
Eckhart:

> There is another power, immortal too, proceeding from
> the Spirit. . . . Aye, in this power is such poignant joy, such
> vehement, immoderate delight as none can tell. . . . I say,
> moreover, if once a man in intellectual vision did really
> glimpse the bliss and joy therein, then all his sufferings would
> be a trifle, a mere nothing. . . .[13]

It was this 'fiery joy' that Seuse set out to capture.

The value of such extremes, of course, lies in the vitality
of the Will behind them; if they were undertaken merely as a
penance, a deliberate burden, they might be useless or even
harmful. It is the Will that matters.

The argument of this book has come almost its full circle. It
is not my aim to propound a complete and infallible solution
to 'the Outsider's problems', but only to point out that traditional solutions, or attempts at solutions, do exist. Before we
turn to T. E. Hulme and his prediction of 'the end of humanism', there is one more modern attempt at a solution which is
far too important to exclude from a study in the Outsider's
problems. This is the 'system' of that strange man of genius,
George Gurdjieff.

Gurdjieff died comparatively recently, in 1950, at about the
age of seventy (his exact age was not known). He had spent
some forty years of his life teaching his 'system' to his pupils.
Our knowledge of Gurdjieff is not very great; we know he was a
Caucasian Greek, who did most of his teaching in Moscow
and Petersburg, and later in Europe and America. Of Gurdjieff's major exposition of his system, *All and Everything*, only
the first part has to date been printed in England; this is over
twelve hundred pages long, and it is hardly unfair to its
author to say that it is almost unreadable—hardly unfair since

it seems to have been a part of his aim to make sure that no dilettante could dip into it and then claim to 'understand Gurdjieff'; his efforts to achieve this effect have made the first volume rather less comprehensible than *Finnegan's Wake*.

Fortunately (or unfortunately, Gurdjieff would say), there are simpler expositions of his philosophy; there is the absorbing introduction by Kenneth Walker, *Venture With Ideas*, and the brilliant exposition by Gurdjieff's chief follower, P. D. Ouspensky, *In Search of the Miraculous*, which tells the story of Ouspensky's period as Gurdjieff's pupil; Gurdjieff played Socrates to Ouspensky's Plato.

Gurdjieff's system can be regarded as the complete, ideal *Existenzphilosophie*. It is not interested in ideas for their own sake, but only in results. Therefore, the 'system' itself consists of various disciplines and exercises, which, at the moment, are only known to Gurdjieff's pupils and followers. It is only with some of the 'theoretical' part of the 'system' that we are concerned here.

Gurdjieff's starting-point is the completely deluded state of man; man, he claims, is so completely embalmed and enmeshed in delusions that he cannot even be considered as a living being; he can only be regarded as a machine. He has, in other words, absolutely no free-will.

This seems to be no more than the blackest pessimism, but this is not the whole. Having emphasized that men are virtually asleep, mere sleep-walkers without real consciousness, he goes on to state that man *can* attain a degree of freedom and 'awakening': but the first step in attaining 'freedom' is to recognize that you are not free. Since we have spent some nine chapters listening to Outsiders emphasizing just this fact, this should present no difficulties to us. A part of Gurdjieff's system is a method of observing oneself and other people, and recognizing how many actions are habitual, mechanical.

One of the most interesting points in Gurdjieff's system, from our point of view, is his exposition of 'three ways', the way of the fakir, the way of the monk, the way of the yogi. For these are the three ways we established in Chapter IV: discipline over the body, the emotions, the mind. But what is most interesting is that Gurdjieff claims that his system is a *fourth way* which involves all the other three. Gurdjieff's 'school' in the South of France was called 'The Institute for the Harmonious

Development of Man', harmonious development of the three parts. Obviously, Gurdjieff's system and the Outsider have the same aim.

In my own copy of Ouspensky's book, I have gone through the Contents list, labelling various chapters 'philosophical' or 'psychological'. The 'philosophical' parts may or may not be 'true'; it is impossible to say. Such a statement, for instance, as that the moon is a younger earth, and the earth a younger sun, and that the planetary bodies are living beings, just as we are, can be taken with a pinch of salt or not, according to the reader's inclination. But there can be no doubt whatever about Gurdjieff's astounding penetration as a psychologist; and it is here that he touches the field of this book.

Gurdjieff teaches that there are four possible states of consciousness. The first is ordinary sleep. The second is the condition in which the ordinary bourgeois spends his life, the state which is called—ironically, Gurdjieff thinks—'waking consciousness'. The third state is called 'self-remembering' (which we shall define in a moment), the fourth, 'objective consciousness'.

From our point of view, 'self-remembering' is the most important state. We have seen in the course of this study many Outsiders experiencing this state. Perhaps the best example is Steppenwolf in bed with Maria; Yeats in the 'crowded London shop' is another.

Ouspensky explains 'self-remembering' with great clarity. Normally, when you are looking at some physical object, the attention points outwards, as it were, from you to the object. When you become absorbed in some thought or memory, the attention points inwards. Now sometimes, very occasionally, the attention points both outwards and inwards at the same time, and these are moments when you say, 'What *I*, really *here*?': an intense consciousness of yourself and your surroundings. (A fine example in literature is Olenin's first sight of the mountains in Tolstoy's *Cossacks*, a moment of complete self-remembering.) Ouspensky says: 'Moments of self-remembering came either in new and unexpected surroundings, in a new place, among new people, while travelling for instance . . . or in very emotional moments, moments of danger, etc.'

Self-remembering can be produced by a deliberate discipline, but it is very difficult. Try, as an experiment, looking at your watch, and then, while your attention is concentrated on seeing the time, try to become aware of yourself looking at the watch. A moment will come during which you are aware of both the watch and yourself, but it will not last more than a few seconds. You will either become aware only of yourself looking, or only of the dial of the watch. That moment of self-awareness, looking at the watch and at yourself, is Gurdjieff's third state. (And, of course, people who are incorrigible self-dramatizers, like the young Nietzsche, are only trying to get themselves 'outside' the situation, and to see themselves in the situation objectively.) To express it in the Outsider's way: we identify ourselves with our personalities; our identities are like the pane of a window against which we are pressed so tightly that we cannot feel our separateness from it. Self-remembering is like standing back, so you can see 'yourself' (the window-pane) *and* the outside world, distinct from 'you'. Ouspensky relates how deliberate exercises in self-remembering produced strange intensities of feeling. Obviously, he had found one solution that the Outsider has overlooked.*

Gurdjieff also points out that man wastes an appalling amount of energy in what he calls 'negative emotion', like fear, disgust, anger, and so on. These emotions, he claims, are completely unnecessary to the economy of the human machine, and are as wasteful as tossing a match into a heap of

---

* 'I was once walking along the Liteiny towards the Nevsky, and in spite of all my efforts, I was unable to keep my attention on self-remembering. The noise, movement, everything distracted me. Every minute I lost the thread of attention, found it again, and then lost it again. At last, I felt a kind of ridiculous irritation with myself, and I turned into the street on the left, having determined to keep my attention on the fact that *I would remember myself* at least for some time, at any rate until I reached the following street. I reached the Nadejdinskaya without losing the thread of attention, except, perhaps, for short moments. Then I again turned towards the Nevsky still remembering myself, and was already beginning to experience *the strange emotional state of inner peace and confidence which comes after great efforts of this kind.* [My italics.] Just round the corner, on the Nevsky, was a tobacconist's shop where they made my cigarettes. Still remembering myself, I thought I would call there and order some cigarettes.

'Two hours later, I *woke up* in the Tavricheskaya, that is, far away. I was going by carriage to the printers. The sensation of awakening was extraordinarily vivid. I can almost say that I *came to*. I remembered everything at once. How I had been walking along the Nadejdinskaya, how I had been remembering myself, how I had thought about cigarettes, and how at this thought I seemed all at once to fall and disappear into a deep sleep.

'At the same time, while immersed in this sleep, I had continued to perform consistent and expedient actions. I left the tobacconist, called at my flat in the Liteiny, telephoned to the printers. . . . On the way, while driving along the Tavricheskaya, I began to feel a strange uneasiness, as though I had forgotten something. *And suddenly I remembered that I had forgotten to remember myself.*' (Ouspensky: *In Search of the Miraculous*, p. 120.)

gun-powder. Negative emotion is just an accident that sabotages the human energy-factory.

Man also has various 'centres': an emotional centre, a 'moving' centre (which does all the work connected with the body's movements) an intellectual centre and an instinctive centre. He also has a sexual centre, and two higher centres of which he knows almost nothing, since they work deep in the unconscious mind (although mere glimpses of these centres have been the 'visions' of saints). Man tends to mix up all the centres, and to use the energy intended for the moving centre on emotions, or that of the emotional centre on intellect, or that of the instinctive centre on sex; and, apparently, all the centres tend to steal the energy of the sexual centre, and give it in return a type of energy that is practically of no use to it ('It is a very great thing when the sexual centre works with its own energy,' Gurdjieff told Ouspensky). An important part of Gurdjieff's system is his method for observing the centres, and recognizing what should be the distinctive work of each.

But the main difficulty which the system must combat is man's tendency to sleep, to do things mechanically. The world has no meaning for us because we do all things mechanically. One day we are inspired by some poem or piece of music or picture, and the whole world is suddenly ten times as real, as meaningful, for us. The next day we re-read the poem, or hear the music again, and we have got used to it and hear it 'mechanically'. But other actions in everyday life are best done mechanically. I can type this page at a reasonable speed because the work has been taken over from my intellectual centre (which did all the work of learning to type) to my moving centre, which does it far more efficiently. If all the centres did their own work there would be no waste of energy, and maximum intensity of consciousness could be achieved.

The final 'maximum intensity' would be the limit of man's possible evolution (*q.v.* Ouspensky's slim volume, *The Psychology of Man's Possible Evolution*). In its aim (higher consciousness) and the primacy it gives to the concept of evolution, Gurdjieff's philosophy has obvious features in common with Shaw's, the difference being that Shaw sets no limit to possible development: 'As to what may lie beyond, the eyesight of Lilith is too short. It is enough that there is a beyond'. One day 'ages yet', pure mind 'might roll unchecked over the place where the

material world had been, and God would move upon the face
of those waters'. This is T. E. Lawrence, and it is pure Shavian-
ism, but it is not Gurdjieff. Gurdjieff deliberately limits the aim:
the first step is to break the sleep of hypnosis under which all
men live. He has a parable to illustrate it:

There is an Eastern tale that speaks about a very rich
magician who had a great many sheep. But at the same time
this magician was very mean. He did not want to hire
shepherds, nor did he want to erect a fence about the pasture
where the sheep were grazing. The sheep consequently
often wandered into the forest, fell into ravines and so on,
and above all, they ran away, for they knew that the
magician wanted their flesh and their skins, and this they
did not like.

At last the magician found a remedy. He hypnotized his
sheep and suggested to them, first of all, that they were immortal and that no harm was being done to them when they
were skinned; that on the contrary, it would be very good
for them and even pleasant; secondly he suggested that the
magician was a *good master* who loved his flock so much that
he was ready to do anything in the world for them; and
in the third place, he suggested that if anything at all were
going to happen to them, it was not going to happen just
then, at any rate not that day, and therefore they had no
need to think about it. Further, the magician suggested to
his sheep that they were not sheep at all; to some of them
he suggested that they were lions, to some that they were
eagles, to some that they were men, to others that they were
magicians.

After this all his cares and worries about the sheep came to
an end. They never ran away again, but quietly awaited the
time when the magician would require their flesh and skins.

This tale is a very good illustration of man's position.[14]

And in an earlier passage, Gurdjieff speaks with the authentic accents of mystical religion:

[Man] is attached to everything in his life; attached to his
imagination, attached to his stupidity, attached even to his
suffering—possibly to his suffering more than anything else.

He must free himself from attachment. Attachment to things, identification with things keeps alive a thousand 'I's' in a man. These 'I's' must die in order that the big I may be born. But how can they be made to die? . . . It is at this point that the possibility of awakening comes to the rescue. To awaken means to realize one's nothingness, that is, to realize one's complete and absolute mechanicalness, and one's complete and absolute helplessness. . . . So long as a man is not horrified at himself, he knows nothing about himself.[15]

And again:

One must die all at once and forever. . . .

St. John of the Cross expresses it:

> *Vivo sin vivir en mi*
> *Y de tal manera espero*
> *Que muero porque no muero.*

> I live, but there's no life in me
> And in such a hopeful way
> I die because I do not die.[16]

In *All and Everything*, Gurdjieff explains man's bondage in a slightly more complex way, but it is significant for us because it is obviously an attempt to recreate a legend of Original Sin. He explains that some cosmic catastrophe knocked two pieces off the earth, which became two satellites, the moon and another smaller moon which men have forgotten (although it still exists). These two moons, as part of the parent body, had to be sustained by 'food' sent from the earth (I have mentioned that Gurdjieff considers the heavenly bodies to be alive), and this 'food' is a sort of cosmic ray manufactured by human beings. In other words, the only purpose of human beings is to manufacture 'food' for the moon.

But human beings were, not unnaturally, irritated by this completely subject-role they were expected to play in the solar system. As they began to develop 'objective reason' (Gurdjieff's fourth state of consciousness), their chafing became a danger to the existence of the moon. A special commission of archangels decided to put a stop to the development of object-tive reason. So they implanted in man an organ, called *Kundabuffer*, whose special function was to make men perceive fantasy as actuality. And from that day onward men have been enmeshed in their own dreams, and admirably serve their function of providing food for the moon. Unfortunately, their inability to see things objectively is leading them to self-destruction at an appalling pace. It is necessary for at least a few men to develop a new type of consciousness, to develop it slowly, painfully, instinctively, without understanding what is happening to him. Would not such a man be a complete Outsider?

They are all asleep. This is the point to which Gurdjieff returns again and again. *They must be made to feel the urgency of the need to wake up.* And after the legend of the magician, to call the mass of contented bourgeois 'sheep' has a new and terrible significance. At the end of *All and Everything*, the grandson of the 'all-wise Beelzebub' (Gurdjieff's mouthpiece) asks whether it is still possible to save mankind and 'direct them to the becoming path'. Beelzebub answers: 'The sole means of saving the beings of the planet Earth would be to implant again into their presences a new organ . . . like *Kundabuffer*, . . . of such properties that everyone should sense . . . the inevit-ability of his own death, as well as the death of everyone upon whom his eyes or attention rest.'[17]

It is again the religious injunction: Remember thy last things. . . . But we can see now just how irrelevant is the idea of 'an allegorical abode where existence hath never come'. It is existence that counts. Man must live more; he must *be* more. And for this, he must be endlessly conscious of the principle of limitation. 'There is a definite time, a definite term, for every-thing,' Gurdjieff told Ouspensky. 'Possibilities for *everything* exist only for a definite time.'

It will be seen that our study has led us to formulate a number of conceptions which are indubitably religious. We have, as it were, run over the area of human life, and re-chalked the demarcation lines of religion. We have not mentioned a great many conceptions which many sincerely religious people take to be absolutely essential to religion—God and heaven and hell among them—and what we have constructed can be called the bare necessities of religion, the absolute, essential framework. This, I believe, is the framework of religion as it first existed for the human race. Continual intellectual rigour is necessary to stop these lines from getting vague. Our criterion has been this: that any 'truth' of religion shall be determinable *subjectively*. When we normally speak of the truth of an idea, we mean its correspondence with some outside fact. 'Truth is subjectivity', Kierkegaard said. That is the Existentialist concept. 'The dog is blue.' Is that, *could* it be, a religious truth? No; even if it is objectively true that the dog is blue, it is an objective truth; therefore it could not be religious truth. 'There is a spirit world where we all go when we die.' That may be true, in the same sense that the dog is blue; but in that case it is a truth about the external world, and not therefore a religious truth. Religious truth cannot exist apart from intellectual rigour, apart from the individual effort to realize it. When Eckhart wrote, 'Man cannot live without God, but God cannot live without man either. Without man, God wouldn't know he existed', he was speaking a subjective truth, but when the Brethren of the Free Spirit made this an excuse for complete relaxation of the will and of all moral standards, it ceased to be true as far as they were concerned. The most absolute and rigorous intellectual truth ceases to be true when there is no life to affirm it. In Boehme, a student asks: 'Where does the soul go after death?' and his master replies: 'There is no need for it to go anywhere. Heaven and Hell are universally co-extensive'; and this is apparently an attempt at an 'objective' statement of truth. Yet it is Boehme who warns his reader with Nietzschean vigour, in his first work: 'If you are not a spiritual self-surmounter, let my book alone. Don't meddle with it, but stick to your usual nonsense.' This is the essence of religion.

When T. E. Hulme was killed in France in 1917, he left the elements of an immense task behind him. It was a task that Nietzsche had already begun for him, philosophizing 'with a hammer'. The first step in re-defining religion is to knock some of the fungus off the old values, and try to discern their shape as they existed for the men who made them.

But for a hundred years or more, Outsiders have been swinging the hammer, without consciously realizing what they were doing, and slowly creating new values by implication. Forty years after Hulme's death, we can begin to see the results of the hundred years of intellectual questioning. Hulme regarded his *Speculations* as a preface to Pascal's *Pensées*, but it would perhaps be more accurate to regard them as the epilogue of a certain indispensible body of Outsider literature, beginning with Dostoevsky's *Notes from Under the Floorboards* and including *Steppenwolf*, *The Secret Life*, Nijinsky's *Diary* and *Mind at the End of Its Tether*.

We might preface an analysis of the *Speculations* with a few words on the development of Existentialism. Hulme's thought is not systematically set out, and the simplest way of understanding his attitude, his feeling about philosophy, is to approach him via Kierkegaard.

When Kierkegaard expressed his revolt against Hegel in the *Unscientific Postscript*, he was making a philosophical stand against philosophy; but let us not get confused about the meaning of what he was doing. Some two thousand four hundred years before, Aristophanes had thrown mud at Socrates in exactly the same spirit, with the dislike of the poet for the logician. Western civilization has been too hasty in condemning Aristophanes. The real issue is not whether two and two make four or whether two and two make five, but whether life advances by men who love *words* or by men who love *living*. The Socratic conception of history (propagated in our time by Professor Whitehead) is that civilization advances in proportion as its thinkers are interested in abstractions, in knowledge for its own sake. Aristophanes deplored the heresy and exposed Socrates to ridicule at every opportunity. For him, as for Nietzsche, knowledge is merely an instrument of living; there is no such thing as abstract knowledge; there is only useful knowledge and unprofitable blatherskite. And it is likely that if Aristophanes had ever been pressed for a definition of useful knowledge, he would have answered: Whatever enables a man to live more. So much can be gathered from the spirit of the plays.

Kierkegaard felt the same. As an intensely living, intensely suffering individual, he was not concerned about whether man in the abstract fitted into a great Abstract Universal System; he only knew about the simple, finite, guilty and suffering creature called Søren Kierkegaard, who had to make a decision in the face of God, and who needed to feel that that decision mattered, ultimately, absolutely; not that the Universal Scheme could get on very well whether he decided for God or the Devil.

In view of the gradual change in the meaning of Existentialism with Sartre and Heidegger, we should understand this:
that Kierkegaard's protest was a protest on behalf of the
suffering and involved, against the abstract and impersonal.
Sartre's endless tergiversations about the *pour-soi* and the
en-soi (in *L'Etre et le Néant*) would have annoyed him as violently
as Heidegger's hair-splitting about Existence and Time.
Kierkegaard would have preferred James Thompson's *City
of Dreadful Night* or Eliot's 'Ash Wednesday'; and there can be
no doubt that the Outsider shares his preference. Kierkegaard's
attitude is so Existential that his Christianity is a religion that
regards God as the intermediary between himself and his
fellow human beings, and cannot even accept their existence
without first accepting the existence of God. He is an extreme
case of the poet who says, 'I will *not* serve'—*Non Serviam*—like
Stephen Dedalus. I will serve nothing but God and my own
soul; perish all such conceptions as knowledge and civilization
and social causes and being a do-gooder.'

It is necessary to emphasize this extremist attitude so that we
can be quite clear about what constitutes the essence of religion.
It does not deny knowledge and civilization and doing-good;
it only denies their primacy. The attitude of Leigh Hunt's
Abou Ben Adhem, who admits that he does not love God, but
tells the Angel, 'Set me down as one that loves his fellow men,'
is loathesome to it as a sentimental sophistry.

Hulme was like Kierkegaard; religion was instinctive for
him. He is a poet, and his approach to religion is a poet's. He
does not (like Plato) compare a child to a star; he compares the
stars to children:

> A touch of cold in the Autumn night
> I, walked abroad
> And saw the ruddy moon lean over a hedge
> Like a red-faced farmer.
> I did not stop to speak, but nodded,
> And round about were the wistful stars
> With white faces, like town children.[18]

His approach to religion is like G. K. Chesterton's. Chesterton has a hero who loves London so much that he would not

dream of saying, 'A taxicab came round the corner like the wind,' but rather, 'The wind came around the corner like a taxicab.'[19] That is the Existentialist approach. The way of Alienation (Hegel's phrase) points outward, towards abstraction; the way of mysticism points inward, towards the concrete.

Hulme expressed his dislike of the outward way, the romantic way, in the essay on 'Romanticism and Classicism':

> The Romantic, because he thinks man infinite must always be talking about the infinite. . . . [He] is always flying, flying over abysses, flying up into eternal gases. The word Infinite is in every other line. . . .
> Here is the root of all romanticism: that man, the individual, is an infinite reservoir of possibilities; and if you can so rearrange society by the destruction of oppressive order then these possibilities will have a chance, and you will get Progress. . . .[20]
> One can define the classical quite clearly as the exact opposite to this. Man is an extraordinarily fixed and limited animal whose nature is absolutely constant. It is only by tradition and organization that anything decent can be got out of him.[21]

This distinction lies at the root of all that Hulme has to say. For instance, on modern art (modern, for Hulme, meant Picasso and Gaudier-Brzeska):

> There are two kinds of art, geometrical and vital, absolutely distinct in kind from one another. These two arts are not modifications of one and the same art but pursue different aims and are created for the satisfaction of different necessities of the mind. . . . Each of these arts springs from and corresponds to a certain general attitude towards the world. . . .[22]

Now, it must seem to the reader that what Hulme has actually done is to create a distinction between the optimistic way of viewing the world, the humanistic, and the pessimistic, and that he has called the pessimistic view 'religious'. But this fails to do justice to the subtlety of Hulme's thought. It can best be made clear, perhaps, by referring to Nietzsche's development of Schopenhauer's view of the world (*Weltanschauung*). Schopenhauer's essentially Buddhistic view recognized Will as the underlying reality of the world, but considered that Will is the servant of the world of idea, illusion, in that it can only be roused to act by some purpose outside itself and in the world of idea. Man's freedom lies in refusing to act. Nietzsche's deeper experience of the Will, his vastations, made him reject Schopenhauer's conclusions, without rejecting his analysis of the world as Will and the world as idea. Nietzsche's great concept of Yea-saying gave him a notion of purpose that is seen as positive. Nietzsche, in short, was a religious mystic.

Before quoting the key-passages in the *Speculations*, it may perhaps be as well here to aim at clarifying this disagreement between Nietzschean Vitalism and Hulme's religious attitude. The rift is not as wide as it seems at first sight. Hulme was unwilling to dwell on the similarities because Nietzsche enthusiasts and Shaw enthusiasts were advocating a vitalist extremism that amounted to humanism. Now Shaw is dead, and Nietzsche hardly ever read in England, Mr. Eliot has further obscured the fundamental agreement by a campaign of literary sniping at them that has temporarily made them 'unfashionable' within the sphere of his critical dictatorship. Hulme's influence on Mr. Eliot is well known, and their attacks on vitalism tend to follow the same line. Here is Mr. Eliot:

> Mr. Babbitt says: 'To give the first place to a higher will is only another way of declaring that life is an act of faith. . . .' This is quite true, but if life is an act of faith, in what is it an act of faith? The life forcers, with Mr. Bernard Shaw at their head, would say, I suppose, 'In life itself,' but I should not accuse Mr. Babbitt of anything so silly as that.[23]

And here is Hulme:

> Biology is not theology, nor can God be defined in terms of 'life' or 'progress'. . . .[24]

In the first passage, Mr. Eliot has simply misrepresented Shaw, while in the second Hulme's statement is true, but again, does not apply to Shaw or Nietzsche. Hulme's desire not to be thought a Nietzschean in any sense has led him to make certain inaccurate statements about the relation of his own views to Nietzsche's; for instance, in a long section dealing with a 'Critique of Satisfaction', he uses a vivid simile to express his suspicion of philosophers and their 'Systems':

A man might be clothed in armour so complicated and elaborate, that to the inhabitant of another planet who had never seen armour before, he might seem like some entirely impersonal and omnipotent mechanical force. But if he saw the armour running after a lady, or eating tarts in the pantry, he would realize at once that it was not a god-like or mechanical force, but an ordinary human being extraordinarily armed.[25]

This is the essence of Nietzsche's criticism of philosophers in the first section of *Beyond Good and Evil*, 'Prejudices of Philosophers'. But Hulme has no wish to be thought a Nietzschean, and states:

... I do not want to imply any scepticism as to the possibility of a really scientific philosophy. I do not mean what Nietzsche meant when he said, 'Do not speculate as to whether what a philosopher says is true, but ask how he came to think it true.' This is a form of scepticism that I hold to be just fashionable rubbish. Pure philosophy ought to be, and may be, entirely objective and scientific.[26]

Hulme failed to grasp, or did not wish to grasp, that Nietzsche never denied the possibility of an objective philosophy; he only denied that a non-Existential philosophy can be valid. Nietzsche and Hulme meant precisely the same thing by their criticism of philosophers. This might have been clearer to Hulme if he had known the work of Kierkegaard.

To non-philosophical readers, all this may seem to be hair-splitting that has come a long way from our analysis of the Outsider, but let me try to get the matter straight with a few sentences. The Outsider's problem amounts to a way of seeing the world that can be termed 'pessimistic' (*q.v.* Roquentin). I have tried to argue that this pessimism is true and valid. It therefore discounts the humanistic ideals of 'man rising on stepping stones of dead selves to higher things, etc.', and criticizes philosophy by saying that there is no point in the philosopher's trying to get to know the world if he doesn't know himself. It says flatly that the ideal 'objective philosophy' will not be constructed by mere thinkers, but by men who combine the thinker, the poet and the man of action. The first question of philosophy is not 'What is the Universe all about?' but 'What should we do with our lives?'; i.e. its aim is not a System that shall be intellectually consistent, but the salvation of the individual. Now, I assert that this formula is a religious formula, whether we find it in St. Augustine or Bernard Shaw, and an important part of my aim in this book has been to try to point this out.

Hulme is unprecedentedly clear on the subject of the distinction between the philosopher's view (humanism) and the religious view, and we can pick up the basis of his disagreement with Nietzsche from the opening pages of the *Speculations*, where he divides reality into three realms: the physical, the vital, the religious:

> Let us assume that reality is divided into three regions; separated from one another by absolute divisions, by real discontinuities. (1) The inorganic world, dealt with by mathematics and physical science, (2) the organic world, dealt with by biology, psychology, history, and (3) the world of ethical and religious values.[27]

Nietzsche is at one with Augustinian theology in seeing the world as made up essentially of matter and spirit, and seeing life as the region of the interaction of the two. There is no absolute gulf. Inorganic matter is being continually transformed into organic. Hulme recognizes this in another essay on Bergson:

> The process of evolution can only be described as the gradual insertion of more and more freedom into matter. . . . In the amoeba, then, you might say that impulse has manufactured a small leak through which free activity could be inserted into the world, and the process of evolution has been the gradual enlargement of this leak.[28]

Here, as elsewhere, Hulme uses the term 'evolution' without any implied criticism. The essence of his criticism of humanism and romanticism is contained in the sentence (describing classicism): 'You are always faithful to the conception of a limit.' He says:

> The amount of freedom in man is much exaggerated. That we are free on certain rare occasions both my religion and the views I get from metaphysics convince me. But many acts that we habitually label free are in reality automatic.[29]

There is no need to point out the similarity to Gurdjieff's vitalism. There is a conception of the limit there. And Hulme summarizes:

> You could describe the facts of evolution, then, by saying that it seems as if an immense current or consciousness had traversed matter, endeavouring to organize this matter so that it could introduce freedom into it.
>
> But in doing this, consciousness has itself been ensnared in certain directions. Matter has captured the consciousness which was organizing it, and entrapped it into its own automatism. In the vegetable kingdom, for example, automatism and unconsciousness have become the rule. In the animals, consciousness has more success, but along the whole course of evolution, liberty is dogged by automatism, and is, in the long run, stifled by it. One can get a picture of the course of evolution in this way: It is as if a current of consciousness flowed down into matter as into a tunnel, and, making efforts to advance on every side, digs galleries, most of which are stopped by rock which is too hard, but which in one direction at least has broken through the rock and back into life again. . . . The passage through matter may give to a part of the current of consciousness a certain kind of coherence which enables it to survive as a permanent entity after its passage.[30]

We might compare this with Lilith's speech at the end of *Back to Methuselah*, with its sentence, 'I brought life into the whirlpool of force, and compelled my enemy Matter to obey a living soul; but in enslaving Life's enemy, I made him Life's master, for that is the end of all slavery. . . .' And Lilith's speech contains the Outsider's credo: 'I say, let them dread above all things stagnation. . . .'[31]

There is in Shaw, as in Gurdjieff and Nietzsche, a recognition of the immense effort of Will that is necessary to express even a little freedom, that places them beside Pascal and St. Augustine as religious thinkers. Their view is saved from pessimism only by its mystical recognition of the possibilities of pure Will, freed from the entanglements of automatism. (Mr. Eliot's line in the *Family Reunion*, 'And partial observation of one's own automatism', places him with Hulme and Gurdjieff and Bergson, in the same way that his 'Make perfect your will' in 'The Rock' emphasizes the affinity of his thought with Nietzsche as well as with Boehme and Eckhart.)

Hulme predicted the end of the present humanist epoch, an epoch that, as he pointed out, was inaugurated with the Renaissance and its discarding of the dogma of Original Sin, the absolute limiting principle. He believed that this dogma cannot be discarded without blurring all lines of clear thinking, and throwing open the doors to sentimentally optimistic modes of thought. He recognized that:

> A new anti-humanist ideology could not be a mere revival of medievalism. The humanist period has developed a certain honesty in science, and a certain conception of freedom of thought and action that will remain. . . .[32]

A gradual change in the intellectual climate since Hulme wrote these words vouches for his penetration.

The new anti-humanist epoch will be the consequence of the rigorous questioning of such men as Blake, Nietzsche, Dostoevsky, Shaw. Humanism is only another name for spiritual laziness, or a vague half-creed adopted by men of science and logicians whose heads are too occupied with the world of mathematics and physics to worry about religious categories. For such men, it is only necessary to make the outlines and derivations of these categories clear and graspable. They cannot be expected to sort out all the rubbish left over from the Renaissance. That is the concern of men who are deeply enough touched by religious issues to get to work with a pick and shovel. Shaw had put his finger on the real need in the *Back to Methuselah* Preface:

> Let the churches ask themselves why there is no revolt against the dogmas of mathematics though there is one against the dogmas of religion. It is not that the mathematical dogmas are more comprehensible. The law of inverse squares is as incomprehensible to the common man as the Athanasian Creed. It is not that science is free from witchcraft, legends, miracles, biographic boosting of quacks as heroes and saints, and of barren scoundrels as explorers and discoverers. On the contrary, the iconography and hagiology of science are as copious as they are mostly squalid. But no student of science has yet been taught that specific gravity consists in the belief that Archimedes jumped out of his bath and ran naked through the streets of Syracuse shouting Eureka, Eureka, or that the Law of Inverse Squares must be discarded if anyone can prove that Newton was never in an orchard in his life. . . . In mathematics and physics, the faith is still kept pure, and you may take the law and leave the legends without a suspicion of heresy. . . .[33]

Let us couple this with Hulme's disclaimer of the 'sentiment' of religion in *Speculations*:

> I have none of the feeling of *nostalgia*, the reverence for tradition, the desire to recapture the sentiment of Angelico, which seems to animate most modern defenders of religion. All that seems to me to be bosh. What is important is what nobody seems to realize—the dogmas like that of Original Sin. . . . That man is in no sense perfect, but a wretched creature who can yet apprehend perfection. It is not, then, that I put up with the dogma for the sake of the sentiment, but that I may possibly swallow the sentiment for the sake of the dogma.[34]

The understanding of the attitude behind this paragraph is, I believe, one of the most important needs of our time.

Hulme regarded his *Speculations* as a prolegomena to the reading of Pascal. It was my ambition, in writing this study in the Outsider, to serve as a prolegomena to an even wider field, to a field bounded by Shaw and Gurdjieff on the one hand, and on the other by an orthodox Protestant like Kierkegaard or an orthodox Catholic like Newman. In this aim, I have admittedly covered a great deal of the ground already brilliantly dealt with in Reinhold Niebuhr's *Nature and Destiny of Man*, and in various works of Berdyaev, and I must acknowledge my indebtedness to them, as also (in common with many others of my generation) to Mr. Eliot's penetrating essays on humanism and the religious attitude. In retrospect, I feel that probably no book running to a hundred thousand words could achieve this aim. If the present book could serve as a stimulus to the re-reading of Shaw, it would have more than served its purpose. At the time of writing this, Shaw is passing through a period of undervaluation that is without parallel since Shakespeare was forgotten in the seventeenth century. Such an undervaluation of a major religious teacher would be the worst possible symptom of our age, if it were not for the increasing interest in Existentialist thinkers like Berdyaev, Kierkegaard, Camus. If Hulme's 'new religious age' is to be born before our civilization destroys itself, it may require an intellectual effort of gestation that will involve the whole civilized world.

There are still many difficulties that cannot be touched on here. The problem for the 'civilization' is the adoption of a religious attitude that can be assimilated as *objectively* as the headlines of last Sunday's newspapers. But the problem for the individual always will be the opposite of this, the conscious striving *not* to limit the amount of experience seen and touched; the intolerable struggle to expose the sensitive areas of being to what may possibly hurt them; the attempt to see as a whole, although the instinct of self-preservation fights against the pain of the internal widening, and all the impulses of spiritual laziness build into waves of sleep with every new effort. The individual begins that long effort as an Outsider; he may finish it as a saint.

NOTES

All page references are to British editions

Chapter One

page 11. 1. Barbusse, Henri: *L'Enfer* (tr. John Rodker, London, Joiner & Steele, 1932; New York, E. P. Dutton & Company, Inc., under the title *The Inferno*), p. 72.
page 12. 2. Ibid., p. 12.
    3. Ibid., p. 9.
    4. Ibid., p. 15.
    5. Ibid., p. 39.
page 13. 6. Ibid., p. 243.
    7. Ibid., p. 22.
page 16. 8. Wells, H. G.: *Mind at the End of Its Tether* (Heinemann, 1945), p. 1.
    9. Ibid., p. 2.
   10. Ibid., p. 3.
page 17. 11. Ibid., p. 4.
page 18. 12. Ibid., p. 34.
page 22. 13. Sartre, Jean-Paul: *The Diary of Antoine Roquentin* (tr. Lloyd Alexander, London, John Lehmann, 1949; New York, New Directions under the title *Nausea*), p. 8.
   14. Ibid., pp. 12ff.
page 23. 15. Ibid., p. 17.
   16. Ibid., p. 31.
   17. Ibid., p. 34.
page 24. 18. Ibid., p. 169.
page 25. 19. Ibid., pp. 170ff.

Chapter Two

page 27. 1. Camus, Albert: *The Outsider* (tr. Stuart Gilbert, London, Hamish Hamilton, 1946; New York, Alfred A. Knopf, Inc., under the title *The Stranger*), p. 9.
    2. Ibid., p. 9.
page 28. 3. Ibid., p. 23.
    4. Ibid., pp. 40ff.
page 29. 5. Ibid., p. 81.
page 30. 6. Ibid., pp. 102ff.
    7. Ibid., pp. 103-4.
page 31. 8. Hemingway, Ernest: *First Forty-Nine Stories* (Cape, 1944), p. 137.
page 32. 9. Ibid., pp. 142ff.
page 33. 10. *The Essential Hemingway* (Cape, 1947), p. 15.
page 34. 11. Hemingway, Ernest: *A Farewell to Arms* (London, Cape, 1953; New York, Charles Scribner's Sons), p. 17.
   12. Ibid., p. 33.
page 36. 13. Ibid., p. 329.
   14. Hemingway, Ernest: *First Forty-Nine Stories* (Cape, 1944), p. 247.
   15. Ibid., pp. 457-8.
page 37. 16. Ibid., p. 412. (First published as a chapter of *Death in the Afternoon*.)
   17. Ibid., p. 413.
   18. Ibid., p. 416.
page 39. 19. Sampson, George: *Concise Cambridge History of English Literature*, p. 996.
page 40. 20. Granville-Barker, Harley: *The Secret Life* (London, Sidgwick & Jackson, 1928; Boston, Little, Brown & Company), p. 12.
   21. Ibid., p. 14.
page 41. 22. Ibid., p. 31.
page 42. 23. Ibid., p. 33.
page 43. 24. Ibid., p. 31.

page 43. 25. Granville-Barker, Harley: *The Secret Life* (London, Sidgwick & Jackson, 1928; Boston, Little, Brown & Company), p. 88.
    26. Ibid., p. 87.
    27. Ibid., pp. 87ff.
page 44. 28. Ibid., p. 86.
page 45. 29. Ibid., p. 152.
    30. Ibid., p. 158.
    31. Ibid., p. 118.
page 46. 32. Ibid., p. 113.

Chapter Three

page 48. 1. Sir John Suckling.
    2. Novalis: *Heinrich von Ofterdingen.*
page 49. 3. Joyce, James: *Portrait of the Artist as a Young Man* (London, Cape, 1952; New York, The Viking Press, Inc.), pp. 72ff.
page 50. 4. Ibid., p. 271.
page 53. 5. Hesse, Hermann: *Demian* (Holt, 1948), pp. 2-3.
    6. Ibid., pp. 4-5.
page 54. 7. Ibid., pp. 5-6.
    8. Ibid., p. 28.
page 58. 9. Hesse, Hermann: *Steppenwolf* (tr. Basil Creighton; London, Secker, 1929; New York, Henry Holt and Company, Inc.), pp.. 55, 57.
page 60. 10. Ibid., p. 93.
    11. Ibid., p. 94.
    12. Ibid., p. 95.
    13. Ibid., p. 96.
page 61. 14. Ibid., p. 96.
    15. Ibid., pp. 96, 97, 98.
    16. Ibid., p. 101.
page 62. 17. Ibid., pp. 210, 211, 212.
page 63. 18. Ibid., p. 322.
page 66. 19. Hesse, Hermann: *Magister Ludi* (*The Bead Game*) (tr. Mervyn Saville; London, Aldus Publications, 1949; New York, Henry Holt and Company, Inc.), p. 38.
page 67. 20. *Steppenwolf* (ed. cit.), pp. 47-8.

Chapter Four

page 73. 1. *T. E. Lawrence by His Friends* (Cape, 1937), p. 272.
page 74. 2. Lawrence, T. E.: *The Seven Pillars of Wisdom* (Cape, 1952, New York, Doubleday & Company, Inc.), p. 37.
    3. Ibid., p. 38.
page 75. 4. Ibid., p. 41.
    5. Ibid., p. 41.
page 76. 6. Ibid., p. 527.
    7. Ibid., p. 117.
page 77. 8. *T. E. Lawrence by His Friends* (Cape, 1937), pp. 284ff.
    9. Lawrence, T. E.: *The Seven Pillars of Wisdom* (London, Cape, 1952; New York, Doubleday & Company, Inc.), p. 580.
    10. Ibid., p. 284.
    11. Ibid., p. 521.
page 78. 12. Ibid., p. 582.
    13. Ibid., p. 566.
page 79. 14. Ibid., p. 421.
    15. Ibid., p. 461.
page 80. 16. Ibid., p. 477.
    17. Ibid., p. 477.
page 93. 18. Ibid.
page 94. 19. *Diary of Vaslav Nijinsky* (London, Gollancz, 1937; New York, Simon and Schuster, Inc.), p. 64.
page 97. 20. Nijinsky, Romola: *Nijinsky* (London, Gollancz, 1933; New York, Simon and Schuster, Inc.), p. 408.

21. *Diary of Vaslav Nijinsky* (London, Gollancz, 1937; New York, Simon and Schuster, Inc.), p. 21.
22. Ibid., p. 60.
page 98.   23. Ibid., p. 44.
24. Ibid., p. 45.
25. Ibid., p. 49.
26. Ibid., p. 54.
27. Ibid., p. 47.
28. Ibid., p. 54.
page 99.   29. Ibid., p. 49.
30. Ibid., p. 66.
31. Ibid., p. 40.
page 100. 32. Ibid., p. 22.
33. Ibid., p. 202.
34. Ibid., p. 196.
page 101. 35. Ibid., pp. 201-2.
36. Ibid., p. 136.
page 104. 37. Hulme, T. E.: *Speculations* (London, Kegan Paul, 1926; New York, Harcourt, Brace & Company), p. 53.
38. Ibid.
page 106. 39. *Diary of Vaslav Nijinsky* (London, Gollancz, 1937; New York, Simon and Schuster, Inc.), p. 197.

Chapter Five

page 107. 1. James, William: *The Varieties of Religious Experience* (Longmans, Green, 1903), pp. 132ff.
page 108. 2. 'Death's Jest Book.'
page 109. 3. 'Ode to a Nightingale.'
4. 'City of Dreadful Night.'
5. 'The Waste Land.'
page 110. 6. *Youth and Other Stories* (Blackwood, 1922), p. 170.
page 111. 7. James, William: *The Varieties of Religious Experience* (Longmans, Green, 1903), pp. 158ff.
8. *Society the Redeemed form of Man* (Boston, 1879), p. 43ff.
page 117. 9. *The Varieties of Religious Experience* (ed. cit.), p. 160.
page 118. 10. Kafka, Franz: *In the Penal Settlement* (Secker & Warburg, 1949).
page 122. 11. *q.v.* Conrad Bonifazi's *Kierkegaard and Nietzsche* (Rockliff, 1953).
page 123. 12. James, William: (op. cit.), pp. 173ff.
page 124. 13. Nietzsche: *Joyful Wisdom* (tr. T. Connor; London, T. N. Foulis, 1910; New York, The Macmillan Company), p. 7.
page 125. 14. Reyburn, H. A.: *Nietzsche* (Macmillan, 1948), p. 66.
page 126. 15. Halévy, D.: *Life of Nietzsche* (Fisher-Unwin, 1914), p. 53.
page 127. 16. Nietzsche: *Birth of Tragedy* (tr. W. A. Hauseman; London, Allen & Unwin, 1909; New York, The Macmillan Company), p. 26.
page 131. 17. Ibid., p. 232.
18. Nietzsche: *Joyful Wisdom:* (ed. cit.), p. 1.
page 132. 19. Ibid., p. 5.
20. Ibid., p. 7.
21. Ibid., p. 9.
page 138. 22. Blake, William: *Complete Works* (Nonesuch Edition, 1927; New York, Oxford University Press), pp. 322, 603.
23. Nietzsche: *Thus Spake Zarathustra* (tr. A. Tille and M. M. Bozman, London, Everyman, 1946; New York, The Macmillan Company), p. 6.
page 139. 24. Ibid., p. 7.
25. Nietzsche: *Ecce Homo* (tr. Anthony M. Ludovici, London, T. N. Foulis, 1911; New York, The Macmillan Company), p. 2.

page 140. 26. *Thus Spake Zarathustra:* (ed. cit.), p. 7.
27. Ibid., p. 9.
page 141. 28. Rilke, R. M.: *Malte Laurids Brigge* (tr. J. B. Leishman; London, Hogarth Press, 1950; New York, W. W. Norton & Company, Inc.), p. 99ff.
page 142. 29. *Thus Spake Zarathustra:* (ed. cit.), p. 54.
30. Ibid., p. 55.
31. Ibid., p. 102.
page 145. 32. Ibid., p. 129.

Chapter Six

page 149. 1. Tolstoy, Leo: *War and Peace* (tr. L. and A. Maude; London, World's Classics, 1922-3; New York, Heritage Press), Vol. 1, p. 460.
2. Ibid., Vol. III, p. 194.
3. Maude, Aylmer: *Life of Tolstoy* (London, World's Classics, 1930; New York, Oxford University Press), Vol. I, p. 384.
4. Ibid., p. 385.
page 150. 5. *q.v.* Aylmer Maude's *Life* (London, World's Classics, 1939; New York, Oxford University Press), Chapter XI.
page 151. 6. Tolstoy, Alexei: *Memoirs of a Madman* (tr. A. Maude; World's Classics), pp. 210ff.
7. Ibid.
page 152. 8. Maude, Aylmer: (op. cit.), p. 385.
9. Tolstoy, Alexei: *The Death of Ivan Ilytch* (tr. A. Maude, London, World's Classics, 1935; New York, Dodd, Mead & Company), pp. 1ff.
page 154. 10. Newman, J. H.: *Apologia* (Sheed & Ward, 1946).
page 158. 11. Dostoevsky, Fiodor: *Notes from Underground* (tr. C. J. Hogarth, London, Everyman Library, 1953; New York, E. P. Dutton & Company, Inc.), p. 12.
12. Ibid., p. 15.
page 159. 13. *A Treasury of Russian Literature* (tr. B. G. Guerney, London, Bodley Head, 1948; New York, The Vanguard Press), p. 460.
page 160. 14. Blake, William: 'Marriage of Heaven and Hell,' *Collected Works* (ed. cit.), p. 191.
15. Blake, William: *Collected Works* (ed. cit.), p. 564.
page 161. 16. Quoted from *Dostoevsky* by N. Berdyaev (Sheed & Ward, 1936), pp. 53ff.
17. Dostoevsky, Fiodor: (op. cit.), p. 41.
page 163. 18. Dostoevsky, Fiodor: *Crime and Punishment* (tr. Constance Garnett, London, Heinemann, 1945; New York, The Macmillan Company), pp. 138-9.
page 164. 19. Berdyaev: *Dostoevsky* (ed. cit.), p. 97.
page 166. 20. *Crime and Punishment* (ed. cit.), p. 457.
page 172. 21. Dostoevsky, Fiodor: *The Devils* (tr. D. Magarshack; Penguin, 1953), pp. 665ff.
page 173. 22. *Crime and Punishment* (ed. cit.), p. 142.
page 174. 23. *The Devils* (ed. cit.), p. 612.
page 175. 24. Ibid., p. 243.
25. Revelation x.5.
26. Dostoevsky, Fiodor: *The Idiot* (tr. E. M. Martin, London, Everyman, 1953; New York, E. P. Dutton & Company, Inc.), p. 224.
page 176. 27. *The Devils* (ed. cit.), p. 589.

Chapter Seven

page 180. 1. Dostoevsky, Fiodor: *The Brothers Karamazov* (tr. Constance Garnett, London, Heinemann, 1948; New York, The Macmillan Company), p. 235.

page 181. 2. Ibid., p. 236.
page 182. 3. Ibid., p. 253.
page 184. 4. *The Devils* (ed. cit.), pp. 613-14.
page 186. 5. *The Brothers Karamazov* (ed. cit.), p. 297.
page 191. 6. Ibid., p. 537.
    7. *Crime and Punishment* (ed. cit.), p. 142.
page 195. 8. *The Brothers Karamazov* (ed. cit.), p. 683.
page 198. 9. Blake, William: *Collected Works* (London, Nonesuch, 1927; New York, Oxford University Press), p. 1068.
page 199. 10. Mann, Thomas: *Doktor Faustus* (tr. H. T. Lowe-Porter, London, Secker & Warburg, 1949; New York, Alfred A. Knopf, Inc., under the title *Doctor Faustus*), p. 147.
page 200. 11. *Thus Spake·Zarathustra* (ed. cit.), p. 64.
page 201. 12. Hemingway, Ernest: *Short Stories* (ed. cit.), p. 78. (In the original *Esquire* publication of the story (1936) Hemingway wrote: 'Poor Scott'. Later, for book publication, this was changed to 'Poor Julian'.)

Chapter Eight

page 203. 1. Blake, William: *Collected Works* (ed. cit.), p. 844.
page 205. 2. Sartre, Jean-Paul: *Existentialism and Humanism* (London, Methuen, 1948; New York, Philosophical Library), p. 31.
page 206. 3. Fox, George: *Journals* (Cambridge, 1950), pp. 71ff.
page 208. 4. Ibid., p. 3.
    5. Ibid., p. 3.
page 209. 6. Ibid., p. 4.
    7. Ibid., p. 4.
page 210. 8. Ibid., p. 5.
    9. Ibid., p. 6.
page 211. 10. Ibid., p. 10.
    11. Ibid., p. 11.
    12. Rilke, R. M.: *Duino Elegies* (tr. Leishman and Spender, London, Hogarth Press, 1939; New York, W. W. Norton & Company, Inc.), p. 91.
page 212. 13. Fox, George: (op. cit.), p. 12.
page 214. 14. Ibid., p. 16.
    15. Ibid., pp. 12-13.
page 215. 16. Ibid., p. 44.
page 216. 17. Ibid., p. 15.
page 220. 18. Reyburn, H. A.: *Nietzsche* (Macmillan, 1948), p. 66.
page 222. 19. Dowson, Ernest: *Poetical Works* (Cassell and the Bodley Head, 1934), p. 3.
page 225. 20. Blake, William: *Collected Works* (ed. cit.), p. 127.
    21. Ibid., p. 78.
page 226. 22. Ibid., pp. 148-9.
page 227. 23. Ibid., p. 202.
    24. Ibid.
    25. Ibid.
    26. Ibid., p. 563.
page 228. 27. Ibid., p. 267.
    28. Ibid., p. 214.
page 230. 29. Ibid., p. 197.
page 231. 30. Ibid., p. 232.
    31. Ibid., pp. 207ff.
page 233. 32. *A Buddhist Bible* (ed. Dwight Goddard; New York, E. P. Dutton & Co., 1952), p. 235.
page 234. 33. Blake, William: *Collected Works* (ed. cit.), p. 173.
page 235. 34. Ibid., p. 220.
page 236. 35. Ibid., p. 235.
page 237. 36. Ibid., p. 554.
page 238. 37. Ibid., p. 108.

page 242. 38. Ibid., p. 842.
   39. *Steppenwolf* (ed. cit.), p. 97.
   40. Newman, J. H.: (op. cit.), Book V.
page 243. 41. Blake, William: *Collected Works* (ed. cit.), p. 240.
page 244. 42. Eliot, T. S.: *Four Quartets* (London, Faber, 1939; New York, Harcourt, Brace & Company), p. 10.
   43. Yeats, W. B.: *Collected Poems* (Macmillan, 1950), p. 283.
page 246. 44. Kierkegaard, Søren: *Either/Or* (The Rotation Method): *A Kierkegaard Anthology* (ed. R. Bretal; Princeton, 1946), pp. 22ff.

Chapter Nine

page 247. 1. Translation taken from the last chapter of Edmund Wilson's *Axel's Castle* (Scribner's, 1931).
page 248. 2. Traherne, Thomas: *Centuries of Meditation* (Dobell, 1948), p. 152.
   3. Ibid., pp. 155ff.
page 249. 4. Yeats, W. B.: *Collected Poems:* (ed. cit.), p. 62.
   5. Traherne, Thomas: (op. cit.), p. 284.
page 250. 6. Yeats, W. B.: *A Vision* (Macmillan, 1936), p. 33.
page 252. 7. *Life of Ramakrishna* (Anonymous) (Ramakrishna Math, Madras, 1929; Hollywood, Vedanta Press), p. 20.
page 254. 8. Ibid., pp. 71ff.
page 257. 9. *The Gospel of Shri Ramakrishna* (Mylapore, Madras, 1947; Ramakrishna-Vivekananda Center (tr. Swami Nikhilananda) 1942); *q.v.* Index of Hymns, p. 1,043.
page 259. 10. *The Gospel of Shri Ramakrishna* (Mylapore, Madras, 1947; Ramakrishna-Vivekananda Center (tr. Swami Nikhilananda) 1942); *q.v.* Index of Hymns, pp. 170, 305-6.
page 260. 11. James, William (op. cit.), p. 262.
page 262. 12. Woodward, F. L.: *Sayings of the Buddha* (Oxford, 1939), pp. 14ff.
page 263. 13. Eckhart (ed. Pfeiffer; Watkins, 1947), p. 37.
page 268. 14. Ouspensky, P. D.: *In Search of the Miraculous* (London, Routledge and Kegan Paul, 1950; New York, Harcourt, Brace & Company), p. 219.
page 269. 15. Ibid., p. 218.
   16. *Poems of St. John of the Cross* (tr. E. Allison Peers; Burns, Oates and Washburne, 1948), p. 28.
page 270. 17. Gurdjieff, George; *All and Everything* (London, Routledge and Kegan Paul, 1950; New York, Harcourt, Brace & Company), p. 1,183.
page 273. 18. Hulme, T. E.: *Speculations* (London, Kegan Paul, 1926; New York, Harcourt, Brace & Company), p. 265.
page 274. 19. Chesterton, G. K.: *The Napoleon of Notting Hill* (Penguin, 1946).
   20. Hulme, T. E.: (op. cit.), p. 119.
   21. Ibid., p. 116.
   22. Ibid., p. 77.
page 275. 23. Eliot, T. S.: *Selected Essays* (London, Faber, 1932; New York, Harcourt, Brace & Company), p. 440.
   24. Hulme, T. E.: (op. cit.), p. 8.
page 276. 25. Ibid., p. 19.
   26. Ibid., p. 17.
page 277. 27. Ibid., p. 5.   28. Ibid., p. 208.
page 278. 29. Ibid., p. 123.   30. Ibid., p. 210.
page 279. 31. Shaw, G. B.: *Collected Plays* (London, Odhams, 1950; New York, Dodd, Mead & Company), p. 962.
   32. Hulme, T. E.: (op. cit.), p. 57.
page 280. 33. Shaw, G. B.: *Prefaces* (London, Odhams, 1938; New York, Dodd, Mead & Company), p. 541.
   34. Hulme, T. E.: (op. cit.), p. 70.

POSTSCRIPT TO THE OUTSIDER

THE OUTSIDER first appeared eleven years ago, in 1956, and achieved a success that made one critic write: "Not since Lord Byron woke up one morning and found himself famous has an English writer met with such spontaneous and universal acclaim." It was true, and it was hard luck on me, for reasons I shall try to explain.

I was born in 1931 into a working-class family in Leicester; my father was a boot-and-shoe operative who earned £3 a week. This meant that education was hard to come by. I realize this sounds absurd at this point in the twentieth century. But what has to be understood is that English working-class families—particularly factory workers—live in a curious state of apathy that would make Oblomov seem a demon of industry. My own family, for example, simply never bother to call in a doctor when they feel ill; they just never get around to it. One family doctor—an old Irishman, now dead and probably in Hell—killed about six of my family with sheer bumbling incompetence, and yet it never struck anyone to go to another doctor.

This explains why, although I was fairly clever at school and passed exams easily enough, I never went to a university. No one thought of suggesting it. Anyway, my family wanted me to bring home a weekly wage packet. So I left school at sixteen. (My brother left at fourteen.)

In a way, this was a good thing. Ever since I was twelve, I had been preoccupied with the question of the meaning of human existence, and whether all human values are not pure self-delusion. (No doubt this feeling was intensified by my dislike of the vague, brainless, cowlike drifting of the people around me.) My main interest was in science—particularly atomic physics—so that I was obsessed by the idea that there must be a scientific method for investigating this question of human existence. At fourteen, I discovered Shaw's *Man and Superman*, and realized, with a shock, that I was not the first human being to ask the question. After that, I discovered Eliot's *Waste Land,* Goethe's *Faust* and Dostoevsky's *Devils* in quick succession, and began to feel that I was acquiring the basic data for attacking the problem. Since no school or university in England provides courses in this problem, it is probably as well that I set out to work on my own at sixteen.

For the next eight years I worked in various jobs—mostly unskilled labor—and continued to accumulate data. I also did a good deal of writing—I kept a voluminous journal, which was several million words long by the time I was twenty-four. It was an extremely hard and discouraging business, for I knew no one whose interests overlapped with mine. I married when I was nineteen, and a wife and child added to the problems. But at least it meant that I got used to working completely and totally alone, and not expecting encouragement. Later on, reviewers and critics were outraged by what one of them called "his stupefying assurance about his own genius." But it would have been impossible to go on working without some conviction of genius—at least, of certainty about the importance of what I was doing, and the belief that it wouldn't matter if no other human being ever came to share this certainty. The feeling of alienation had to be totally accepted. Luckily, I've always had a fairly cheerful temperament, not much given to self-pity. So I went on working, reading and writing in my total vacuum, without contact with any other writer or thinker. I finally came to accept that I might spend all my life working in factories, and that my writing might never see print. It was hard to swallow, but I swallowed it, feeling that if Blake and Nietzche could do without recognition, so could I.

Then a publisher to whom I sent the first few pages of *The Outsider* accepted it. And when I was nearly twenty-five, there came that shattering morning when I woke up and found press men banging at the door and television and radio demanding interviews. It was such a total change that it was like a bang on the head. *The Outsider* shot to the top of the nonfiction best-seller list in England and America, and was translated into fourteen languages within eighteen months. It so happened that a number of young writers made their appearance at this time, including John Osborne, John Braine, and my friend Bill Hopkins. The press labeled us "Angry Young Men." In my case, nothing could have been more grotesquely inappropriate. I was aggressively nonpolitical. I believed that people who make a fuss about politics do so because their heads are too empty to think about more important things. So I felt nothing but impatient contempt for Osborne's Jimmy Porter and the rest of the heroes of social protest.

The tide turned very quickly. It was the highbrow press that made us successful. England has a large number of critics who delight in nothing so much as the discovery of new artistic talent. But they tend to turn very peevish if their enthusiasms are taken out of their hands and accepted by the popular press. This is what happened with the Angry Young Men. But my case was extreme. I had nothing in common with the others anyway. Osborne and Braine had a streak of self-pity that appealed to these highbrow critics, most of whom believed that the accident of a public-school education had destroyed their creativity and ruined their lives. Besides, I had written a book of ideas, and every critic in England felt that my success was monstrously unfair, in that it really belonged to himself—for a critic is, after all, a professional man of ideas.

The experience was vertiginous. After a month of the noisiest and gaudiest kind of success, in which popular reviewers compared me to Plato, Shelley, Shaw and D. H. Lawrence, the merry-go-round came suddenly to a halt, and then began to to revolve in the opposite direction. My name became a kind of dirty word to serious critics, and the ones who had "discovered" me winced when they remembered their praises. Every Christmas in England, the "posh" Sunday papers run a feature in which eminent men and women are asked their opinion of the best books of the year. Not one mentioned *The Outsider*, except Arthur Koestler, who went out of his way to refer to it as the "bubble of the year," "in which a young man discovers that men of genius suffer from *Weltschmerz*."

If *The Outsider* was an unprecedented success, my next book, *Religion and the Rebel*, was an unprecedented failure. The highbrow critics seized the opportunity to go back on their praise of *The Outsider*. And the popular press joined in like a gang of Indians invited to a massacre. *Time*, with its usual awe-inspiring vulgarity, ran a kind of obituary on me headed "Scrambled Egghead."

It was then I was grateful for my ten years' training in standing on my own feet. I had disliked the success of *The Outsider*.

I don't much like people anyway, so the endless succession of parties and receptions, and the hordes of new acquaintances, left me with a strong feeling of "people poisoning." Six months after *The Outsider* came out, I moved as far away from London as I could get, to a cottage in Cornwall. There I plunged into the world of religious mysticism—of Eckhart and Boehme, Pascal and Swedenborg—of which I wrote in *Religion and the Rebel*. Success or failure didn't matter all that much, provided one had enough money to live. *The Outsider* made me less money than might be expected—taxes took a lot of it, and I spent the rest pretty quickly—but I lived frugally anyway. The sheer malice of some of the attacks on me was difficult to swallow. But I felt I held a final card—my long practice in working alone, which probably meant that I could go on writing longer than my critics could go on sneering. The prospect of continuing the battle until I was ninety gave me a certain grim satisfaction. When my second book was hatchetted, I shrugged and went on working. The attacks didn't worry me too much. I know enough of success to know that it is meaningless unless it is based on real understanding. I recognized that such understanding would probably take twenty years to grow. I was right. After ten years, it seems to be developing in countries where I would have least expected it—Japan, India, France, Spain, Arabia (the Arabs have translated seven of my books in the past year). Even in America. It may happen in England if I can live to be ninety or so.

In the past ten years, I have written 21 books, eight of them novels, and seven in my "Outsider series." In this time, I had developed the ideas of *The Outsider* to create a philosophy that I sometimes refer to as "the new existentialism." (I prefer to call it "phenomenological existentialism," but the word worries most people.) While I felt that I had stumbled upon a particularly fruitful and exciting line of investigation, I was not certain of the general importance of these ideas—being naturally modest and lacking in self-assurance—until I came to America to lecture in 1961, and again in 1966. Their reception by audiences of American students all over the country convinced me that I had not been too conceited in suspecting that they constituted a kind of revolution in philosophy.

For anyone who is interested in following them up in detail, I recommend the six volumes of the Outsider series: *The*

Outsider, Religion and the Rebel, The Stature of Man, The Strength to Dream, Origins of the Sexual Impulse and *Beyond the Outsider*. For readers who would prefer a clear and fairly short summary, I suggest my *Introduction to the New Existentialism*—perhaps the best introduction to my ideas. For readers who haven't time for any of these, I'll attempt to sketch them in the remainder of this postscript.

The basic problem of "The Outsider" is his instinctive rejection of the everyday world, a feeling that it is somehow boring and unsatisfying, like a hypnotized man eating sawdust under the belief that it is eggs and bacon.

All major poets and philosophers have had this feeling as their starting point, the feeling, expressed by Axel, that living itself is a trivial and repetitive task, fit only for servants. This led many philosophers to reject the "real world"—Plato is an example—and to believe that there is somehow another world —of ideas, of the spirit, which is the true "home" of the poet. This is the feeling behind Keats' "Ode to the Nightingale" as well as Wagner's *Tristan*.

In the nineteenth century, this kind of world-rejection came to a head in poets who called themselves "romantics." Most of them believed that the poet was never intended for "this world," dreary and heartbreaking as it is. And yet he has certain moments when he feels curiously immortal, god-like, as if hovering above the world, untouched by its dullness. Is this feeling an illusion, like an opium dream? The romantics were obviously inclined to believe so, for large numbers of them committed suicide or died of tuberculosis.

In the twentieth century, romanticism revived under another name. It called itself "existentialism." But its basic question was still the same. Which of the two worlds is real: that world of supreme, godlike detachment and power, or the world in which we feel victimized, helpless, "contingent"? Which is true: man's experience of his freedom, or of slavery to his body and the world?

Existentialism was not quite so pessimistic as romanticism. Its position tended to be stoical. It is summed up in that phrase of Hemingway from *The Old Man and the Sea*—"A man can be destroyed but not defeated." Not very hopeful, yet asserting the "eternal spirit of the chainless mind" all the same.

I could not accept either the death-worship of the romantics, nor the stoical defeat of the existentialists. For various temperamental reasons—partly because I am an Englishman—I do not share the tendency to gloom and defeat that pervades so much modern literature. I felt that I had no intention of being either defeated or destroyed. On the other hand, neither have I any sympathy for that lazy and intellectually timid school of English philosophers, led by Professor Ayer, who assert that the whole problem is meaningless, and we had better accept our pathetic little limitations. The problem ought to be solvable *in its own terms*, not by turning away and pretending it doesn't exist.

It seemed to me that a solution must be found. Here, my natural optimism was to my advantage. For when I read Sartre or Camus or Graham Greene, I experienced a *temperamental* rejection of their pessimism. I suspected that their ultimate picture might be distorted by a certain self-pity or lack of discipline—or, in the case of Greene, by a certain congenital lack of vitality. I suspected that if the problem left them defeated, it was because they had not attacked it hard enough.

I saw, even at this early stage, that it was a problem of *consciousness*. For what it amounts to, after all, is whether these strange moments of *freedom* can be recalled at will. The romantics were gloomily inclined to believe that they were some form of "grace"—or perhaps even something to do with the chemistry of the body or brain, so that the "glory and the freshness of a dream" vanish inevitably as one grows past childhood.

And here I made my first important observation—the one that has been the foundation stone of all my subsequent thinking. I called it "the St Neot margin." It is the recognition that man's moments of freedom tend to come under crisis or challenge, and that when things are going well, he tends to allow his grip on life to slacken. Auden wrote:

> Put the car away; when life fails
> What's the good of going to Wales?

I should explain how I became aware of this problem of the "St Neot margin." One hot day in 1954, I was hitchhiking up the Great North Road to Peterborough, in a state of fatigue and "life-devaluation." I didn't want to go to Peterborough—it was a boring duty call—and neither did I particularly want to return to London, where I was working in a dreary plastic

factory and quarreling with my landlady. I felt so depressed
that I did not even feel grateful when a truck finally stopped
for me. After a mile or so, there was a knocking sound from his
gearbox, and the driver explained that he would have to pull
into a garage to have it repaired. So I got out and went on
thumbing lifts. A second truck stopped for me. Again, I felt
no gratitude or relief. But after ten minutes or so, an absurd
coincidence happened; there was an odd knocking noise from
his gearbox too, and he said: "It looks as if I'll have to drop you
off at the next garage." And for the first time that day I felt a
positive emotion, a feeling of "Oh *no!*" However, he drove on
cautiously, and found that the noise stopped when he drove at
less than 20 miles an hour. After half an hour of this—both of
us listening with strained attention for the noise—he said:
"Well, I think we'll make it if we keep going at this speed."
And I suddenly felt an overwhelming sense of relief and delight. And I caught myself feeling it, and noticed its absurdity.
Nothing had been "added to me" in the last half hour, nothing
given. All that had happened was that I had been threatened
with inconvenience, and the threat had been removed. The
threat had stimulated me, aroused my latent will power. I
formulated this recognition rather clumsily, in the words:
"There is a margin of the human mind that can be stimulated
by pain or inconvenience, but which is indifferent to pleasure."
And as we were passing through the town of St Neots, I labeled
it "the St Neot margin," so I wouldn't forget it.

It was an absolutely fundamental recognition. It meant that
"life-devaluation"—the opposite of freedom—is due to our curious laziness, to a childish "spoiledness" that gets resentful and
bored in the face of minor problems. And freedom—the moment of vision, of poetry—is due to a certain *unconscious* discipline of the will.

The vision, the freedom, comes from a subconscious region
inside us. And yet, in an odd way, we have power over this
subconscious region. Discipline and effort are all-important.

Once I had my clue, other things began to fall into place.
There was Ramakrishna, who received his first "vision of God"
when about to plunge a sword into himself. There was Raskolnikov, with his thought that he would prefer to live on a
narrow ledge forever rather than die at once. There was
Graham Greene, who tells how in his teens he suffered from a

perpetual and total boredom, which he would dissipate by taking his brother's revolver on to Berkhamstead Common and playing Russian roulette: that is, he inserted one bullet, spun the chambers, pointed it at his head and pulled the trigger. When there was only a click, "it was as if a light had been turned on.... I felt that life contained an infinite number of possibilities." And Sartre was getting at the same thing when he said that he had never felt so free as under constant threat of death during the German occupation.

All this, of course, is inherent in *The Outsider*. But when I wrote this book. I could still see no answer. My novel, *Ritual in the Dark,* is an exploration of the same problem. (All my novels are based upon my recognition that there are things that can be said in fiction that are unsayable in a work of philosophy.) The hero, like Rilke's Malte or Sartre's Roquentin, sits in his room and hurls his mind at the problem of the *negative nature of freedom*. It is absurd—like buying an expensive car and discovering that it will do 90 miles an hour *in reverse,* and only ten miles an hour going forward.

Gradually, it became clear to me that what we are dealing with is a problem of evolution. In this book, I have compared outsiders to fast trains who are likely to go off the rails. An even better comparison is with the problem of airplanes and the sound barrier. When an airplane travels at a speed approaching that of sound, the air cannot get away from in front of its wings quickly enough, and builds up into a kind of concrete barrier. In the early days of jet travel, planes tended to disintegrate against this concrete barrier of air. But even when the designers had succeeded in making a plane that would smash through the "sound barrier" (with the supersonic "bang") , the problem was not solved. The planes always went into a steep dive, and crashed, and the harder the pilot pulled on the stick, the steeper became the dive. And then one day, an exceptionally gifted test pilot tried doing something absurd. Instead of frantically pulling back the stick, he tried pushing it forward—which, logically ought to have made the dive steeper than ever. Instead, the plane straightened out. At speeds greater than that of sound, some of the usual laws of nature get reversed.

This, it seemed to me, is a picture of the "outsider" problem. One might say that evolution has been trying to create a human being capable of traveling faster than sound. Capable, that is, of a seriousness, a mental intensity that is completely foreign to the average human animal. The nineteenth century is covered with the wrecks of the unsuccessful experiments. Yet this does not mean that the problem is insoluble. I knew that I had found more than half my answer in my concept of the "St Neot margin." The main trouble is our ignorance of the strange laws of supersonic travel.

The evolutionary aspect interested me. There is a passage at the beginning of Wells' autobiography in which he argues that certain men of today are trying to become pure creatures of the mind, as a fish is a creature of the water or a bird of the air. There are men—like Wells himself—to whom you can say: "Yes, you love, you hate, you work for a living... but what do you really *do*?" They possess imaginative and creative interests that make everyday life boring to them. (I had written of the hero of *Ritual in the Dark*: "There was a futility about physical existence that frightened him.") Wells had gone on to compare men to the earliest amphibians, who dragged themselves out of prehistoric seas and wanted to become land animals; but they only possessed flippers, so that a short period on land would exhaust them, and they would have to get back to the comfortable, sustaining medium of the sea—which they hated. Here it is again, the outsider problem, the Faust problem, the St Neot margin. So man wishes to become a creature of the mind, of the imagination—but a few hours in this inner land, and they have to get back to the physical world, with its stupid, repetitive problems. The world of the mind exhausts them.

Before I go on, let me make an important observation. I say: "Man wishes to become a creature of the mind." But *how many* do? That problem can be answered with some accuracy. It was my friend Robert Ardrey who pointed out the answer. In the Korean war, the Chinese discovered that they could prevent the escape of American soldiers by segregating the "leader figures" and keeping them under heavy guard, and leaving the others without any guard at all. *The leaders were always precisely five percent of the total number of soldiers.* And it so happens that this figure holds good for most species of animals too. The "dominant minority" is always five percent.

This does not mean that mankind consists of five percent "outsiders." Most of the five percent is made up of other dominant types—soldiers, politicians, businessmen, sportsmen, actors, clergymen, and so on—that is to say, of people whose "dominance" is by no means intellectual. The difference between these men and Wells' "amphibians"—the *intellectual* dominant minority—is that soldiers, actors and the rest *need other people to express their dominance*. A Napoleon without his army, an actor without his audience, is a nobody. The peculiarity of the poet, the man of creative imagination, is that he doesn't need other people to express his dominance. The great writer or thinker isn't writing *primarily* for other people; he is exploring the world of his own being. The huntsman needs a fox to give the chase excitement; the philosopher pursues an abstract fox across the landscape of his own mind.

And yet he is not yet capable of remaining in that mental universe for more than an hour or so. After that, he becomes tired, bored, depressed; he has to get back to the physical world and his ordinary little concerns. Everyone has at some time noticed this odd inability to remain in the world of the mind. If you try to finish a long book in one sitting, you not only find your eyes getting tired; you feel yourself sinking morally lower, getting somewhat sick and depressed. We cannot stay in the world of the mind for long.

This is a fascinating problem. Julian Huxley suggested in 1913 that just as there is an obvious difference between dead matter and living matter (say a piece of protoplasm), so there is the same *basic* difference between animal material and human material. One might compare dead matter to a straight line, which has length but no thickness—that is, which has *existence* but no freedom. In that case, you could say that animal material is like a square, for it has an extra dimension of freedom. And, according to Huxley, you could go on to compare man to a kind of cube, for he has yet another dimension of freedom—this mental realm. The animal is stuck in a perpetual present. It has no mind to speak of—its mental processes are a mere reflection of its environment.

I believe Huxley is mistaken (although he and I have argued about it). Man *does not yet* possess this third dimension. The black room experiments prove this. If you put *any* human being in a totally black and soundless room, he goes to pieces after a day or so, because his mind is totally dependent on the outside world, upon external stimuli. (The Chinese are said to use the black room for brain washing—it is far more effective than torture.) In other words, because man is still an amphibian, a sea creature with flippers instead of legs. IF he was truly a creature of the mind, the black room wouldn't worry him. In short, *man does not yet exist*. He is still a mere animal.

And yet the problem now becomes so serious that it threatens his existence. Why is the crime rate rising so steadily? Why has juvenile delinquency become such an acute problem? Why is the suicide rate climbing? Why are mental homes overcrowded? The answer to all these questions is the same. Because the modern world provides no outlet for a large number of the dominant minority. A hundred years ago, there were a hundred ways in which a dominant person could express himself—the chief one being fighting, for there was always a war going on somewhere. Today we cannot afford war, and our civilization has become so complex and mechanized that there is simply nothing for the dominant person *to do*. This is why our civilization is bursting at the seams with crime and neurosis. Man must learn to express his dominance in a new way—in the realms of the mind. But at present, even the most imaginative and creative men are not truly "creatures of the mind."

There are a number of possible answers. I thought I had discovered one when I first read Aldous Huxley's *Doors of Perception*, describing how mescalin plunged him into this "world of the mind," and made him aware of its immensity. You could put a man in the black room with mescalin, and the blackness wouldn't worry him in the least; he'd simply plunge like a diver into his own mind.

And yet I was suspicious of this answer. Huxley admitted that mescalin destroys will power; one is so delighted with this strange and beautiful world that one has no desire to do anything but sit still and stare. Huxley concluded: "A world in which everyone took mescalin would be a world in which there are no wars" (and so the basic problem of the dominant minority would be solved), "but it would also be a world in which there is no civilization, for we just couldn't be bothered to build it."

I verified this when I took mescalin in 1963. (I have described it at length in an appendix to *Beyond the Outsider*.)

Mescalin plunged me into a fascinating world in which I was aware of a kind of basic universal benevolence. But it was like becoming a baby again; you are ecstatically happy—and also helpless and defenseless. It reduces you, in a way to an animal level. I tried to explain this by saying that mescalin destroyed my mental VHF system. (Radio sets have a VHF attachment so that you can pick up a single station clearly, without getting 20 other stations interfering.) My mind became a kind of giant receiving set, with 20 stations all clamoring away together. My capacity for concentration is usually excellent—I have, for example, been able to write this postscript in a single sitting; mescalin destroyed this. So while it was a superb mental holiday, destroying all the mind's tensions, turning one truly into a "creature of the mind," it was useless and dangerous. (It can cause complete mental breakdown in a neurotic or morbid person.)

But clearly, this is the direction in which the answer must lie. Mescalin is no answer. We need to get its advantages—the sense of deep vision, the connection with the deepest sources of one's vital powers—without its disadvantages.

Let me try to explain a little more fully. Suppose you are driving down a road at night with your headlights on. Apart from the narrow beam of light ahead of you, you feel completely isolated in your narrow world of blackness. And you can't really *see* anything in your headlights, for you are moving too fast. Now if you turn off your headlights and drive on your sidelights, an interesting thing happens. Your world expands. You become aware of the shapes of trees and houses looming in the darkness. You can look out of your side windows, and see things going past. It is a far more interesting world. But *you are forced to drive at five miles an hour*.

This expresses the problem of mescalin. It plunges you into a delightful world of twilight where you become aware of some of the strange fish that inhabit the depths of your own mind. But you become a drifter.

But now supposing someone invented a kind of open spotlight that went on the roof of your car. You could now see ahead of you *and* around you—and behind, if necessary. It would, of course, be somewhat inconvenient for other motorists—but then, in the world of the mind, this objection obviously doesn't apply. Can we, in other words, create forms of mental discipline that will produce some of the effects of mescalin—that sense of contact with our inner source of power, meaning and purpose—without impairing our ability to concentrate?

There are such disciplines, and, to a certain extent, I have discovered how to use them. I can create in myself most of the effects of mescalin by purely mental disciplines. I am not speaking of yogic disciplines, but of processes of thought, of what Husserl calls "phenomenological disciplines." Primarily, they are concerned with the creation of new language, a new conceptology; for our problem is that we spend too much time looking at the external world to make any close acquaintance with the world of the inner mind. We have no maps, no geography, no signposts, of this inner world. But my own work has been a consistent attempt to create such a geography.

This is obviously the point where I should be starting this postscript, not finishing it. I can only suggest that interested readers follow me through the remaining books of the Outsider sequence, and through such novels as *Necessary Doubt* and *The Sex Diary of Gerard Sorme*. (The title is not mine; it was chosen by the American publisher.)

Let me offer one more clue, concerning how the "St Neot margin" notion can be applied. (For *this* is the core.) De Quincey tells an interesting story about Wordsworth. He had asked Wordsworth how he came to write poetry, and Wordsworth's answer was not satisfactory. But later in the day, they went to meet the mail cart, which was coming from Keswick. Wordsworth knelt down with his ear to the ground to listen for its rumble; when he heard nothing, he straightened up, and his attention was caught by an evening star, *which suddenly appeared to him to be intensely beautiful*. Wordsworth said: "Now I can explain to you how I come to write poetry. If ever I am *concentrating* on something that has nothing to do with poetry, and then I suddenly relax my attention, whatever I see when I relax appears to me to be beautiful."

This is obviously another version of what happened to me in the truck—the threat of inconvenience causing a certain concentration of the attention, and then the removal of the threat, which allows the senses to expand with relief, causing a sensation of delight, of life-affirmation.

Try a very simple experiment. Take a pencil and hold it in

front of your eyes, a few feet away. Narrow your attention to the pencil itself, so you cease to be aware of the room. Then let your attention expand, so you become aware of the room as its background. Then narrow your attention again. Do this a dozen times. At the end of this time, you will begin to experience a curious mental glow, not unlike what happens if you exercise your muscles. Because, in fact, you *are* exercising a muscle of whose existence you are normally unaware. You take your perception for granted, as something that merely "happens" when you open your eyes. But, as Husserl knew, *perception is intentional*. You would not see anything unless you made a subconscious effort of will to perceive.

Freedom and imagination are also muscles that we never exercise; we rely upon external stimuli to make us aware of their possibilities. We tend to be trapped in a world of everyday premises that we take for granted. (Husserl calls this "the natural standpoint.") The problem is to use the mind in such a way that we become detached from this world of the natural standpoint, able to criticize it *and analyze it*. This latter is the key to the phenomenology.

I have taken more than ten years to create my "new existentialism," and it seems to me that I am working upon the most interesting problem in the world, the *only* interesting problem. In America, there are others who are working along similar lines—Hadley Cantril and Abraham Maslow, for example (both experimental psychologists). England is totally unaware of these problems; intellectually, we have always been the most backward country in the world. Europe has little to offer, besides the dead philosophy of Sartre and Heidegger. And yet in spite of this, I feel that immensely exciting things are about to happen, that we are on the brink of some discovery that will make our century a turning point in human history.